D1603481

WHERE
THEY ARE NOW

WHERE
THEY ARE NOW

The Story of
the Women
of Harvard Law
1974

JILL ABRAMSON AND
BARBARA FRANKLIN

1986
Doubleday & Company, Inc.
Garden City, New York

Library of Congress Cataloging-in-Publication Data
Abramson, Jill, 1954–
  Where They Are Now.
  1. Lawyers—United States—Biography. 2. Women
lawyers—United States—Biography. I. Franklin,
Barbara, 1953–   . II. Title.
KF372.A27   1986   349.73′092′2 [B]   85–15923
ISBN 0-385-19432-3   347.300922 [B]

To Cornelia, William and Henry L. Griggs III

To Michael H. Franklin

We began working on this study of seventy fascinating women in the spring of 1983. As staff reporters for *The American Lawyer*, a monthly magazine covering the legal profession, we set out to do a story about the status of women lawyers. With invaluable guidance from our editor, Steven Brill, we hit upon the women in the Harvard Law School Class of 1974 as the perfect group for our study. The resulting article: "Are Women Catching Up?", published in the May 1983 issue of *The American Lawyer*, received wide attention and was the inspiration for this book.

Without the cooperation of the women from this watershed law school class, however, there would have been no article and no book. They invited us into their offices and homes and gave generously of their time—which, given the billable hourly rates of successful lawyers, is their most precious commodity. Most not only agreed to let us use their thoughtful observations, but also their names, which we truly appreciate. We are also grateful to many other Harvard Law alumnae who granted our requests for interviews, and to many male Harvard Law graduates who did likewise.

The support of the editors and staff of *The American Lawyer* was instrumental to this project. We wish to thank in particular Ellen Joan Pollock, Pamela Brown and Katherine States for their insights and assistance.

Jill Abramson wants to thank Steven Brill for his enlightened and generous sabbatical policy which allowed her to spend the summer of 1984 behind a typewriter working on this book.

Barbara Franklin expresses thanks to Carl Liggio and Henry Kellerman for their support and interest in this project.

Harriet Rubin of Harper & Row gave direction to our work in its early stages, while our agent, Carol Mann, gave us hope. At Doubleday, we wish to thank our editors Loretta Barrett and Cynthia Barrett for their intelligence and encouragement for the past two years.

We express gratitude to our former colleague and friend, James B. Stewart, Jr., whose wit, savvy and writing about the legal profession are a continual inspiration.

During our research, various members of the Harvard Law School faculty and administration were extremely helpful. We also express our thanks to the organizers of the Tenth Year Reunion for the class of 1974, who permitted us to take part in the festivities and to those who attended and so graciously accepted our intrusion.

Several friends and colleagues read our manuscript at various stages and we thank them for their thoughtful contributions: Lynne Griggs, Jane O'Connor, Norman and Dovie Abramson, James Cramer, Joan Kenyon, Howard Franklin and Jill Harris.

Lisa Hill Fenning, Patricia Schnegg, Timi Hallem, Judith Bain and, in San Francisco, the members of Downtown Women Lawyers were eager to help us put our material into a broader perspective. We appreciate their input.

The reporters and staff of the San Juan *Star,* Mary Meagher, Georgette and Robert Essad, and Pat Hartley and Dick Fontaine generously gave us places to hang our hats during our travels.

Finally, without a lot of give and take, a sense of humor and mutual trust, this collaborative effort might have collapsed, so we each thank the other.

Jill Abramson
Barbara Franklin
New York City
August 1985

CONTENTS

WHERE
THEY ARE NOW

1

Harvard Law's New Breed

In the brilliant April sunlight the law school is preening for its returning alumni, radiating the same air of permanence and authority that both thrills and intimidates each new generation of One Ls, as first-year students at Harvard Law School are known. Even Austin Hall, a sooty, dungeonlike structure on the southern rim of campus, looks resplendent. The powerful and self-satisfied lawyers who now pass before it were all, long ago, part of the nervous mass huddled in Austin for the dean's traditional welcome: "There is no glee club at Harvard Law School," words that perfectly summed up the school's notoriously competitive atmosphere.

We are in Cambridge to attend the tenth-year reunion of the Harvard Law School class of 1974. For the past year, as journalists, we have been tracking down the seventy[1] women who were members of this watershed class. In the past decade the legal profession, which for centuries operated like an elite gentlemen's club, has been shaken by an unprecedented influx of women. For more than a year we have been exploring what impact these women are having on the law and, even

[1] According to Harvard Law's alumni records, sixty-seven women registered in 1971 and seventy-one earned JDs in 1974. For convenience, we have used an average of seventy.

more important, what impact the profession is having on them. For a case study, we picked the 1974 alumnae of Harvard Law School, who stood a better chance of finding success than any other group of women lawyers in the country. They joined the profession with the best possible credentials when it was possible, for the first time, for women to have the same expectations of professional and personal fulfillment as men. The question on our minds today is: have they found it?

Harvard Law School is the oldest, largest and most influential American law school, "the high citadel,"[2] of the legal profession. These seventy women, in an entering class of 563, arrived at Harvard at an important moment in the law school's history. Nineteen seventy-one, their first year, marked the first time any Harvard Law School class was more than ten percent female. It was the first year the law school had anything approaching "a body of women," as then dean Albert Sacks puts it, rather than a token few. There were 800 female applicants for admission in 1971, a record for Harvard, which had only begun to admit women in 1950, the last Ivy League law school to surrender. (Yale Law had admitted women in 1918, the same year the American Bar Association took in its first female members.)

Between 1963 and 1978 there was a veritable explosion in the legal population and law school enrollment more than doubled nationwide, from 49,000 to 122,000. Female enrollment rose even more dramatically during this period, mushrooming from just 2,000 (4.1%) to 37,000 (30.3%).[3] A growing commitment to the ideals of social justice and desire to influence the nation's power structure, heightened by the protest over the Vietnam War (and a related desire to avoid the draft), propelled thousands of young people into law school during the early 1970s. Many of the women who were

[2.] Joel Seligman, *The High Citadel: The Influence of Harvard Law School* (Boston: Houghton Mifflin Company, 1978).
[3.] Cynthia Fuchs Epstein, *Women in Law* (New York: Basic Books, 1981), p. 53.

involved in the antiwar movement as undergraduates were also swept up by the burgeoning women's movement, and a legal education provided the ticket to a high-powered career in an exclusive, male-dominated profession. If law was among the most challenging careers a woman could choose, Harvard Law School was surely the most challenging proving ground.

The women of Harvard Law 1974 were in the vanguard of this revolution, although they still comprised only twelve percent of their incoming class. From 1971 on, the law school rapidly increased the number of acceptance letters going to women and by 1974, the year they graduated, the incoming class of One Ls was twenty-two percent female. When we catch up with the class of 1974 ten years later the citadel has been stormed: women, who make up more than one third of the student body, are visible everywhere. When the women of 1974 began their legal education no women at Harvard Law School held either tenure or tenure-track positions on the faculty. Now, the faces of two tenured female faculty members peer out from a line of portraits decorating the walls of Pound Hall where the tenth reunion is scheduled to begin. As One Ls, the women of 1974 were among the first female bodies ever to shower in Hemenway Gym. According to a newsletter we are given by the Harvard Women's Law Association, a group that some of the women from the class of 1974 helped launch, "women only" hours are being set aside in the gym's weight room.

Arrows point the way to the tenth reunion and when we arrive there are about thirty men and women from the class clustered around several tables, munching doughnuts, drinking coffee and playing catch-up. Roscoe Trimmier, one of the organizers of the event and a partner at Ropes & Gray, the Boston firm that represents Harvard, has warned us not to expect a big turnout, that there is a certain degree of "apathy" among his former classmates. Harvard Law alums usually turn out in droves for a twenty-fifth reunion. After only a

decade in the profession, it is much more difficult to lure
young lawyers in their mid-thirties, who have only begun to
make their way in the profession.

One of the 1974 alumnae seated at our table is Marley Sue
Weiss, best remembered by her classmates as the most vocal
feminist in the class. Recovering from a recent knee injury,
Marley had, moments earlier, hobbled into the room assisted
by crutches, obviously enjoying being the focus of attention.
Since graduation she has been dispensing legal advice at the
United Auto Workers union. Near the doorway to the room
stands Mary Brody, who, like so many women in her class,
headed to a law firm following graduation. She is now a partner at a small Boston firm and has a newborn baby daughter
strapped to her chest in a Snugli. Marley and Mary are symbolic of the two main "types" of women who were in their
law school class: those who used their law degrees to promote social change and those who went the establishment
route. What both groups shared was the belief that a woman's career should be a top priority and a determination to
succeed on the same terms as men. Our hope is to find out
how they, and the others, have made out in the past ten years.

For the past year we have traveled the country tracking
down the women from the Harvard Law School class of
1974. Our journeys have taken us from Cape Cod to Seattle
as well as to Puerto Rico and London. By the time of the
April 1984 reunion we have already interviewed about half
the women from the class. Our mission has been to find out
how the realities of being in the profession have corre-
sponded to the high expectations these women had on commencement day, 1974. Has a Harvard Law degree opened
the same doors for women as it always has for men, functioning like Gatsby's white card in the Fitzgerald novel, as one
woman from the class, Alice Young, so eloquently put it?
Have the women stayed on the fast track to power and influence in the past ten years? If so, how have they coped with

the problems of burnout and juggling their careers against family demands? Did the women who went the law firm route achieve the goal of partnership? Have the women who went into public interest work remained true to their ideals, given the increasing conservatism of the Me Decade 1970s and Reagan 1980s? As a group, have they found some measure of success and happiness as lawyers? How have they, and along with them their profession, changed in the past ten years?

The changing culture of Harvard Law School deeply influenced these seventy women and shaped their attitudes as they entered the legal profession, full of hope and ambition. Our goal in Cambridge is to soak in the law school atmosphere and try to recapture what Harvard Law School must have been like in the early 1970s. The reunion begins with a class symposium, led by Marley Weiss. Back in 1971 Marley was part of a new, vocal group of feminist law students who were making their presence felt at Harvard. Only weeks into first semester Marley was leaping up from her seat in class to hassle her professors about their use of sexist hypotheticals in case studies, including dizzy women drivers in torts and batty dowagers in trusts and estates. "I think I made a vivid impression," she tells us. "I took on the faculty over women's issues. There were not a lot of women with the nerve to do that." She also launched a petition drive to get the faculty to address the women in their classes as "Ms." Both efforts had negligible effect.

Like many of her classmates who attended college during the late 1960s, Marley was deeply affected by the activism of the times and remains committed to social change. Although she is leaving the UAW to teach at the University of Maryland Law School, she is not one of the members of the class who have used their Harvard Law degrees as tickets to material success. The 1974 crimson class report that is handed out to the alumni as they register for the reunion reveals that the average income for those working in large law firms, a large percentage of the class, is $115,000. Marley will probably be earning less than half of this as a law school professor. The women's movement is still an important part of her life and she remains outspoken on feminist and other political issues. But it must be startling for some of her classmates to see this husky, dark-haired woman dressed in a lawyerly tweed suit, a very different image than the one she cultivated in law school. The 1974 yearbook catches Marley in a characteristic pose, perched on a motorcycle, with a heavy metal chain dangling around her shoulders, clasping a helmet in her lap.

There was a significant countercultural contingent on campus in the early 1970s. Many of Marley's friends were charter members of a group called the Freaked Out Friends, which rebelled against the cutthroat competition of the law school. They held free-for-all rap sessions, sitting in a circle on the lawn outside Pound Hall, the building where some of the Freaked Out Friends would meet, more than a decade later, as more sedate lawyers gathered for their tenth reunion. "Freaked Out?" the flier announcing their very first rap session had asked. "Isolation can be very heavy, especially when you're up against a mythical institution. In an atmosphere of smiling immorality, required competition and assigned seats, isolation is not an easy thing to overcome." Instead of studying round the clock, Marley and other members of the Freaked Out society partied in their dorm rooms, walked along the banks of the Charles River analyzing the lyrics of Bob Dylan songs and formed a motorcycle club as a spoof on the more serious-minded organizations at Harvard Law School, like the Marshall and Learned Hand clubs, named after famous judges.

By the time she arrived at Harvard Law School, Marley Weiss's life already revolved around the women's movement. As an undergraduate she had been a founding member of a Barnard College women's liberation group. In 1970 she was one of two hundred feminists who stormed and occupied the offices of the *Ladies' Home Journal* for eleven hours. At Harvard Law School a Women's Law Association had been launched the same year. Alice Ballard, a member of the class of 1973, who was one of the leaders of the WLA, as the group was called, remembers Marley's arrival on campus vividly. "Marley was like a breath of fresh air. She was fun and kind of crazy. She called her own shots and she wasn't afraid of anyone." Ballard, a blue-blooded Philadelphian whose father and grandfather were both pillars of the city's legal establishment, and Weiss, the daughter of a Jewish garment worker and furrier, were two of the most vocal members of the Women's Law Association.

The Harvard Law School administration grudgingly gave the WLA a dingy little office in the basement of Austin Hall. There were two grimy sofas and a membership-donated library consisting of well-worn copies of *Our Bodies, Ourselves* and *Sisterhood Is Powerful,* the bibles of the women's movement. The WLA agitated on several different fronts. Some of their concerns were practical—like getting more ladies' rooms. During exams it was a common spectacle to see women dashing through the tunnels that connected the lecture halls, searching for the nearest toilet facilities. Getting more women students admitted and more women faculty members were the larger issues on the WLA's wish list.

With only seventy women in the class, split among the four One L sections, Marley complains, "We were drowning in a sea of men." Ellen Marshall, one of Marley's classmates, had already described these feelings of isolation to us during an interview in Los Angeles. "As you sat in the amphitheaters," she says, "every time a woman was called on you kind of held your breath, thinking, 'She'd better do well for all of us.' Often, she didn't, and you'd feel embarrassed." The WLA hoped to ease the isolation of women students by upping female enrollment. They printed a special brochure aimed at female applicants and sent foot soldiers on recruiting missions to women's colleges.

The law school was desperately hunting for a female tenure prospect when Marley and the other women from the class of 1974 were One Ls. In a scathing editorial that pounded the administration on its dismal record in attracting women professors, the *Harvard Law Record* asked, sarcastically, "Which is harder to find, a qualified woman candidate for the Supreme Court of the United States or a qualified woman candidate for a professorship at Harvard Law School?" In 1971 one contender appeared, Ruth Bader Ginsburg. Already a tenured professor at Rutgers Law School, who had argued several landmark sex discrimination cases, Ginsburg was invited to teach a Women in the Law course at Harvard.

When she finished teaching the fall course the law school was still unsure whether she met its lofty standards for tenure. She was invited back, as a guest lecturer, to teach in the spring. But Columbia Law School broke in with an offer of tenure, and with a bird in hand, Ginsburg decided not to hang in limbo at Harvard. Instead, she headed to Columbia, leaving Harvard's administration embarrassed and empty-handed as far as a female tenure prospect was concerned. Elisabeth Owens, a tax specialist who had worked in obscurity for more than fifteen years at one of the law school's research institutes, was drafted to teach the now popular Women in the Law course. "She was like the invisible woman of the law school," is how one member of the class of 1974 described her. Marley took the course with Owens and thought she "tried very, very hard. Betty Owens learned the material right along with the rest of us." During the summer of 1972, with little fanfare, Dean Sacks announced that Owens, after years of service to the law school, was being promoted to full professor. The WLA, meanwhile, drafted a sex discrimination complaint against Harvard, arguing that the law school's requirements for tenure were sexist. An initial investigation by what was then H.E.W. never went anywhere.

"These women were still hearing some echoes from the past," admits former dean Sacks. But during the years the women of 1974 were in law school Harvard was changing. While some members of the faculty were still obviously less than thrilled by the burgeoning number of women on campus, most were resigned to, and some even enthusiastic about, the presence of more women. A younger group of professors, with more progressive social values, was also having an impact, making the atmosphere at the school a bit looser. In his popular constitutional litigation course, for example, Charles Nesson told Lenny Bruce jokes and also ran a legal clinic for soldiers in Vietnam who needed civilian defense lawyers to help them with discharge and court-martial proceedings. One member of the class of 1974, Susan Thorner, spent a year in Saigon working for Nesson's group. Derrick Bell, a black lawyer who had worked for the NAACP Legal Defense and Education Fund, was teaching a course on racism in the law. Gary Bellow, a veteran of the war on poverty, had been snatched away from the University of Southern California to launch a serious clinical law program at Harvard.

By 1974 the law school had made dramatic leaps since the year it began accepting women. When they were finally admitted in 1950, women met with a chilly reception from the administration, faculty and fellow students. The issue of whether or not to admit women had deeply divided the faculty and administration for almost a century and continued to be a source of strife. In 1899, and again in 1915, after bitter debates, the university's governing corporation[4] had turned thumbs down on having women join the law school's

4. Stevens, Robert, *Law School*, University of North Carolina Press, Chapel Hill, 1983, p. 83.

student body. Several short-lived, all-female law schools had sprouted up in the Boston area in the meantime. It took nearly four more decades to resolve the issue. When then Dean Erwin Griswold finally announced the decision to admit women on October 11, 1949, Wesley Sturges, the dean of Yale Law School, sent a congratulatory telegram: "The Yale Law faculty and student body are deeply moved by the action of Harvard Law School in admitting women. Feel it quite possible Harvard may make contribution to womanhood. Doubt many adverse consequences to Harvard faculty and student body. Our many generations of women graduates are of course a pride and joy."

Gaining real acceptance was an almost impossible task for the women who began arriving on campus in the early 1950s. During the era of Dean Griswold, who ruled Harvard Law School with an iron grip from 1946 to 1967, when he left for Washington to become President Lyndon Johnson's Solicitor General, women were accepted to the law school in token numbers. We interviewed many of the women who graduated from the law school during the pioneer era of the 1950s and early 1960s and virtually all of them remembered being treated like members of an alien species. Beginning in 1950, Griswold, perhaps with good intentions, hosted a reception for every incoming class of female One Ls. The faculty was usually invited, stag. The women gathered around Griswold on folding chairs while he asked each the same question: why was she at Harvard Law School occupying the seat of a man? "When my turn came," recalls Ruth Bader Ginsburg, one of the women clustered around the dean in 1956, "I wished I could have pressed a button and vanished through a trapdoor." Nearly thirty years later Griswold, 80, practicing law in Washington, remembers these parties vividly. He says he asked each woman why she was at Harvard Law School, "because there was some concern among the faculty that a fair proportion of the women wouldn't use their degrees. I wanted to get their reaction and to encourage them to develop the idea that they should make use of their educations."

Ladies' Days were reserved by a few members of the faculty as occasions for the women in their class to perform like circus animals. Only women were called on. "All the women were made to look very smart," recalls Hope Eastman, a member of the class of 1967. "The professor would gently guide the women through the Socratic analysis, the point being—'If these dumb women can do it, how come you gentlemen can't?' " In the mid 1960s, according to Carolyn Clark, class of 1968, Ladies' Day met a sudden death in the classroom of property professor Barton Leach, who had been the tradition's greatest enthusiast. Leach had asked the eight women in his class, including Clark, to recite a case in which the chattel in question was ladies' underwear. They had prepared themselves ahead of time and each came to class dressed in black, wearing horn-rims and carrying a briefcase. After making their presentation from the front of the classroom, the women opened their briefcases and showered a red-faced Leach with a cascade of frilly lingerie. The professor called off Ladies' Day for good.

Other professors only called on women to recite the most grizzly rape cases, or when the subject at hand had some potential for female degradation. When her torts professor asked Ruth Baker-Battist, class of 1958, why a husband and not his wife had sued in a fourteenth-century dispute, she correctly responded that, if the case was so old, women were considered chattels and had no legal rights whatsoever. The professor promptly responded that this was probably the way things should have stayed. "The thing that's so shocking is not the story," Baker-Battist told us nearly thirty years later, "the thing that is so shocking is that I sat down. I don't think there is any woman in any law school today who, faced with any professor in the world, would have done what I did. And perhaps what is more shocking is that no one thought it was surprising that I sat down."

The male student body was often no more enlightened than the faculty. Congresswoman Patricia Schroeder (D, Colo.), who arrived at Harvard Law School in 1961, remembers finding "a kind of preppie mafia. The women in the law school were treated like Amazons. Men wanted cute blondes from Lesley [a junior college near Harvard]. Among the men there was a feeling that Harvard Law School had been ruined because they let girls in." The Amazon stereotype persisted into the seventies. Several women from the class of 1974 complained to us about the graffiti on bathroom walls and in the tunnels connecting the law school buildings. One mainstay was a drawing of "the typical Harvard Law coed," replete with pimples, Coke-bottle glasses and extensive underarm growth. Carolyn Daffron, a member of the class, says a fellow who sat next to her in one of their first-year classes complained that he was getting lonely for women and informed Daffron that he was going out to Wellesley to meet some. "Because we were fledgling lawyers," Daffron explains, "we weren't women."

Like Marley Weiss, Daffron became involved in the WLA. Since graduation she has worked in poverty law and taught and is now teaching and writing a novel, one of six women who have not made law their primary focus. Many of the feminists in the class have pursued "alternative careers" in poverty or public interest law and government, hoping to use their legal educations to foster social change. Ann Greenblatt, another kindred spirit, is still in the trenches working in legal aid. At the reunion, her clothes—black turtleneck and black slacks—are a stark contrast to the silk dresses worn by most of the wives of the men who were once Greenblatt's classmates. Some of the more idealistic feminists from the class are less tenacious than Ann Greenblatt and have lost heart in the intervening ten years since graduation. "A lot of us thought we'd change the world in five years," Marley laments during the class symposium discussion that officially launches the reunion. "A lot of us burned out in the process." This is true of herself. "I'm overworked and I'm leaving the practice of law," she announces. "I want a schedule I can predict, a more controllable lifestyle." What happened to the other left-leaning women from the class—Judith Berkan, Renee Chotiner and others—who were all so determined to go out and change the world?

And what about the larger group of women—sixty percent —who started their careers at big law firms? Mary Brody is part of a select group who achieved the goal of partnership. Yet, even though she is a partner, Mary speaks candidly about the difficulties of trying to operate at the top level of her profession while she raises two small children. "Having children slows you down," says Mary, who wrote her firm's maternity leave policy. "That's part of the choice. It doesn't make it easy. Women who really work at their careers are also competitive and ambitious, so it's hard for them to have this slowing down." The difficulty of raising children and making the law firm climb had prompted several women in the class to leave private practice and the profession altogether. Others simply burned out, tired of the grind and discouraged by the dim prospects for partnership.

After commencement day, 1974, for the first time in any Harvard Law School class, more women than men went to work at large, elite firms. In the past, finding the doors to most firms shut, women had been forced to accept do-good and lower-paying jobs in government and poverty law. Why did so many women from the class gravitate toward firms? First, Harvard Law School inculcated in generations of its students the belief that corporate law was the most challenging and rewarding way to use their degrees. And in the early 1970s firms were under court-ordered pressure to hire more women. The women of Harvard Law 1974 were positioned perfectly to take advantage of the changing times, and they flocked to the male-dominated bastions of Wall Street, Los Angeles, Chicago and Boston.

The more conservative political orientation of the mid-1970s was another reason more 1974 Harvard Law graduates than ever—men and women—went to established firms. The riotous atmosphere that prevailed during their undergraduate years had been replaced by a more sober career orientation. Before the reunion we met Molly Munger, a member of the class whose evolution seemed to symbolize the changing times. "Through most of my college years," Munger told us, "I really thought my job was to find a husband." At Radcliffe during the late 1960s Molly fought against the stereotype of the "California airhead." The fight, she says, helped to raise her consciousness. One of her economics professors had once scrawled across her exam, "I guess you're not such a dumb blonde after all." During her first year at law school she flirted with feminism and joined the WLA, helped organize the first women in the law course and volunteered to hand out fliers for the militant Red Stockings collective. She remembers turning up for duty wearing "the 1970s equivalent of Jane Fonda—turtleneck, bell-bottoms, hiking boots, no makeup." But the head of the Red Stockings unit refused to give the all too perfect-looking Californian the address of the group's storefront, growling, "How do I know you're not CIA?" By the end of law school, Molly says, she was turned off by the more militant, orthodox tone of the movement. In 1974 this self-described "conservative girl from Pasadena" left Harvard Law School and headed to a respected Los Angeles firm. Other women from the class were also turned off by the increasingly strident tone of the Women's Law Association. "Its style and philosophy were different than mine and I just didn't feel comfortable with it," says Margaret Morrow. "From their side we probably looked like namby-pamby little wimps who couldn't get with the program." Ellen Marshall also steered clear of the WLA because she didn't want to be categorized as "one of those girls." Marshall adds, "The only thing the WLA could offer me was the name of a gynecologist." Morrow and Marshall, like Molly Munger, headed to respected Los Angeles firms after graduation. All three are partners.

Going head to head in competition with men at law firms was a fitting conclusion to "basic training" the women of 1974 received at Harvard Law School, where the dog-eat-dog philosophy was carried to extremes. Although most of the student body arrive at the law school as chronic over-achievers, at Harvard the competitive spirit is carried to new heights. The very nature of education there—the Socratic method—is based on a quasi-adversarial relationship between the professors and the students. And the women from the class of 1974 had a far more negative reaction to the cracking of the Socratic whip than the men.

The Socratic method was developed by Harvard Dean Christopher Columbus Langdell in the late nineteenth century. It is vividly portrayed in John Osborn's novel, movie and television series, *The Paper Chase.* The movie was being filmed in Cambridge in 1971 with a number of women from the class of 1974 playing extras. Using the method,[5] the professor usually begins by selecting a student at random from the seating chart and asking the student to "state the case"— to recite the information contained in the assigned case brief. The professor then follows up with questions, pressing the student to make his or her answers more and more precise, narrowing the legal issues in the case. When the student is unable to answer, the professor either calls on another student at random or chooses from a group of raised hands. Some professors may interrogate each student for only a few minutes. Others, in the tradition of Osborn's dread Professor

[5]. A good description of the Socratic method is found in Scott Turow's *One L* (New York: Penguin Books, 1978), p. 41.

Kingsfield, for whom several Harvard professors claim to be the inspiration, delight in keeping the same poor soul on the hot seat for an entire class.

"I think the first student to be called on felt like everyone in the class was there to pick on him and humiliate him," Mary Nelson, another member of the class, explained to us. "And the professor was the cheerleader, sort of cheering on the students to destroy the first one's argument. The women were more sensitive to the humiliation than the men. I don't think women saw it as beneficial in the end. I think a lot of men saw it as boot camp—you're going through a hellish experience, but you're going to come out a real tough soldier on the other side." It wasn't the Socratic method itself that many of the women objected to, but the way it was used by certain professors to degrade and humiliate. As a minority, the women felt on display to begin with. The added pressure of being called on at random and the risk of public humiliation were too much for some. Several of the women from the class of 1974 told us that they "back-benched" their way through classes, sitting out of their assigned seats to avoid being called on. Several professors, including contracts scholar Clark Byse and civil procedure expert Arthur Miller, brilliant and witty on his television program "Miller's Court," were known to be devastating to students who were unprepared for their classes. (Both were also rumored to be inspirations for Professor Kingsfield.) Vern Countryman, who was known outside Harvard Law School for his valiant defense of victims of McCarthyism, was called "Stern Vern" by the students in his bankruptcy law classes. And many students avoided Archibald Cox's labor course, passing up an opportunity to study with one of Harvard's most famous lawyers, because he was a notoriously low grader.

Women at Harvard Law had a poor track record for making *Law Review,* where precious slots were awarded to the students with the highest first-year grades. Thus competition to get on the prestigious journal reached a feverish pitch right before spring exams. "Tell me, why do women always do so poorly at the law school?" a professor asked one woman from the class, Bari Schwartz, at a faculty party for One Ls during reading period. "Here was this professor prejudging how all of us would do," Schwartz complains. In the end, only one woman in the class, Toby Hyman, did make *Law Review* at the end of their first year. Most members of the class are at a loss to explain why so few women made *Law Review*. At the tenth reunion Richard Levine, now an attorney with the Justice Department, recalls that the women in his class were less inclined to become narrowly focused grinds. "The women had broader interests before coming to law school," he says. Fear of success, the psychological theory about women propounded by Radcliffe president Matina Horner, may also have come into play. "It was unacceptable for women to make, even to themselves, such a clear statement of ambition," claims Jane Eng, who met us in New York's Chinatown, where, ten years after graduation, she serves on the board of a health clinic.

The pressure of exams, which determined grades, was so intense that several students, men and women, collapsed under the strain. Because make-up exams were forbidden, several of those with jagged nerves sought refuge in the school's infirmary, remaining in isolation until they steadied themselves enough to face their blue books. Others found different ways to cope. Rosemary Williams Hill, a member of the class, became "born again" right before one of her exams. She babbled to everyone about her religious conversion and when she explained her transformation to Professor Bell he calmly responded, "Some people have nervous breakdowns. Others turn to drugs. This is your way of dealing with Harvard." When we caught up with Hill ten years later she still described herself as a "born again" Christian and was working in a public defender's office in Boston's Roxbury ghetto, work, she says, that God has directed her to do.

Tragically, not everyone in the class of 1974 was able to cope with the pressure. During reading period, when everyone was frantically preparing for first-year exams, there was a suicide. A gentle red-haired boy from Kansas was found by a maid who had come to clean his dorm room. He had been dead for several days. The carefully planned suicide of the popular student stunned the rest of the class, and several professors allowed their students to vent their feelings in class. Many students began echoing the rhetoric of the Freaked Out Friends, openly questioning the values of the law school. One confessed that he had left on a tape of a typewriter clacking in his room all weekend, not wanting to let on that he had gone away in order to keep up the stoic pretense of studying round the clock. As a memorial to their classmate, a petition demanding pass-fail grading circulated through the school, but exams took place, and were graded, as usual.

The three years of Harvard Law School were, for most of the men and women, a harrowing boot camp. It had been the custom of one of the law school's deans to announce on opening day, "Look to your right and then look to your left. One of you will not be here on graduation day." This same warning was often given in the military at the start of basic training. If it taught anything, Harvard Law prepared its students how to survive and compete against the best, a prerequisite for making it in the legal profession. And it gave them an entrée to power and influence. Most of the women from the class of 1974 left the law school just as determined as the men to use their newly earned Harvard JDs to get to the top, to exercise power and influence, whether in law firms or public interest jobs.

By commencement day in 1974 these seventy-one women had shared many experiences—learning the Socratic method, the sadness of a classmate's suicide, the frenzy for grades, then for jobs. And, as they stood up in Harvard Yard to receive their degrees in June, what they shared most of all was a sense of new horizons for women lawyers. "The women before us had to fight against impossible odds," says Alice Young, who left Harvard to begin a career as an international specialist at a New York firm. "My group had a lot of hope and certain expectations, but we did not expect the world to lay anything at our feet."

We leave the reunion knowing a lot of work lies ahead. We have been peppered with inquiries from practically all of the reuniting members of the class of 1974 when they learn that we are in the process of writing about their female classmates. "What happened to So-and-so?" "Where is So-and-so practicing?" "Did So-and-so ever make partner?" "Is So-and-so married? Does she have kids?" On and on. We happily oblige when we can, but our research is still incomplete.

We must return to the task of tracking down the women of Harvard Law 1974 individually, for we know their story is an important one. By the time our research is completed we will have talked in person with more than fifty women from the class and interviewed almost all the others by telephone. Their views will have been compared to those of women from earlier classes and to the views of some of the men in their class. But rather than present a collective class portrait, we have chosen to tell the story of the class through the personal stories of twelve women whose lives and experiences are reflective of the group. Each of these twelve has tackled a key issue facing young professionals and women everywhere: how to crack into the corporate arena as a young woman; how to make an impact in the lower-paying but equally important public interest sphere; how to deal with the problem of career burnout; how to deal with the even more critical problem of balancing career and family; how to confront the demon of sex discrimination and the lack of women partners at major law firms; and, for the select few who have already made it to the top, what it takes to stay there. The twelve women whose lives are chronicled in this book were and most still are among those most determined to conquer what may be the last great male bastion: the practice of law.

2

Corporate
Climb

During the Griswold era Harvard Law School's primary mission was to fill the nation's leading law firms with young associates. To this day, virtually all of the most prestigious firms, including Boston's Ropes & Gray and Wall Street's Sullivan & Cromwell, are heavily populated by Harvard Law alumni. (Ropes derives sixty percent of its 200-plus attorneys from Harvard.) By the mid-1950s, with Griswold's enthusiastic welcome, hundreds of law firms were coming to Cambridge to conduct on-campus interviews and to recruit new associates, and in 1956 the director of the school's placement office hailed the dawning of an era in which there would be "jobs for all."[1] There was, however, one notable exception: for the law school's small cadre of female alumnae, the doors to law firms were still closed.

By 1974 the situation had changed so dramatically that the women in the class were actually receiving as many offers from the top-tier firms as the men, if not more. In large part the reason for the turnabout was simple: in the late 1960s and early 1970s a series of embarrassing sex discrimination suits had been filed against the most prestigious firms, including New York's Sullivan & Cromwell and Rogers & Wells, by

[1] Seligman, Joel, *The High Citadel,* ibid p. 91.

disappointed female job seekers from New York University and Columbia law schools. In all, ten suits were filed, challenging the firms' dismal records on hiring and promoting qualified women. The suits were eventually settled, with the firms pledging to increase dramatically the number of women in their ranks. (Rogers & Wells even agreed to set aside twenty-five percent of its associate positions for female applicants and Sullivan & Cromwell offered to cease holding firm-wide functions at clubs that excluded women.) Their collective attitude seemed to be, "If we must hire women, at least let's get them with a Harvard Law pedigree."

The practical result of this new recruiting drive was that in 1974, for the first time in Harvard Law School's history, a higher percentage of women (sixty-nine percent) than men (fifty-eight percent)[2] in a graduating class started their careers at private firms. The 49 women in the class of 1974 who went to firms were acutely aware of the new possibilities and challenges that lay before them, so different from the dead-end situations that their counterparts from the 1950s and 1960s faced. But few were under the illusion that, once in the door, the corporate climb to partnership was going to be easy.

"There was a wave of armchair liberalism at the time," says Ellen Marshall, a member of the class who signed on at Los Angeles' McKenna, Conner & Cuneo. "One of the easier things to do was hire some women and minorities." Roslyn Daum carefully scrutinized the firms at which she was interviewed. Boston's Choate, Hall & Stewart, where she accepted an associate's position (and eventually rose to partnership), had two women partners and a number of female associates. "It seemed to convey a real acceptance of women," she says. "That was not so apparent at the other firms where I interviewed. I got the feeling I'd be a novelty,

2. Figures for the men in the class supplied by Harvard Law School. Statistics for the women corrected by authors.

the first woman lawyer. They seemed to be terribly anxious to hire a woman to fill their woman quota."

Whatever their true motives, the very fact that the firms were hiring so many women from the class was a revolutionary development, particularly when compared to the situation that existed in the 1950s. Loretta Holway, class of 1956, remembers standing outside one of her classrooms with a group of other third-year women discussing the difficulty of obtaining job interviews. Their professor overheard them. "Nonsense," he told them. "Why, none of you is going to have any trouble getting jobs whatsoever. Any of you will get jobs as legal secretaries at any firm."

"We just stood there with our mouths open," Holway recalls. "He thought he was being kind and reassuring. It was amazing how we accepted those kinds of putdowns."

Despite membership on *Law Review,* Ruth Bader Ginsburg, class of 1959, could not get a foot in Wall Street's door. "They all thought women would leave to marry and have babies," Ginsburg explains. She finally landed a job clerking for a judge and is now, following a distinguished career in academia, a federal judge on the prestigious D.C. Court of Appeals. The few women who did manage to land jobs as associates were shuttled into the trusts and estates departments, mostly drawing up wills. They dealt with family-oriented legal matters rather than corporate work and toiled for years as "permanent associates," never put on the same track to partnership as the men who graduated from law school with them. Ruth Weinstein, class of 1957, knew she wanted to specialize in corporate law, but at the few downtown firms that deigned to grant her an interview she was immediately steered toward trusts and estates. At one Wall Street interview, she recalls, "I was sent out to lunch with a lady from the trusts and estates department. She was of indeterminate age, probably in her fifties, with steel-rimmed glasses and a gray suit. She worked in a windowless office with estate ad-

ministration files and she took me to lunch in the basement of
Schrafft's, which was also windowless, with four other ladies
of similar appearance, similar occupation, similarly dressed.
When the check came they divided it to the penny among the
five of them, being, I guess, very familiar with numbers from
estate administration. I took a look around the table and I
said, 'If this is it, I'm not going to practice law.' '' Weinstein
eventually found a job at a small midtown firm where she
could do mainstream corporate work. She is now a partner.

Sexist episodes were still common during the interviewing
season for the class of 1974 nearly twenty years later. When a
member of the class, Sandra Froman, expressed her prefer-
ence for litigation to one firm's hiring partner, he brusquely
informed her that the few women his firm hired did exclusively trusts and estates work. A partner from a San Francisco
firm told her, "We hired a woman last year," as if they had
filled a quota. Another member from the class was asked to
stand up and turn around during an interview with a New
York firm, and still another was discouraged from pursuing a
specialty in labor law because, she was warned, "our clients
like to cuss and drink beer."

Most of the firms were more careful about how they presented themselves at interviews. The year before the women
of 1974 arrived at the law school, one well-known New York
firm, Parker Chapin & Flattau, was banished from interviewing on campus for a year because of remarks made by one of
its recruiting partners. Two female students complained to
Harvard's placement office that the partner had told them the
firm hired neither blacks nor women because one of the senior partners did not believe in hiring them. Parker, Chapin's
exile from Harvard Law School recruiting, while temporary,
sent a stern warning to other firms.

The ill-advised comment made by the Parker, Chapin
recruiting partner may have reflected the unfortunate reality
at several firms. Despite the fact that young women were in

demand for the first time in the legal profession's history, there were many senior partners at firms across the country who still felt that women did not belong in the profession. The women of Harvard Law School 1974 set out to prove them wrong, and Susan Chan and Deborah Fiedler, who arrived at Harvard Law School from completely different backgrounds, left three years later with the same goal: to break through the sex barrier of the elite corporate firm.

Susan Chan McCarthy felt a sense of pleasant anticipation as she strode through Graham & James's elegant reception area, with its lush oriental carpets and gleaming mahogany furniture. The simply framed navigation maps on the wall and the foreign newspapers and magazines neatly arranged on the coffee tables underscored the firm's burgeoning presence in the Far East and in maritime law. It was exciting to be starting her job as a first-year associate. Launching her career at one of San Francisco's most respected law firms, Susan felt that she and her husband, Mike, whom she had married after her second year at Harvard Law School, were starting to build a future in San Francisco. Her mood was still up from the previous day, when she had celebrated her twenty-fifth birthday.

The fact that Susan was beginning her career at Graham & James was in and of itself an astonishing accomplishment, given her journey from childhood. She grew up in San Francisco's crowded Chinatown. Her family fled to the city after the Communist takeover of China, where Susan was born in September 1949, a month before the coup. Her grandfather had been a peasant landowner, and the family owned the silk, goldsmith and pharmaceutical shops in their village. Practically everything the family owned was confiscated during the "liberation." When Susan was just a year old her mother fled to Hong Kong with her and her older brother, where they waited until Susan's father was able to send for the family to join him in San Francisco.

Her Chinese name was Chen Li-ling but she entered the United States at the age of two as "Susie Mak." Her father had adopted the new name when he immigrated, a fictitious "paper name" used for entry into the United States. A nurse gave her the name "Susie" when she arrived in San Francisco, because her mother didn't know what to call her. Then, about ten years later, during what the Chinese refer to as a "confession period," the United States Government permitted the family to take back the name Chan, and she was naturalized as Susie Chan.

Life in California was difficult and confusing for the new arrivals, who spoke no English and had few local contacts. While her father spoke some English, he seldom lived with the family because of chronic illness. Although he had previously found work as a laborer, he contracted tuberculosis and was confined to a sanitarium soon after her arrival and during most of the time she was in elementary school. A younger sister was born in 1954. Then, in a tragic twist of fate, her father developed leukemia in the late 1950s and was hospitalized on the public roll at San Francisco General Hospital. Too young and healthy to visit the wards, Susan, her brother and little sister stood outside the hospital and waved up at their sick father from the hospital courtyard. He died when she was twelve, and because he had been sick during so much of her childhood, she felt she had never really known him.

Susan's mother, on the other hand, was a strong Cantonese woman. She struggled to raise the children with what work she could find, usually piecework in the little garment factories of Chinatown at the prevailing sweatshop wages. It was a rude awakening for a woman who had had her own maid in pre-Communist China. Through her mother's example, Susan concluded it was necessary for a woman to work. "Without ever being lectured at, it just sort of crept in under my skin that I would expect to find work in due course and that I would be able to take care of myself and those around me," Susan recalls, sitting in the newly planted garden behind her house in a suburb of San Francisco. "I always saw that she had to struggle for a living, and that education was extremely important to what you could do."

Susan Chan attended predominantly Chinese elementary and junior high schools, where most children arrived speaking no English and were confronted by a painful social hierarchy. "In junior high school the kids categorized others according to when they arrived and whether they spoke English," she remembers. " 'FOBs' were 'fresh off the boat.' And then there was 'ABC,' which was the American-born Chinese, who knew English and was considered more 'with it.' At that time, in the early sixties, the Chinese government was not recognized as a nation and not mentioned in the press, except disparagingly. There wasn't a great deal of stock then in identifying yourself as being Chinese."

As one of the brightest students, Susan easily gained entry to Lowell High School, one of the best public schools in San Francisco. Almost all of her Chinese friends aspired to attend Lowell, which had a rigorous college preparatory program and was, at the time, eighty percent white. With a Lowell background, admittance to a reasonably good college was almost guaranteed and Susan, with her excellent academic record at Lowell, not only was admitted to Wellesley College but also was awarded the Procter & Gamble scholarship for her class. To this day she jokingly urges her friends to buy Procter & Gamble toothpastes.

Susan loved her years at Wellesley. To fill in her roots, she studied Mandarin and pursued a joint major in Chinese and political science. Wellesley also provided her with her first glimpse into the professional class, and she liked the idea of having a "career." The foreign service had the most dramatic appeal to her young mind, but she scrapped that idea after spending the summer of 1970 working in the State Department, in the Intelligence and Research Section for Communist Chinese Affairs. At the time, William Rogers was Secretary of State. The State Department's power was at a low ebb, its influence preempted by that of Henry Kissinger and the National Security Council. She was shocked that those on the Cambodia and Vietnam desks at State seemed as surprised as the public to learn about the 1970 Cambodian "incursion." Also, Susan noticed that there were very few senior women in the service. It was apparent that a female foreign service officer on assignment would need to be able to move her family frequently. Few men with careers would pick up and follow a wife.

During her sophomore year Susan began dating Michael McCarthy, a first-year student at Harvard Law School, and at Mike's suggestion she attended a few classes at the law school. It was her first exposure to the law, since she had never known any lawyers while growing up, and she found the subject matter surprisingly interesting; law certainly seemed more appealing to her than an academic career in Chinese affairs, another potential career choice. When her own acceptance letter from Harvard Law School arrived she was certain that she wanted to pursue law too.

As Mike began his career at an old-line firm in New York, Breed, Abbott & Morgan, Susan buckled down to the first-year grind at Harvard. When she wasn't in New York on weekends she was studying. Like most of her classmates, she rarely volunteered in class. Somewhat shy by nature, Susan was relieved to discover that she would not be graded on the number of times her hand shot up in the air. Nevertheless she made sure she was always prepared, just in case she was called on. She read more than she had ever read in her life, so much that she had to switch from hard to soft contact lenses because her eyes began bothering her.

Although she was aware women constituted a small minority at the law school, Susan was not particularly attuned to women's issues or even ethnic ones. The women who served as role models in her life were strong individuals, like her mother, and only once had Susan felt the sting of being doubly in a minority. At Wellesley she had overheard a classmate from the South refer to her as "that little Chinese girl." The woman didn't mean to hurt her feelings but, coming from cosmopolitan San Francisco, Susan was surprised to be identified by her race. She did attend one of the meetings of the Women's Law Association but she didn't empathize with its aims. One of the speakers was raving about how terrific she thought it was that a professor's new book used a woman as the criminal, how marvelous it was for women to have the active roles, not always to be the victims.

She was aware of how different her background was from her classmates', some of whom were at Harvard Law School almost by birthright. Many were the children of the rich and influential. One of the students in her section was the son of a federal judge. Her friend Wendy Singer had lived in Europe and spoke fluent German and French. "They were the children of newspaper editors and professionals and they had dinner table conversations about the great issues of the day. I was still pretty dense then, not thinking much about how different I was from many of the other people at college and in law school," Susan recalls.

Nevertheless Susan was not intimidated by the self-assurance and superior airs of some of her Harvard Law classmates. She was used to stiff competition, and in her own quiet way she was just as determined to succeed as anyone else at the law school. She didn't walk around the campus with that "I am the best" swagger that some students had when they arrived in Cambridge. Most of them lost that desperate need to impress after the first year, anyway. The One L experience was a humbling one for almost everyone.

Perhaps because she had lived under pressure at an earlier

age and had survived, law school was sometimes even enjoyable for Susan Chan, who always flourished when she was intellectually challenged. Being able to talk with Mike, who had been through the experience of Harvard Law School, helped. Mike was practicing in corporate law, the field Susan, too, chose for concentration. Although she took a few courses in Harvard's world-famous East Asian Legal Studies program, under the direction of China scholar Jerome Cohen, she stuck to the law school's core curriculum, which provided the basics for a corporate practice—tax, commercial transactions, corporations and contracts. She knew she wanted to launch her career in a business practice at a law firm. "I always had this fascination about it [business], not having been involved with any family business. It always seemed to me that that was sort of the economic engine for society. I think I just assumed I would go into a law firm because that's where you represented the major business clients," she explains.

After law school she returned to her home turf, depending on the same toughness and confidence that had carried her through Harvard to bring her through her first year as a Graham & James associate. She had clerked at Graham & James the summer after her second year at law school. When the firm offered her the summer clerkship she accepted provided she be allowed to clerk half of the summer at New York's Sullivan & Cromwell. She had wanted the option of taking a job in New York, where Mike was working. But during the course of her second year Mike had grown restless with his work at Breed, Abbott, which consisted mainly of handling "blue sky" work, involving technical state securities laws for one major client, Avon Products. They both agreed that San Francisco would be a better city than New York to raise a family, and they decided to move to California. Accordingly, Susan accepted an associate position when Graham & James extended her an offer at the end of the summer.

Mike landed a job in the legal department of Bank of America. Having watched Mike put in punishing hours at Breed, Abbott, Susan knew she was probably in for a difficult time that would make the rigors of Harvard Law School seem mild by comparison. But she was ready for a new challenge and anxious to build their new life in her old hometown.

The world of corporate law was as far removed from Susan Chan's background as anything could be, which was, in large part, why she was so attracted to it. Other women in the class were drawn to corporate law firms not through a conscious decision, like Susan's, but because at Harvard going the corporate route represented the path of least resistance. The firms had the resources to come to campus to interview and then pay to fly potential recruits to the home office for more intense wooing. The law school's curriculum was also heavy on the essentials of corporate practice, and corporate law was billed by many members of the faculty as being the most intellectually challenging. The $15,000-plus starting salaries offered by most firms was also part of the magnetism. Given all these factors, it is hardly surprising that many of the men and women who came to Harvard Law School during the early 1970s with ill-defined notions of what kind of lawyers they wanted to be left, three years later, with their noses pointing toward Wall Street and State Street.

Deborah Fiedler was typical of those who drifted toward law firms without knowing precisely why. Throughout law school she worried that law was an "uncaring" profession. Her ambivalence became so perplexing that she dropped out of Harvard for a number of months to ponder whether she had made a mistake in choosing law school over attending medical school. But when she finally returned to the law school Debbie decided to work at a firm, even though some of her happiest moments were spent working in the law school's legal aid program. Although she was a child of privilege—her father was the famous Boston Pops conductor Arthur Fiedler—Debbie, like Susan Chan, had not been exposed to the business world and she was curious about it. Harvard Law School provided an easy route to Wall Street.

The Wall Street firm was, and is, a species all its own, where bloodlines sometimes matter more than brains. It is an intensely masculine world, where the very word "partner" is still spoken in reverential tones, as if synonymous with blood brother. Despite the fact that there were more than 13,000 women lawyers in 1970, about five percent of the legal population, fewer than one percent of the lawyers on Wall Street were women. By 1974, the year Debbie and nineteen other women from the class headed to Wall Street (joining some of the very firms that were targets of the recently settled sex discrimination suits), most of the major firms still had only a tiny sprinkling of female associates and lacked a single woman partner. The firm that Debbie decided to join, Cleary, Gottlieb, Steen & Hamilton, was a bit looser than some of the older Wall Street firms. Although Cleary did not have any women partners, there were more women in the associate ranks, and practice areas traditionally closed to women, such as litigation and corporate law, were opening up. Debbie was eager to take advantage of the changing times.

Cleary, Gottlieb occupied several floors of a gleaming, modern tower at 1 State Street Plaza, and many of the offices had panoramic views of Battery Park and the Statue of Liberty. Debbie had weighed Cleary's offer against an equally tempting one from another Wall Street firm. Both firms had offices overseas, and Debbie thought that at some point she would like to spend time abroad working for an American law firm.

Cleary, Gottlieb, one of the few ethnically mixed firms on Wall Street, represented a wide array of powerhouse clients, including the investment banking firm, Salomon Brothers,

Inc. and Pan American World Airways. The law firm had been founded in 1946 by a group of defecting partners from the old Root, Clark, Buckner & Ballantine firm, the predecessor of the famous Wall Street firm, Dewey, Ballantine, Bushby, Palmer & Wood. The reasons for the split had been shrouded in mystery, but the Cleary, Gottlieb contingent took many key clients, including Salomon Brothers, with them. Rumor had it that Leo Gottlieb, then the most prominent Jewish lawyer on Wall Street, who represented several Guggenheims and Lehmans, as well as Federated Department Stores, had wanted his name on the shingle at Root, Clark and that the blue bloods there had refused. Others attributed the split to a fight over money.[3] Whatever the reasons, Gottlieb's new firm quickly became one of the top international firms in New York. Partner George Ball, who later served as Under Secretary of State during the Kennedy and Johnson administrations and as a U.S. representative to the United Nations, brought in such clients as the French government. At the time Debbie joined, the firm had an activist reputation, sending its associates into the ghettos to handle pro bono landlord-tenant disputes and civil rights cases, as well as teaching them to handle complex corporate transactions and multimillion-dollar financings. Like so many women in her class, Debbie thought she wanted to be a corporate lawyer and believed Cleary would provide her with excellent corporate law training.

Her path to corporate law had been bumpy. First she had to put up a fight with her father just to get to law school. As the beloved conductor of the Pops, Fiedler projected a jolly, grandfatherly image, with his white hair and mustache. The public adored him. He had introduced two generations of Bostonians to classical music, with his summer concerts on Boston's Esplanade. In private, however, he could be a stern

[3] Paul Hoffman, *Lions in the Street* (New York: Saturday Review Press, 1973), p. 63.

perfectionist who had trouble showing the love he had for his family. He had married at fifty, after what he often described as "a charming bachelorhood." Because his three children had come late in life, and because he had a busy career that often kept him on the road, he did not devote a lot of time to them.

Having a famous father made Debbie all the more determined to have a career of her own. Also, she felt that having a profession was a way for a woman to gain "respect and an entry ticket" to influence. "I picked law because it was intellectually challenging and because in those days it was considered to be a way of changing society within a legal, or nonrevolutionary, framework." But "Papa" did not believe that his two daughters should have careers and he thought the law was a boring profession. When Debbie made it known she might want to attend law school in California after graduation from Radcliffe, her father exploded. He told her in no uncertain terms that if she went to California he would not contribute a penny toward her education. Papa's theory, which Debbie thought had some practical basis, was that a Harvard degree would serve her better than a Boalt (University of California at Berkeley) or Stanford degree. "In addition, that was the late 1960s, and I think he was worried about all of the campus unrest at the universities out in California during that time," she recalls. "Now, on a deeper level, I think it was more a matter of his wanting to have his children around him." During the summer after graduation from Radcliffe, Debbie finally decided to follow her father's advice and she accepted Harvard's offer.

After battling to get to law school, Debbie hated it almost from the start. It was difficult for her to believe that Harvard Law School, located just a few blocks away from Radcliffe, could be so totally different from the undergraduate college. "I remember feeling overwhelmed, that it was a huge place, larger in feeling than Harvard had been during my Radcliffe years," she recalls. Her undergraduate professors had been genuinely interested in her intellectual development, and she hadn't hesitated to speak out in class. In contrast, the students at the law school were alienated from one another, suspicious and competitive.

In class the professors acted like disapproving fathers and, like many of her fellow students, she felt that volunteering in class was just an invitation to a verbal dressing down. She sat in the huge lecture halls, staring at the gloomy portraits of old English judges that decorated the walls, with a growing sense of discontent. "At Radcliffe you just went off and did your own thing. You weren't compared to anybody else. But in law school you had this feeling everybody was in there kind of running for the same carrot, and I didn't like that because you can't help but compare yourself to other people. I have my own standards and I do pretty well by them ordinarily, but I remember feeling very uncomfortable about the peer competition at Harvard."

For Debbie, like many first-year students, the Socratic method was hard to follow, and it was the first time in her life that she didn't easily master the course material. The professors took hours just to get relatively simple points across, and the adversarial teaching methods used by some of them were not to her liking. "I don't react well to the whip," she explains. The competitive atmosphere did frighten her into studying hard, but she did not do very well on her first-year midterm practice exams. She was feeling somewhat panicked and her contracts professor, Jack Dawson, tried to reassure her. "First-year students always feel that way," he patiently told her. "All of you learn at different paces, but by the end of the year the material will fall into place for you," Dawson promised.

If the Socratic method was supposed to teach One Ls how to think like lawyers, the Ames Competition held the fall of first year, commonly known as Moot Court, was supposed to teach them how to perform like lawyers. As part of the competition, which was required of all first-year students, One Ls argued appellate cases in pairs before a judicial panel comprised of senior faculty members, prominent practitioners and real judges. The teams, which were arbitrarily assigned to argue on the plaintiff or defendant side, were supervised by third-year students, who helped prepare them for the grilling they would get from the panel during oral argument. After hearing each side's argument, the judges ruled for one side or the other. Rumor had it that some students, driven by the intense competition, sliced pages out of case reports that were needed by their opponents to prepare their arguments.

When it came time for Moot Court, Debbie had the bad luck to end up with a partner who she felt was a goof-off who refused to take responsibility for his share of the work. She went to see Vice Dean William Bruce to complain about the situation. As they talked in his office Debbie raised the possibility of taking time off from law school. Bruce launched into a patronizing speech about the rigors of the first year. He seemed to be thinking, "Here we go again, one of *these* women, we let them in and then they go and let us down." Bruce told her that she could postpone Moot Court but warned her that if she took a leave of absence from Harvard he could not guarantee her a place if she decided to return. Also, he stressed, she had to make good use of her time off. "You can't just go and smoke pot in Katmandu," he told her. Under the threat of eternal banishment, she decided to opt out of Ames but continue at the law school, at least for the time being.

Professor Dawson was right—the class material did begin to fall into place during the spring semester and she felt confident going into her final exams. In the end her studying paid off—she ended up with As and Bs in her courses. Feeling relieved to have made it through first year, Debbie took off for Washington, D.C., for the summer, where she worked at the U. S. Department of Housing and Urban Development, in preparation for a second-year seminar on housing law problems organized by one of her professors.

But despite the successful denouement of her first year, Debbie was still unsure whether she really wanted to study law when she returned to Cambridge to begin her second year. After completing the first semester she decided that taking a leave was her best course of action. The break gave Debbie time to think about what she wanted to do with her life. She flirted with the idea of going to medical school, but since she did not have a science background she thought starting a full premedical course load, from calculus to chemistry, would only further postpone her career. Besides, she did not want to be a dilettante who drifted from one career idea to the next. Although she still had doubts about whether she wanted to be a lawyer or even finish Harvard Law School, she decided to return to complete what she had started.

When Debbie came back she found to her surprise that she liked law school better. She concentrated on her studies and worked hard at the Harvard Legal Aid Bureau. The cases at the Bureau were difficult and sometimes depressing but also challenging. She handled routine uncontested divorces and landlord-tenant cases, and defended psychiatric patients contesting involuntary hospitalizations or transfers. Although she found the work interesting, she ruled out becoming a litigator. "I really hated court," she recalls. "Unlike my father, I am not a performer, and it just didn't appeal to my personality to be a litigator."

With its combination of high-powered corporate practice, international work and pro bono reputation, Cleary, Gottlieb was a good spot for an intense, idealistic young woman like Debbie. It was a relief to be leaving Boston, where her name was practically a household word, and the insularity of Harvard. In the end Debbie graduated from Harvard Law School cum laude. *Harvard Law School Magazine* carried a picture of her sitting next to Papa at the graduation luncheon. Though her path to this world had been a little less surefooted than those of some of her classmates, Debbie Fiedler had finally gained back her enthusiasm for law. It helped to know that Papa, who had originally opposed her choice of careers, was now obviously pleased with her achievement. At last she felt she had earned his respect.

With a sense of excitement, she and classmate Christine Hickman packed up a truck and drove to New York. Debbie was moving into her aunt's empty apartment in Murray Hill, catercorner to the prim Martha Washington Hotel for women, with an old friend from prep school. For two bedrooms and two baths, the women would pay a mere $175 a month. Splitting the rent, Debbie would be living in relative luxury on her $19,500 salary. Now, if Cleary only proved to be half as exciting as she hoped, life in New York held infinite promise.

Beginning the corporate climb, Debbie Fiedler and Susan McCarthy shared the same professional goal. They wanted to pay their dues as associates at large firms and aim for partnership. And for these bright, capable women of a new generation partnership was, for the first time, a reasonable hope. In all but token cases partnership at major firms was totally out of reach for the Harvard Law women of the 1950s and 1960s. During this era many extremely qualified women lawyers dutifully accepted jobs as permanent associates with no real hope of career advancement. Judith Leonard, Harvard Law School class of 1954, has been an associate in the trusts and estates department of New York's Shearman & Sterling for the past twenty-eight years. Realizing that her partnership chances were nil, Leonard tailored her ambitions to fit the male-dominated culture of the firm and settled into estate administration. "I had a feeling it might be dull," she recalls, "because they shuffled women into it." But she found the work to her liking and the more regular hours made it possible for Leonard to raise four children and continue working. Although her father was a partner at Cravath, Swaine & Moore and her husband is a senior partner at Wall Street's Davis Polk & Wardwell, Leonard claims she has been content with her lesser status. "I didn't have that much fiery ambition, I guess. I really didn't expect it," she explains. "I think when I came out of law school, basically the feeling was that one was very grateful to have a job much less ever be considered for partnership. You really felt you'd conquered something by being hired. If I were starting out today," she adds, "I suspect I would be more inclined to be swept up in a feeling that one should move ahead."

Loretta Holway, Harvard Law class of 1956, has also worked as an associate her entire career. At Boston's Ropes & Gray, where she works in the firm's labor department, Holway says she admires the younger women who are gunning for partnership. "I don't have that kind of energy," she says. "My compromise is a satisfying one. You had a very different expectation of what women could achieve coming out of Harvard Law School in 1956 than you do today." Holway was less complacent when she began her career at a much smaller Boston firm. When she found out, after five years of service, that the firm was paying a brand-new male recruit more than she was earning, she quit. (When Frederica Brenneman, class of 1953, landed her first job in Boston, she was paid the difference between a lawyer's wage and her husband's weekly salary in the Army. She netted $35 a week.)

Interviewing on Wall Street, Doris Carroll, class of 1960, found expectations for women lawyers just as low. "I wish we could get a girl to just sit in the library and write," one hiring partner told her. "But I suppose if we hired you on that very limited basis the next thing you'd want is to go to court."

Without any job offers, Carroll says she was "so desperate that I would have said yes," but she was never offered the research job. She finally landed a job with a solo practitioner and later joined New York's Paul, Weiss, Rifkind, Wharton & Garrison, where she is a permanent associate.

At least Susan McCarthy and most of her classmates didn't face these extreme obstacles. She had been well treated during her months as a summer associate, rotating among Graham & James's three floors in the Alaska Commercial Bank Building, getting a feel for the firm's different practice areas. In the end she had decided she wanted to specialize in corporate and tax, and the firm honored her request without ever uttering the words "trusts and estates."

Three other associates started with Susan at Graham & James, but she was one of only two women lawyers at the firm. Graham & James had previously hired two other women associates, one who did trusts and estates work, and a second who had started the prior year. Both had left the firm. In checking out what lore she could find about the firm, Susan had heard various stories about why the associates had left. There was the perhaps apocryphal story about the second woman associate, who had written a memorandum for a prominent senior partner; when he criticized it sarcastically she supposedly balled it up and threw it at him. One fairly prominent member of the San Francisco bar, whom Susan had met the previous summer, claimed that when she had applied to the firm while at law school in Boston several years earlier, she had been advised that there was an opening for a librarian.

It struck Susan as a historical accident that she might make history at Graham & James by becoming one of its first women partners. "You get to a point where, you know, you're the first something or other," she reasoned. She did not worry that she would be treated differently at the firm because she was female, or that she would have to work harder than her male colleagues to prove herself. It would take many years for these realities to sink in.

Although the firm gave her work in the practice areas of her choice, it took a year before Susan, who was somewhat insecure as a brand-new lawyer anyway, felt appreciated. The two partners she worked with her first year, she recalls, were renowned for being difficult—Richard Eastman, a corporate partner, and Norman Laboe, a tax partner. Susan had written a long memo for Laboe the previous summer while rotating through his department, and she felt they had "clicked." Now he needed someone to learn the ins and outs of a new federal pension law that had been enacted on September 2, 1974, the day before she started at the firm as an associate. Known as ERISA—the Employee Retirement Income Security Act of 1974—the statute revolutionized pension practice and required changes in all the retirement plans of the firm's corporate clients. When Susan showed up for work Laboe gave her the massive new ERISA bill and told her to memorize it. She did not know it at the time, but she was being steered toward a detail-oriented specialty into which a number of the women in her law school class were automatically funneled. In fact, in the 1970s, ERISA became what trusts and estates was to women in the 1950s and 1960s. "I didn't know whether to object or not. It was all right. I didn't have any preconceptions that I would or wouldn't like it. I was sort of like a blank slate and I was prepared to be written on," Susan says.

Laboe ended up becoming her friend and mentor in tax matters, but Eastman was another story. Charming when he wanted to be, and well regarded for his legal skills, he seemed to have a knack for making his underlings—both men and women—feel totally inadequate. Even some of his partners considered him abrasive and too bearish with young associates, whom he went through at the rate of one each year. In one routine client meeting she had attended with

Eastman, the client had used a French term with which Susan
was unfamiliar. When she asked what the word meant Eastman responded that it was an expression everyone should
know. Although she had long since forgotten the word in
question, she would always remember how embarrassed she
had felt. Susan assumed her progress at the firm depended on
whether or not she was able to please Eastman, and yet time
and again she found him impossible to please. Too afraid to
talk to other partners about the situation, there were two or
three nights when, after a trying day with her boss, Susan
went home to Mike in tears.

There were advantages to working for two of the firm's
toughest taskmasters. The experience of the first few months
turned her into a perfectionist who second-guessed every
move and anticipated every question. At the end of her first
year, when she left Eastman for a new assignment on a different floor, she learned that her hard work at the firm had not
gone unnoticed. "She was terrifically thorough," recalls Al-
exander (Sandy) Calhoun, one of the firm's top corporate
partners. Susan's entire outlook about her future at the firm
brightened. "It was like moving from the storm to the sun,"
she recalls. "It was a wonderful discovery to find that people
liked my work, that I was a good lawyer, I was competent."

There was even a moment of glory at the beginning of her
second year. She was assigned to handle a $4.5-million clos-
ing of a loan from Citibank to a vineyard in Visalia, California. "I was super well prepared," she remembers. "I mean, I
was so prepared that I brought a giant stapler with me so that
all of the essential documents could be bound and distributed
at the closing. I was going to be perfect on the transaction."
A state of emergency was declared almost from the moment
she arrived; at the last minute the other side had lost all the
written consents. These documents had to be presented before the closing papers could be filed. Susan spent three
hours working with the parties to arrange an alternative

method of closing the deal without jeopardizing Citibank's interests. The deal would close on time after all. "I felt like the hero of the day!" she recalls. At a celebratory lunch the Citibank executives told her to upgrade her return ticket to San Francisco from regular coach to first class. "It's that kind of thing, when you're a second-year associate, that makes you feel you're competent, you're good, and you're well respected." Calhoun would remember her work on the deal ten years later as a real standout performance.

Susan continued to handle the meat-and-potatoes work of an associate—drafting memos, licensing agreements and doing research, but she was also getting more up-front client contact and she was developing a niche for herself in the employee benefit/executive compensation area, having become the firm's resident ERISA expert. When the Bank of Tokyo of California, a wholesale bank that was one of the firm's top clients, swallowed Southern California First National Bank, a retail bank operating in Southern California, Susan drafted the employee benefit plans for the multimillion-dollar merger. With Laboe, she flew down to Southern California to meet with actuaries and bank officers, feeling very much the respected legal adviser. A by-product of getting more responsibility was being in the office past midnight on many occasions. But Mike was working long hours too. They had both decided to put most of their efforts into launching their respective careers.

Despite her earlier ambivalence about her choice of careers, Debbie Fiedler also ended up thriving as a new associate. She loved her work and life at Cleary, Gottlieb from the start. While her counterparts at other firms were complaining about getting the drudge work nobody else wanted, Debbie eagerly buried herself in her assignments and felt she learned more in her first three months at Cleary than she had learned in her entire three years at Harvard Law School. "I loved the people at Cleary and I liked the practice a lot. Working in New York that first year at Cleary was an incredibly exhilarating experience," she recalls. "I wanted to know as much as the senior people right away."

The class of associates hired by Cleary, Gottlieb in the fall of 1974 was an unusually high-powered group. Besides Debbie, about half of the new recruits were from Harvard Law School, including two other women, Wendy Singer and Susan Roosevelt. Debbie started out doing work that was typical for first-year associates—researching and drafting memos for partners and senior associates—and she immediately put in a bid for an assignment abroad. London was her first choice and as a result of her request Debbie was picked to work with lawyers who handled international financings, such as Peter Darrow, a senior associate who was close to being considered for partnership. Darrow had been Cleary's first associate in the London office, and his sharp wit made him fun to work with. He was an example of how Cleary treated talented young lawyers. The firm pushed them along as fast as they could go.

Under Darrow's tutelage she researched some interesting bankruptcy questions relating to syndicated loans being arranged for Burmah Oil Company. Cleary, Gottlieb represented the Bank of England as the guarantor of the multimillion-dollar financing. The transaction was interesting because it involved novel questions in bankruptcy law and was completed under tremendous time pressure. The partner in charge of the London office, Lee Hudson, had been reluctant to bring a woman lawyer into that office out of fear that English clients might object to having a woman lawyer handle their affairs. However, Hudson was sufficiently impressed with Debbie's work during the Burmah Oil transaction to be convinced by the firm's Personnel Committee that she was right for the assignment.

Although Debbie Fiedler received good assignments and

did not feel she was treated differently at her firm because of her sex, many of the women from their law school graduating class were not so lucky. They continued to experience problems that lingered from generations past. "The whole time I worked on Wall Street," says one woman from the class, "I felt like a stranger in a strange land."

"When I first came to work here," recalls Anne Redman, now a corporate partner at one of Seattle's leading firms, Foster, Pepper & Riviera, "there were attorneys who just didn't know how to behave and some who had never really had to deal with women in business. They made stupid remarks and stupid jokes and didn't always treat you like an attorney. They've changed their ways. You'd have to say, 'Don't call me Gumdrop in front of the client,' or, 'When I walk into a room, please introduce me as an associate,' because back then lots of people assumed you were a secretary or a paralegal and you really did have to make sure that when you were introduced they understood. There were lots of times they understood and nonetheless assumed that you were going to be a real powder puff."

Shortly after Redman's arrival a partner walked into her office and brusquely informed her that he opposed the idea of hiring women lawyers. "I don't think we should have hired you," Redman says the partner told her. "Everyone disagrees with me, but I thought I should tell you that." Redman describes the incident as "an absurd exchange."

Partners at other firms displayed their discomfort with having young women in their ranks more subtly. At New York's Kaye, Scholer, Fierman, Hays & Handler, Karen Katzman perceived that some senior partners seemed reluctant to take women under their wings in the same way they brought along young male associates. "Those who went in for locker-room chitchat felt very uncomfortable and stifled with a woman sitting in their office," says Katzman. "There were some partners who I think were probably a little uncomfortable dealing with women when I was first an associate," says Mary Nelson of her early career at Boston's Hill & Barlow. "I remember thinking about certain senior people that they seemed a little unsure of how to talk to a woman about corporate matters or client matters or general business subjects. They'd never had dealings with a woman on things like that." In most cases, Nelson believes, the discomfort was "a function of age. The people I have in mind were at least thirty years older than I was." Both Katzman and Nelson made it to partnership.

Many of the women from the class complained of misplaced paternalism in the law firm world, of a kind of overbearing courtliness that was displayed toward young women attorneys. There were also occasional complaints of inferior work assignments. One woman from the class noticed that most of the other women in the litigation department at her Wall Street firm had been assigned to a giant case that had been droning on for several years. "They were stuck in the library for years," she claims, researching briefs, while the men in the department were learning the ropes of motion practice, getting out to take depositions. The assumption was that major clients would not want to be serviced by women lawyers. When the firm refused to reassign her after more than a year and a half on the case, she quit.

Others were content to stay in the back room. Ellen Marshall, who in her early career was the only female associate at Los Angeles' McKenna, Conner & Cuneo, was surprised when, during her second-year evaluation, she was criticized for not having enough client contact. "I thought it was a funny criticism to level at me," she recalls. "But it made me more self-conscious that it would be desirable to spend time with clients. I hadn't thought about that as a plus up to that point because I was a little self-conscious and young and I was just as happy being a back-room lawyer at that stage. I was in no particular hurry to rush out."

To survive at a firm, some members of the class believed that a woman's work had to be impeccable, that a woman might have to work harder than a male associate to stay on partnership track. Molly Munger remembers writing a memo during her first months as a litigation associate at Los Angeles' Agnew, Miller & Carlson on a minor point of civil procedure. "I remember thinking, 'This memo will be the first memo this person has ever received from a woman lawyer.'" She did not want to let the firm down, or other women who might follow in her footsteps. "There was enough pressure without having that kind of thought," she observes.

Debbie Fiedler was one of the lucky few who felt instant acceptance at her firm. With her dark hair, button nose and dark warm eyes, Debbie was extremely popular with the other associates—and often went out for dinner with her young colleagues after a long night of work. It was impossible for many of them to imagine the vivacious, energetic Fiedler as the uncertain and lonely law student that she felt she had been at Harvard. "I finally found a great big happy family, and I was getting paid for it, too!" she reflected years later.

Although she did not know it at the time, she would also find her future husband that first year. She met Ned Stiles, a forty-two-year-old corporate partner, one month after she started work, at a farewall party for one of the firm's associates in Cleary's spacious, sunny library. When Stiles strode into the room she noticed him immediately. He was handsome, with piercing blue eyes, hair that was beginning to turn a distinguished gray, and a trim, athletic build. They chatted briefly. He had a very slight drawl, having grown up, as he told her, in Kentucky. She was very attracted to Stiles but was keenly aware of the taboos against partner-associate romances.

Their first real confrontation came at a firm ritual known as Wranglers, a semiannual dinner party that was a holdover

from the Root, Clark days and an occasion for the initiation
of new associates. At the party each new associate was supposed to get up and make a short biographical speech, during
which the speaker was likely to be subjected to catcalling and
wrangling from the partners and older associates in the audi-
ence. After being teased by the older associates about what to
expect at the Wranglers hazing, Debbie and another female
associate organized the twenty-one new associates to be fully
prepared for the onslaught. Following the example of the
congressional impeachment proceedings in 1974, each new
associate got up, introduced the next new associate and ceded
his or her remaining time to the next. The traditional plan to
"wrangle" the new associates was ruined. Although one of
the firm's senior partners chided Debbie for dashing the
great tradition of Wranglers, several senior associates toasted
her for saving them from a litany of boring speeches.

Toward the end of the evening Stiles approached her for a
casual conversation, but it was obvious to her that he was
being flirtatious. While it might be a boost to her ego to be
wooed by a partner, Debbie knew an affair would be much
too dangerous at this early stage in her career. In fact it
would be a sure way to derail a promising future. She had
heard that other women at the firm had been driven out after
becoming involved in indiscreet relationships. Besides, Ned
Stiles was married and it wasn't her habit to become involved
with married men. She thought such affairs demonstrated an
avoidance of commitment.

However, later that year she began working with Stiles on
a number of public financings. She helped him on an important public financing for a French import-export bank that was
doing a large bond offering in the United States. The assignment was part of her grooming for Europe. Ned was a down-
to-earth lawyer and a good teacher. He was also charming
and fun to work with. For his part, Stiles was captivated by
Debbie's openness. Her liveliness contrasted sharply with

certain other women lawyers he knew, who seemed to stifle their personalities at work. Debbie's enthusiasm was contagious. They found more and more work to do together. For Lehman Brothers, they worked together on a major financing for a large minerals company. By coincidence, she was moved into the small office next to his. They began meeting for dinner after work and soon were involved in an intense love affair.

At Cleary the couple acted with collegial reserve. Debbie was not at all sure where the affair was leading. "I wasn't thinking about marriage or children or any of that. I just wanted to work hard and have as much fun as I could," she recalls. "I think we were both surprised about how involved we got with one another and how quickly it happened."

Her impending transfer to London hastened development of the relationship. They had started seeing one another in the spring, and by summer she had accepted the assignment abroad. Debbie firmly told Ned that he could make up his mind about their relationship before she left for London or afterward, but in any case she was going. She realized her posture was partly a defensive one—a move abroad would be a convenient escape hatch if their relationship lost steam. On impulse, Ned began talking about asking for a London assignment too. But the thought of him following her abroad with his family in tow made Debbie very uneasy. As the summer progressed, neither of them could bear the idea of being separated; Ned decided to leave his wife and Debbie canceled her move to London.

Almost immediately she began to look for a new job. Remaining at Cleary once their relationship was public was out of the question. Even marriage between partners and associates was frowned upon by firms such as Cleary. They both knew it would be better for her to find something quickly, before Ned announced his separation to any of his Cleary partners or news of their plans leaked out, creating the small scandal that was destined to follow. "It wasn't the nice clean story of a divorced guy and a single woman. It was messy," she recalls.

Debbie went back to Davis Polk & Wardwell, one of her favorite firms from her job-hunting days at Harvard. Because lateral transfers among junior associates were rare at that time, she had to explain her situation to the hiring partner, lest he think she was job hunting because she was doing poorly at Cleary. She was not surprised to hear that there were no openings. "You could see him almost blanch when I explained why I was leaving Cleary," she remembers.

Although Debbie had never interviewed at Debevoise & Plimpton, Ned suggested that firm to her as another possibility when the Davis Polk option fell through. Debevoise and Cleary were considered quite similar in environment and very competitive in hiring. After a nerve-racking three-month wait, Debevoise finally came through with an offer in January. Later, Debbie was told that some of the partners were not enthusiastic about taking her in either, given the circumstances.

She gave her notice to the head of the Personnel Committee at Cleary, and Ned began telling his partners about their relationship. Only two of Ned's partners had been told about their plans before Debbie left, so they could serve as job references. As he expected, Ned's relations with some of his partners at Cleary became strained. He thought he might be elected to the firm's Executive Committee—the select group of partners who divided up the firm's income among the partnership the next year. Now he realized that the affair would probably result in a delay in his ability to play a real leadership role at the firm, until the controversy surrounding their affair died down. Although some of his partners had probably had their own affairs, Ned's decision to leave his family for a young associate still shocked some of his colleagues.

Debbie had been very happy at Cleary and worried about

the move to Debevoise, where she would have to prove herself anew. Although she sympathized with Ned's problems, it was she who was risking her career. Shortly after they broke the news to the firm, they flew to Puerto Rico for a much-needed vacation, but both of them were irritable and on edge.

Debbie Fiedler was not willing to sacrifice Ned for her career. Susan Chan McCarthy, on the other hand, knew that reaching her goal of partnership at Graham & James would mean putting her law practice ahead of practically all else. When her husband Mike became restless in San Francisco and put in for an overseas transfer with Bank of America, Susan worried about derailing her career. Mike tried to convince her that working abroad would be an adventure, something they could only do at this juncture of their lives, when they were young and childless. She finally agreed, but only after several of the firm's partners assured her that working abroad would enhance her value to the firm's international practice. In November 1976 they left for Tokyo, where Susan began practicing at a twelve-lawyer Japanese firm, Logan, Okamoto & Takashima.

Under a written understanding with the firm's Executive Committee, the years she logged at the Logan firm would count toward partnership. Working overseas, she would come up for partner after six and a half years, the established partnership track at Graham & James. But she still worried that, away from the firm's San Francisco headquarters, it would be more difficult for the partners to evaluate her work during these critical years of professional development.

Even as a junior associate, Susan put herself under considerable pressure about making partner. Sometimes she wished she could make herself relax and just enjoy life as it came, but she wanted badly to achieve partnership on time with her class. "You have to understand that these strange things motivate these young people," she would laughingly say on reflection years later. "When you look back at it all, what does it matter anyway? But at that time it did seem to matter because we were in a competitive environment and most firms had an up or out policy. There weren't many precedents for taking detours off the track. In fact I still have that personality fault, that sense of not liking to take the slow track. It's hard to give a rational reason why . . . some form of hunger. I don't want to say it's my background. I don't want to make too much of my background. But if I had to speculate about reasons, that's the only reason I can think of—wanting the recognition of being a successful person."

Susan loved her time in Japan. The couple moved into a house in Mejiro, in the Toshima District in Tokyo. The house was in a compound that at one time belonged to the Tokugawa shogun. The main house of one of Tokugawa's descendants, on a massive acreage by Japanese standards, was directly across the street from their house behind high stone walls. Much of the land had been subdivided and most of the houses were occupied by foreigners on corporate expatriate allowances. The trees and small gardens helped make the neighborhood one of the nicer residential areas.

In the two months before she started work Susan immersed herself in the language and culture of Japan. She remembered her Chinese characters from college well enough and with the aid of a dictionary she was able to figure out what most signs meant, even if she could not yet pronounce them. Since the Logan firm was an international law firm, most of the work was done in English. There was not a single Japanese typewriter in the office; Japanese litigation documents were sent out for typing. Even after she started work, Susan was so eager to master the language that she would listen to language tapes in her spare time.

More than half of the Logan firm's practice was advising foreign clients investing in Japan. Susan worked as part of a team, helping prepare for joint ventures between Australian, American and British clients with Japanese companies. The firm also counseled Fortune 500 companies such as Ford Motor Company, Union Carbide Company and Monsanto Corporation on their Japanese joint venture operations and their subsidiaries in Japan. Because she was only permitted to advise on U.S. law, her contributions were somewhat limited and always at the planning stage. As a trade-off, though, she learned how Japanese companies operated, information she figured would be useful to her at some point in her career.

Besides Susan, the Logan firm had another woman lawyer, a senior associate named Itsuko Mori. Susan was intrigued by Mori, who had an uncanny ability to negotiate for her clients without appearing too aggressive. Mori was a few years older than Susan and had been in practice ten years when the firm made her a partner in 1978, during Susan's second year in Japan. As far as Susan knew, Mori was the first and only woman in Japan to become a partner in a major international law firm. As they counseled clients together, Mori explained to Susan the difficulties that women lawyers faced in Japan, where women were not expected to complete a four-year university education or have long-term careers. If a woman was aggressive and assertive (in the manner of some American women lawyers), Mori warned her, the Japanese would regard her as some kind of monster. Clients expected women lawyers to be gracious and to smile and defer to them. While this was Mori's outward demeanor, Susan saw her inner toughness. When it came to sharp legal analysis, Mori deferred to no one and she could hold her own once she had decided on a particular course of action. Her grasp of the law was obvious, and her clients clearly respected her abilities.

Susan would remember how Mori had saved the day during one important negotiation. Name partner Nobuyuki (Bob) Takashima had tapped Susan and Mori to represent Chemed, a subsidiary of W. R. Grace, in discussions with a leading Japanese chemical company, Shin-Etsu, for a joint manufacturing concern in Japan. The negotiations would drag on for at least two weeks. Takashima accompanied Susan and Mori to the first session and introduced them to the lawyers for Shin-Etsu, an older Japanese man named Mr. Ohno and his young associate, Mr. Shibasake. After a day and a half Takashima left the transaction in the two women's hands, throwing the men off balance. "This put the Shin-Etsu negotiating team and their lawyers into a state of shock because then they were dealing solely with two women who were representing the American side," Susan recalls. To make matters worse, the Chemed representatives spoke no English and refused to speak to Mrs. Mori, who was proficient in both Japanese and English. "They kept on trying to talk through Mr. Ohno, whose English was relatively limited, directly to the negotiators for our side. They were trying to ignore us," Susan recalls, "because they just weren't used to negotiating with women. It turned out that they couldn't continue to do that because Mrs. Mori's skills were too great and too needed." The negotiations almost broke off at the end of the first week due to a misunderstanding, and had it not been for an impassioned speech by Mori, who explained the respective cultural differences on both sides that were causing the problem, the deal would have fallen through.

As a celebratory dinner at the end of the negotiations Susan and Mori, tongue in cheek, asked Shibasake, the young associate on the opposing side, if he would ever marry a lawyer. "Never," he replied, looking at them in horror. A colleague of his had married a lawyer and never had his dinner served on time, he explained. His firm had also refused to hire a woman lawyer, on the theory that one of the firm's secretaries, who had graduated in the same law school class as the job applicant, would become jealous and quit. Later Mori confessed that her own daughter, who was then twelve, had told Mori that she, too, considered her mother's work improper for a woman.

In Japan, for the first time, Susan's eyes were opened to how badly some women lawyers were treated, and the consequences of trying to have a traditionally male career in a society that had such stereotypical roles for women. A woman like Mrs. Mori could succeed, but she was a singular example. In many ways Mori was an excellent role model for Susan. Mori had underscored the difficulty of being a woman lawyer and trying to hit on the right style—neither too aggressive nor too diffident. If you came on all business, it was easy to seem humorless. Somehow Mori carried it off. Rather than fight the system, she had learned to work within what her society would accept and to succeed on its terms.

Susan wondered whether she would have been able to put up with the sexism of the Japanese legal and business world as graciously. Back in the states she knew similar problems might confront her. Although she had never felt especially patronized at Graham & James, Susan had feared clients might relate to her as their daughter rather than as a competent attorney. She heard other women lawyers complain about not being taken as seriously as a man, of being "honeyed" and "sweetied" to death. Anne Redman, the classmate who went to Seattle's Foster, Pepper & Riviera, echoed the experiences of several of the women in the class when she talked of her first months as an associate. Redman was taken to lunch by a senior partner at the Rainier Club, which did not admit women into the main dining room at the time. She was ushered in through a side door and when it was time for dessert the partner ordered, "Have some ice cream, dear." She had felt like his granddaughter. "He was very sweet. He bought me a corsage when I was sworn in as a member of the bar. He told me I would be a great judge someday, and he gave me work. But his way of treating me made me feel like a member of the auxiliary."

Susan was far more sensitive to these kinds of problems herself when she returned to the United States. In September 1978, toward the end of Susan and Mike's two-year stay in Japan, their first child, Kathleen, was born. Both she and Mike wanted to start a family. The pregnancy had been a smooth one, although Kate had been born six weeks prematurely in a Tokyo hospital. With the baby in an incubator and not much mothering to do, Susan bypassed maternity leave and in a few weeks went back to work to finish up her last assignments for the firm. When Kate was four months old Susan and Mike moved back to San Francisco. Now she would be adjusting to her new role as mother while facing the final two-year push to partnership. She would have to prove that she had progressed as quickly in Japan as her counterparts in San Francisco.

As Susan McCarthy was honing her legal skills overseas, Debbie Fiedler was trying to prove herself all over again at her new firm and having a more difficult time than she had expected. Her first impression of Debevoise was that it was somewhat colder and more formal than Cleary. Perhaps this was due to the fact that she had arrived a year and a half after her peers and had missed out on the bonding that often takes place between new associates during their first year of practice. She felt like an outsider and quickly sensed that it was going to take longer for her to feel at home at Debevoise than it had at Cleary. Her feelings were compounded by people's natural curiosity about Cleary, Gottlieb and how it compared to Debevoise. The more she was asked to reminisce about her old firm, the more she felt that she was being unwittingly pegged as a Cleary partisan.

She was also discouraged by her early assignments. First she had to learn the Debevoise way of doing things. Because people did not know her work, she dropped back to a level of lesser responsibility and felt as if she was being treated like a brand-new first-year associate. When Debbie started at Debevoise in 1976 the firm's corporate practice was mostly domestic. She missed international work. She tried to get involved in some of the firm's more general corporate work but ended up doing a hodgepodge of different deals. On top of everything else, she felt she was working simultaneously for three difficult partners, making 1977 an especially hard year. When all three of them dumped on her at the same time, she almost walked out for good. Instead she cried in the ladies' room.

Although she missed Cleary, Debbie decided that, since she was at Debevoise, she had to make the best of her situation. She dug into her assignments and tried to integrate herself into the social fabric of the firm by starting up a newsletter. At Cleary she had been a floor reporter for the firm's monthly newspaper, the *Cleargolaw News,* a publication put together by the associates. Debbie thought a similar paper at Debevoise might increase camaraderie among the lawyers and between the legal and nonlegal staffs. She drew up a proposal and presented her plans to the firm's presiding partner, Oscar Ruebhausen, who gave her a cautious go-ahead. Debbie's enthusiasm convinced him that it was worth a try. The new paper was dubbed the *Debevoice,* a pun on both the firm's name and that of the New York weekly, the *Village Voice* (and hers). For the maiden issue Debbie unearthed an amusing letter from one of the firm's senior partners, Francis Plimpton, written for the Root, Clark newspaper when Plimpton was an associate there. The reception of her new publication within the firm was very favorable. It was her first success at Debevoise.

At home Debbie was having to adjust to having a spouse-like creature around the house. Ned was accustomed to a more conventional lifestyle with a nonworking wife and still liked to have his home comforts, although Debbie's hours were often just as long as his. His two sons were splitting their time between Ned and Debbie's apartment and their mother's apartment. Debbie enjoyed being with the boys, and she had always taken her family responsibilities seriously. But stepmotherhood was yet another challenging new role on top of her new job.

The most awesome aspect of home life was Ned's obvious guilt feelings over breaking up his family. He had strong desires for a traditional family life, stemming from his strict, Southern Methodist, rural background. "Despite my previous marital difficulties," says Stiles, "I have a very strong urge for a conventional home with kids, a station wagon and the whole bit." He searched for ways to resolve his internal ambiguities about where he belonged and it took him several years to feel comfortable with his decision to be with Debbie. After attending an EST encounter group retreat in 1978, he even decided to go back to his wife and family, but the reconciliation failed and within months he was back with Debbie. They were finally married later that year and Debbie had new hope that, with her personal life stabilized, she could get her career back on track.

For her final two years as an associate, Susan Chan McCarthy was not going to let anything—even motherhood—get in the way of her goal of becoming a partner. She was offered work in commercial, banking or employee benefits and, characteristically, she picked all three. Cal First, a key client on whose account Susan had worked before leaving for Japan, demanded she do all of the bank's pension work as a condition of the bank keeping the work with the firm. Then, when Richard Eastman, the partner she had worked with her first year, was assigned to Singapore, she was asked to take over the corporate work for his client, R. Dakin & Company, a major distributor of plush toys, and to become the company's corporate secretary.

The split practice meant Susan had to work extremely long

hours, which made the juggle between career and family more difficult than she had anticipated. Her third month back at the firm, she was still breast-feeding Kate and getting up in the middle of the night. Expressing milk into a baby bottle in the Graham & James women's lounge during the workday, Susan ruefully realized what the word "superwoman" meant. It was a blessing that her mother lived nearby and could come to the house and stay with Kate during the day.

She hit an emotional low when Kate was about seven months old. Susan returned from the office late in the evening as usual, and as she went to take Kate from her mother's arms the baby burst into tears. She stopped crying as soon as she was back in her grandmother's arms. Then Susan wanted to cry. "That was when I did a lot of soul searching," she recalls. "I was exhausted. I wasn't able to have the time with Kate that I wanted and yet, from a career point of view, I knew I needed to reestablish myself. And I was worried because one is acculturated to believe that the mother is the closest thing that a child should have. I was nursing Kate despite difficult circumstances. Yet I wasn't getting very much of the satisfaction of seeing Kate develop except on the weekends. So it was bad."

Her mother was supportive of Susan's career and proud of her accomplishments but she could not really understand the degree to which Susan felt she had to compromise her family life. The only people she knew who worked as hard as Mike and Susan were those who worked two jobs because they really needed the money. Susan tried to explain to her mother that a conscientious lawyer who wanted to build a strong client base had to put the client's needs first, and that meant working extra long hours. Most of the women lawyers she knew were showing the same dedication. Mike, who was busy working on a series of securities transactions at Bank of America, understood. He helped with child care and household responsibilities and did not pressure her to cut back her hours at the office. Sometimes she wished he would.

As Kate grew older Susan became a more relaxed mother. By the time the baby was a year old it was obvious her relationship with her parents was not suffering. Susan did not believe in the "quality time" theory of child rearing. She knew children needed quantity, too, and she tried to manage her time more efficiently, delegating more work to younger associates.

Gunning for partnership, it was hard for Susan to relinquish the total control she felt she had to keep over her practice. During the early months after her return from Japan she had assigned a paralegal to fill in the number of shares owned on forms for a corporate client. The paralegal later said she must have been daydreaming, because several of the forms went out with the certificate number posted where the number of shares should have been listed. When the shareholders complained about the error Susan was mortified. She hadn't bothered to check the paralegal's work. "I felt terribly responsible. I felt it reflected on me and that, unless I double-checked and saw that everything was perfect before it went out, I was the one who would be faulted for work that was not correct," she remembers. Later she realized she had over-reacted. All lawyers make mistakes, and this was not a big one. Her feelings, she thought, were part of a historical paranoia shared by women professionals—that they could never permit themselves to make a mistake, that they had to be twice as diligent as men. Many of the male partners for whom Susan had worked as an associate had not bothered to go over all of her work. They trusted her to do everything right. She wished she could adopt their attitude and be more relaxed.

Child rearing did help Susan show more of a human side around the office. She grew more tolerant of other lawyers' imperfections. She did not want to fit the stereotype of the hardworking, dedicated grind. At Graham & James, she wanted her colleagues to see that she was a real person who had a sense of humor and warmth that was sometimes hidden. Still, she didn't feel she could let the pace of her work slacken. Sandy Calhoun tapped Susan to work on the establishment and organization of Oceanic Bank, which was just starting up. Two law firms and a banking consultant were asked to propose an organizational structure, and the bank ended up adopting Graham & James's plan. Susan became a director of the bank, a great honor for a young female associate.

If such accomplishments weren't enough to ensure Susan's partnership, her expertise in ERISA had made her irreplaceable. ERISA had become known as a "full employment act" for lawyers, owing to the constant changes in the law and the development of regulations requiring counseling and compliance. Susan was the resident guru in this area for the firm's other U.S. offices. She had been smart to carve out a niche for herself, even if others found ERISA intolerably dull.

She was feeling increasingly confident about making partner, and her confidence was well founded. The firm was scheduled to elect new partners for 1981 in December 1980. Her annual review the previous year had been excellent, a good sign. If someone was not partnership material, the firm tried to let the associate know before the critical sixth year. One female associate in her class, a lateral transfer, apparently had not recognized the signals and had stuck it out until the final year when she was not put up for election. Susan, on the other hand, had kept track of every sign or possible clue and knew exactly when the partnership vote was scheduled. During a break in the meeting the partners who were close to her began phoning her with their congratulations. She received the news with a great sense of relief, even though she had been fairly certain of the outcome. It was a thrill to be one of the first women ever elected to the partnership.

In the next two years Susan was assigned a larger office but little else changed. Her schedule certainly did not lighten up, despite the fact that she was pregnant again. She was in the middle of two major transactions when her son Matthew was born the following June. Again, she took just a few weeks off after giving birth and then returned to work, beginning her regime of nursing at night and expressing milk during the day to be frozen and later used at home while she was working. One day, while working with a client, she was unable to break away to get to the ladies' room during a marathon negotiating session and the clothing under her vest became drenched. The professional life of a new mother could certainly be awkward. Somehow Susan managed, and her billable hours were so high the year after Matthew was born that the firm's Compensation Committee awarded her a special bonus.

Sitting in her garden in San Francisco on a spring morning in 1984, Susan feels very fortunate. Her hard work has paid off and she has a group of loyal clients. Her practice is less vulnerable than it would be if she were dependent on other partners for work. "If you're a woman and you've got a niche you're okay. If you're a woman and you don't have a niche, then you have to develop your own practice. That's the same for every attorney, but women often have a harder time developing contacts," she observes.

Developing new business is the major challenge that lies ahead. There are no women at Graham & James to serve as role models in this area, known in the legal community as "rainmaking," although Alice Young, one of Susan's Harvard Law classmates, has joined the firm and is succeeding in attracting new clients in New York. Calhoun, suave and sophisticated, is plugged into all the right social and financial networks in San Francisco and abroad. He makes the task seem effortless. But Susan knows how hard it is to cultivate similar contacts. "That's where I think that we, as young partners and as women, need to be a lot more aggressive," she says. "I think my own practice tends to be more related to providing service for those with whom I have contact through the firm. For whatever reason, perhaps lack of time, I haven't gone out to glad-hand or seek publicity or social prominence."

Susan is not embarrassed to admit that she would like to have it all—a happy family life and the status and power of being a competent lawyer and rainmaker. She will have to push herself, make sure that she and Mike socialize more frequently, try to find the time to join seminar panels or write articles for the important law journals. Until the children are a little older and settled in school, it will be a tall order to fill. Despite her efforts to be more relaxed about her timetable for reaching these goals, Susan Chan McCarthy is still very much the driven perfectionist.

As time passed at Debevoise, Debbie Fiedler continued to work toward the goal of becoming a partner and, given the ups and downs of her personal life, the fact that she was even in the running was evidence of the changing times. However, marrying Ned and becoming more involved in her work at Debevoise did not change her belief that there was some-thing missing in her life, some emotional need that was not being met. She began to think that she wanted to have chil-dren, and the desire became even more intense after her father's death in July 1979. Ned, however, was reluctant to be saddled with baby care during what he hoped would be a comfortable middle age. As Debbie pushed the issue, Ned began to realize her desire for children would become even greater with time and he might risk losing her. Still, he didn't want to rush into anything. He told Debbie they could talk more about having a child during his upcoming sabbatical from Cleary. In July, Ned and Debbie left New York for a four-month stay in Paris.

It was a travel and do-nothing vacation, a welcome break from the stresses of New York and their respective law firms. Debbie continued to press Ned on the subject of children, but they both finally agreed to let the issue rest during their time abroad. Meanwhile the Paris sojourn gave Debbie time to resolve another issue that had been on her mind—whether she had in fact chosen the right career or had erred in giving up her earlier plan of going to medical school. It was a decision that increasingly became linked to her discussions with Ned about raising a family. If the option of having children was closed, she thought she might be happier in a more nurturing and caring profession. It seemed like a way to get her personal and professional needs resolved in one package.

In the fall Debbie returned to the United States, resigned from Debevoise and entered a special premed program at Columbia University for late converts to medicine. Although she did not know if she would ever come back to the law, Debbie felt she was leaving the firm in good standing. Several of the partners wished her luck and told her to come back if she changed her mind.

Although she knew that diving into premed courses was not going to be easy, in part because she had never taken a course in quantitative analysis, it became clear over the course of the first six or seven months at Columbia that being a premed and then medical student was even more demanding than practicing law. Being a premed student was a job that never ended and Debbie realized that if she pursued medicine she would have even less time to spend with Ned and his children, let alone a child of her own. Because of her late start in a second career, she also worried that many career options would be cut off to her when she finished medical school in her early forties.

Meanwhile Ned caved on the issue of having a new baby. He realized Debbie would eventually leave him—emotionally, if not physically, over the baby question and, with the issue finally resolved, Debbie began casting about for a job that would combine her interests in law and medicine. The job market was extremely tight, and a headhunter who was helping her suggested she go back to Debevoise at least temporarily. Debbie broached a possible return with several partners at the firm and was told she would be welcomed back on a temporary basis.

As soon as she returned to Debevoise, Debbie learned that she was pregnant. She was ecstatic. Expecting a child made her more purposeful and energetic, and her powers of concentration at work had never been better. Perhaps doing all those calculus and physics problems at Columbia had paid off. She wasn't exactly sure why her work was better. "I had a less neurotic approach to work," she recalls. "I wanted to do the best I could, as usual, but I wasn't worrying about becoming a partner or what the partners would think. I had stepped back psychologically and was less concerned about what people thought about me than about the work product that I was producing."

Her change in mood was perceptible to almost everyone at the firm. One partner joked that he wished he could become pregnant, since it was doing such wonders for Debbie. As her work and outlook improved, so did the corporate assignments that came her way. She enjoyed her status as a senior associate, playing a major role on deals, supervising the work of younger lawyers and trying to take a special interest in the younger women lawyers. She had finally made her peace at Debevoise.

With the child issue settled, life at home with Ned also settled down, and they were both thrilled when their daughter Jessie was born in 1982. Because both Ned and Debbie had to work late so many evenings they hired a live-in housekeeper from Switzerland to help care for the baby. Debbie tried to spend several hours in the early morning with Jessie or to arrive home early enough in the evening to see her.

Interests such as tennis and jogging fell by the wayside. Ned was enchanted with his new little girl but did not plunge into the details of child care. Debbie sometimes joked that Jessie would never have a birthday party if planning arrangements were left to Ned.

Debbie, too, found the combination of a child and work exhausting. Most of her friends had dropped out of practice or business when they became mothers, and Debbie began to sense a split between her friends who were working mothers and those who were not. She organized a play group with some friends and often regretted having to leave to get back to the office. The logistics of getting Jessie to appointments, taxiing uptown to fetch or deliver her, then speeding back to the office, were maddening. Being a working mother in New York City was no easy task.

While Debbie was glad her firm and other firms were talking about the dilemma women in her situation were facing, she thought it was a problem not easily solved. "Most men just don't seem to go through the doubting and the wondering about what's going to happen to their children if they're not around. I think that it's still the exception rather than the rule that the father is the 'primary parent.' What then happens if the woman—the primary parent—is actively involved in her career? Can a child thrive without a full-time primary parent, whether mother or father?" she reflected. "I worry about it a lot because both Ned and I are in this crazy environment. Ned doesn't think for a second about giving up his career. You don't hear of men becoming part-time professionals very often. I'm delighted that firms are offering women the choice, but it's still really a choice that seems to be only the woman's. How does that affect how women are viewed in a professional situation? Are they viewed as not necessarily serious as a result?" she wondered. "I don't see women opting for part-time work as necessarily less serious,

but it's going to take a long time for institutions to compre-
hend that."

Debevoise, meanwhile, was so pleased with Debbie's work
that the firm invited her to return as a permanent associate
following her maternity leave. In spite of the bumps in her
career, the partners in the corporate department assured her
she would still be on partnership track, although her leaves of
absence would put her a few years behind the other associates
from her class. Her last review had been enthusiastic. She
decided to shoot for partnership, fueled, in part, by a stub-
born streak that would not let her be defeated easily.

Relaxing in the firm's conference room one Saturday in the
fall of 1984, Debbie reflects on her future. She is keenly
aware that if she makes it to partnership she will be the first
woman corporate partner in the firm's history. Debevoise has
already accepted two women into the partnership, but they
are in other practice areas. One started her career in the corporate department but after her children were born she
switched to trusts and estates, a practice with more predictable hours.

Debbie is reluctant to speculate on her partnership
chances. It is difficult to gauge what qualities the partners
look for. From his experience at Cleary, Ned has told her the
partnership decision is based on a combination of smarts, personality, client relations and energy, and that the whole process of weeding out the candidates is more subjective than
scientific. With her personality, brains and Boston upbring-
ing, Ned thinks she has a decent chance. Debbie also believes
that the firm is anxious to have a woman partner in its largest
and most visible area of practice. But Debevoise is also conservative, she knows, and there are female corporate associates in the classes behind her who are also good prospects
and who have followed more conventional career paths.

Debbie worries that her outside responsibilities may weigh
against her in the end. Although she is working hard, she just

cannot bill the hours that some of her male colleagues can. Most of them are either single or married to women who tend to household and family. They have the luxury of devoting themselves single-mindedly to work. She is certainly not regretful about her family responsibilities, but she is concerned that Debevoise may, even unconsciously, hold her back because of them. Only when there are more women partners, Debbie says, will there be a real effort to deal with this problem. This is one reason why she wants to become a partner. She wants to encourage other women in her situation to keep trying.

In the winter of 1984 a crisis erupted that made Debbie thankful she had stuck with her career at Debevoise. During a routine physical examination Ned's doctor discovered a spot on his lung. Further tests revealed a tumor lodged in the right lobe. It was malignant. When Ned checked into Sloan-Kettering, New York's renowned cancer treatment center, for surgery, his doctors were not at all optimistic. But they were able to remove the entire tumor; apparently the cancer had not spread. Ned's prognosis for recovery was good.

During Ned's illness Debbie tried as hard as she could to prevent her work from suffering because of the obvious stress she was under. Several partners mentioned how they admired her for carrying on so well during the crisis. Somehow she managed to keep herself on an even keel while continuing to handle a heavy work load. After visiting Ned in the hospital she would head home to play with Jessie, hoping her small daughter would not detect her strain. Between Ned and Jessie and work, she had absolutely no time for herself, but she was determined not to let her exhaustion dampen her spirits.

With Ned fifteen years older, Debbie has always known there is a danger that she may someday be Jessie's sole means of support. Her husband's illness has made this an even starker reality. Whether or not she becomes a partner, she is

confident that she will find another good job. With her training at two of New York's top corporate firms, she could land
an in-house job at a large company or find a slot for herself in
another firm. She is not afraid of what the future may bring.
Debbie has toughened up in the past ten years. Her emotions
are not so brittle, her need for approval less intense. In ten
years she may not have come as far in a law firm as some
women in her class but, measured against herself, Debbie
Fiedler has made great strides.

Though they have different styles of lawyering—Susan
Chan McCarthy single-minded and serious, Debbie Fiedler
more free-wheeling and controversial—both are reaching for
the pinnacle of success in their chosen field. There has never
been a better time for women lawyers to have such ambitions. Slowly, as the most senior, old-fashioned partners retire
and younger partners begin taking leadership roles within
law firms, women at these firms sense that attitudes toward
them are becoming more open. And as some firms have
brought in "classes" of women—as many as four or five new
female recruits in 1974, the numbers rapidly increasing in
ensuing years—and more women have been seen walking the
halls, attending meetings and servicing clients, barriers are
beginning to fall.

But the eight- to nine-year partnership track (in California
and other places it was a more civilized six to seven years)
was an arduous and discouraging one for many of the women
from the class. To stay on track and make it to the top, you
needed the kind of single-minded ambition that Susan Chan
McCarthy displayed. A number of women in the class are still
unsure of the final outcome of their corporate law careers
and, like Debbie Fiedler Stiles, have veered from the straight
and narrow path—taking time off to have children or pursue
other interests. In 1984, ten years after graduation, eight of

the women who are still at firms have not yet achieved the rank of partner. Sixteen are partners.

However, a more interesting and revealing statistic is the astonishingly high dropout rate among the Harvard Law women who began the corporate climb in 1974—more than half of the forty-nine women who launched their careers at firms have opted out in the last decade. Their reasons are varied. At least five were "passed over," failing to make the cut in the final partnership vote. Four women left because of growing family demands that made working the kind of hours that Susan Chan McCarthy, Debbie Fiedler Stiles and all the other law firm holdouts put in intolerable. The majority left for more intangible reasons—they just didn't feel comfortable or fulfilled at the big corporate firms. Debbie Fiedler Stiles herself came close to becoming one of the casualties.

The small number of women in the partnership ranks continues to discourage many young women from making the climb. Susan Chan McCarthy and Debbie Fiedler Stiles are among those willing to put their careers, personal lives and egos on the line for ultimate judgment by a group of older, influential men who continue to dominate the affairs of their firms. For many women in the class of 1974, the stakes required by the corporate climb are just too high and the payoff far too uncertain.

3

High Ideals,
Low Pay

Historically, women lawyers were supposed to take do-good, low-paying jobs and were viewed more like social workers than real attorneys. This stereotype prevailed until the late 1960s, when hundreds of law students, both women and men, enlisted in antipoverty programs, legal aid and public interest groups as an expression of their political activism. Although the legal services movement was larger and better funded than ever before, as the women in the Harvard Law School class of 1974 approached graduation, it was somewhat ironic that the idealism that fed the movement with young workers and fueled a brief, anti-law-firm backlash at Harvard Law School was ebbing. Several women who had set out to become storefront lawyers when they entered law school in 1971 found three years later that, once ensconced at corporate-oriented Harvard Law School, they liked being in the "establishment."

Ellen D'Alelio, who enrolled at Harvard after teaching French literature at New York University, was considering a career as a storefront or legal services lawyer. "What I learned in talking with people at the law school was that apparently the intellectual challenges of storefront or legal services kind of law were not nearly as great as in corporate practice." D'Alelio joined New York's White & Case as an associate after law school, eventually becoming a partner at Washington, D.C.'s Steptoe & Johnson, specializing in securities litigation. Roz Daum, a partner at Boston's Choate, Hall & Stewart, also switched tracks. Daum thought she would take a job with a public agency but decided a law firm job would provide a quicker ticket to power and influence. She admits that the law school, with its emphasis on placing people in the private sector, was partly responsible for her decision.

Nevertheless, fifteen women from the class bucked the ground swell toward corporate law and began their careers in the legal services/public interest sphere. At Harvard Law School, most of them say, they found little support for their goals. "I remember feeling by the end of the first year that if I for some reason was not interested in becoming a securities lawyer there was something intellectually deficient about me," recalls Barbara Sard, an attorney at Greater Boston Neighborhood Legal Services. Bari Schwartz, who has also devoted her career to legal services, adds, "The message consistently from Harvard Law School for three years both from the faculty and from my peers was that, if you were interested in being involved in legal services or public interest law, you were literally wasting a space that could have gone to someone who was going to practice real law."

So all-encompassing was the law school's corporate orientation that even women who were almost certain they wanted to work as poverty lawyers or public defenders felt obliged to take summer jobs at law firms, at least to see what they were like. Some were converted to private practice for good; others managed to resist the generous salaries and other perks of law firm existence and stick to their original goals.

At Harvard the one place these women found a receptive climate was at the student legal aid bureau. Were it not for the Harvard Legal Aid Bureau, which trained student volunteers to handle routine trial work for needy Boston area clients, a few of these women say they would have dropped out of law school altogether. To join the Bureau, members of the class of 1974 were required to devote at least twenty hours per week to working on their cases and to make a two-year commitment—their second and third years of law school—to work in the Bureau. About thirty students in the class participated in the program. Gary Bellow and his teaching fellows, John Bowman and Valerie Vanaman, who were experienced poverty law lawyers on leaves from their jobs, served as role models for their younger, more impressionable students. Following graduation, the women who had worked together in the Bureau remained a tightly knit group, following one another's progress and offering encouragement to "keep the faith."

In previous classes far more women from Harvard Law School went into public interest work and "poverty" law than did the women of 1974. "Legal aid has always been a haven for qualified women attorneys," observes Eve Plotkin, a 1954 Harvard Law graduate who joined the Legal Aid Society after staying out of practice for twelve years to raise her three daughters. Besides government work, legal aid was one area where women won ready acceptance. Representing the poor was considered suitable work for women lawyers, who were supposed to bring a caring, sympathetic ear to their poor clients. The low-paying, low-prestige work was often shunned by male attorneys, who viewed legal aid more as charitable than legal work.

While in Plotkin's era a woman lawyer might well have ended up at Legal Aid because there were few opportunities in traditional law practice, for the women of the class of 1974 this was not the case. They actively chose a different path. The idea of working for social justice was ingrained in many of them early on. "From age ten or eleven, when I watched lunch counter sit-ins and saw black kids in Greensboro getting ketchup dumped on their heads, I became determined to be in the social welfare area," says Bari Schwartz. "There was never any choice. I couldn't live in society with the advantages I had and not address the inequities." Lois Wood, who has worked at Land of Lincoln Legal Assistance Foundation in East St. Louis, Illinois, since graduation, found that legal services was "a way to express my social beliefs through my career. . . ." For these women and others, law firms never entered the picture. "I've never been in a firm and I never wanted to be in one," says Ann Greenblatt, executive director of Massachusetts Correctional Legal Services. "They have little in the way of redeeming social value. . . ."

Given the low salaries, poor working conditions, highly demanding case loads and sometimes difficult clients, it was as hard for the women who swam against the corporate tide to stick to their original career paths as for the women who went the law firm route. Although the burnout rate among legal services and public-interest lawyers is extremely high, the emotional and political commitment that these fifteen women brought to their careers was strong enough to keep ten of them in the field a decade after graduation. Among this group, Judy Berkan and Judith Lindahl display a passionate, all-consuming dedication to their work, in the most trying of circumstances.

Professor Judy Berkan sits atop a table at the front of her classroom at the Inter American University in San Juan, Puerto Rico. Her arms—bare and tanned in a spaghetti-strapped sun dress—seem to conduct a phantom orchestra as she engages in animated dialogue with her students. The Spanish is almost perfect. It is the last class session of the semester in federal jurisdiction, and Judy is talking more than usual in order to cover the final points she wants to make before exam time. She prefers to let the students do the talking as she leads them to ponder the meaning of various laws.

Her style of teaching is far different from that which she grew to detest at Harvard Law School. So, too, the faces that peer back at her are different from those of her classmates of ten years ago. Some are *blanquitos,* or children of wealth, whose grades were not high enough to gain them admittance to the more prestigious University of Puerto Rico. Others live in working-class urban developments and attend school at night on borrowed money, hoping to better their situation. Occasionally a student gives her a poem that she hangs on the wall of her tiny office on the first floor by the school entrance. The ones who dream of working for social change after graduation drop by during office hours in search of advice and inspiration.

After class Judy goes for a run at a nearby park and then drives about ten miles to her house in Cupey Alto, the most rural part of the city. She is training for the New York City marathon scheduled for the fall of 1984, three months from now. The curved roads leading up to her house are shaded by tall trees and at night noisy tree frogs abound. Judy refers to her neighborhood as a "mini-rain forest," because it can be raining at her house and sunny in the city. Her three dogs, which she insists are "Spanish-speaking," and several cats share the lawn with a neighbor's cow. The cabinlike structure was treated for termites, but the house is infested. Judy has decorated her home with political posters, running medals and pictures and drawings of family members back in New York.

Her house, office and car are usually in disarray, with books piled atop papers piled atop more books. Cobwebs are spun across naked light bulbs. A videotape player, a wireless phone and a television set are practically the extent of her possessions. Judy has none of the material desires that have accompanied the $115,000 average incomes that many of her former Harvard Law classmates now earn. She is perfectly happy with her teaching salary of $24,000. She eats out and travels when she pleases and cannot imagine what she would do with the money if someone were to double her salary. "I do not deny myself anything I want," she proclaims.

With her dark skin and hair, Judy, who is in fact of European Jewish ancestry, is often mistaken for a Puerto Rican. She does not affect the style of a native, and is annoyed when North Americans come down and change their names, as from George to Jorge, pretending to be from the island. Still, it is fun when people assume she has Latin ancestry. Growing up in the 1950s in the United States, she had always wanted to be tall and thin with straight blond hair. In Puerto Rico she fits more into the cultural stereotype of beauty.

When Judy moved to Puerto Rico from New Haven in the fall of 1977 she was excited by the political situation on the island. A Spanish colony for four centuries, Puerto Rico was ceded to the United States in 1898 after the Spanish-American War. In 1952 the island became a commonwealth territory of the United States, with local self-government. Over the years the question of its future political status—whether it should become a fifty-first state or an independent nation or maintain the status quo—has been a highly charged issue in Puerto Rico and at times has spawned violence by extremist groups.

Judy early on aligned herself with the minority independence movement. There are other "Independentistas" on the faculty, but she is probably the one most closely identified with the cause. She is also identified with the fishermen of Vieques, a small island off the coast of Puerto Rico, whom she represented years ago in a highly publicized lawsuit against the United States Government. The fishermen were trying to stop Navy target practice on Vieques because they felt it interfered with their fishing. During one of their demonstrations on the island Judy was arrested and subsequently tried and convicted for trespass. While her case was on appeal she became embroiled in a lengthy fight to join the federal bar in Puerto Rico. The events surrounding Vieques and her fight to practice were covered in the San Juan *Star* and other newspapers, making her a minor celebrity of the class of 1974.

Unlike many of the women in her law school class, who dove into big firm practice after graduation alongside the men, Judy Berkan wanted to be an agent for social change and live out principles of justice and fairness that were cultivated in her from an early age. She grew up in an upper-middle-class home on Long Island, but some of her earliest memories are connected with repression. "I don't know why I got it much more than my sisters, but I was very aware of fascism. I remember having dreams about Nazis as a child. I remember seeing people with numbers on their arms. I remember the Rosenberg killings when I was about four . . . the McCarthy hearings . . . I remember sympathizing greatly with the civil rights struggles of the 1950s when I was eight, nine years old. . . ." At age twelve she was marching in demonstrations on Long Island for Women Strike for Peace, and an interest in the politics of Latin America was sparked when she spent three months in El Salvador as an exchange student during high school.

She continued her political activities at Yale University, where she transferred from Brandeis University after her sophomore year to become part of the first class of women admitted to Yale. In New Haven in 1969 the atmosphere was highly charged. Her friends were being drafted to fight in Vietnam, others were going to jail or Canada. Besides getting involved in antiwar protest activities, Judy also began organizing around women's issues. It wasn't until her junior year at Yale, when she heard a rousing speech by activist lawyer Leonard Weinglass,[1] that law school entered into her plans. "We were all very involved in the Panther 21 trial and

[1] Weinglass was co-counsel with William Kunstler for the Chicago Eight defendants.

this and that. We were organizing. The school had shut down. Leonard Weinglass came and gave a very, very good speech about the Chicago Eight trial and that was sort of like the turning point for me. Here's something I can do in life that's not selling out. . . .'' She chose Harvard, reasoning the greater the status of the school the better the education, and she wanted the best legal training she could get.

When she began law school at twenty-two, Judy was sure she didn't even want the option of a job with a corporate firm dangled in front of her, so she refused to set foot in a corporations or tax class. She joined the Freaked Out Friends and the *Outlaw* newspaper, overlapping groups that included students who shared her leftist sentiments. Still she felt isolated at times. She and one of her classmates, Claudia Angelos, would complain to each other about feeling like token women at the *Outlaw* and, over at the Women's Law Association, like the token radicals. Getting more women into big law firms—a topic of interest to WLA members—just wasn't at the top of their priority list.

She began skipping classes and, when she did go, she usually sat out of her assigned seat. One experience in Professor Clark Byse's contracts class was characteristic of what she detested about Harvard. Byse was reputed to be the toughest in his use of the Socratic method. One day in class while Byse was grilling one of the students, Judy felt a young man next to her jam her with his elbow. "Look how he gets that guy!" the student exclaimed, obviously enjoying the sacrifice. While he may have been enjoying it, the spectacle was making her sick.

A few weeks later Judy was invited to a traditional reception for new students at the dean's house. As they sat around the living room, Dean Albert Sacks asked her whether she was enjoying Harvard. "I really have some question about the teaching method," she politely replied. "I think it makes us all hostile to each other. I think we should all be sharing and trying to learn together." To illustrate her point, she recounted for Sacks the incident in contracts. Although she did not identify Byse, everyone at the party—including Byse —seemed to know what she was referring to. Later in the semester Byse called her over after class and showed her a flattering letter written to him by a former student who had moved on to become an associate at Cravath, Swaine & Moore. The letter urged Byse not to relax his teaching methods. "I wanted to tell her there were reasons for it whether she believed it or not," the emeritus professor explained years later. Judy thought the professor was just making a pathetic attempt to justify his behavior.

By the second year she was so deeply depressed that she was stuttering and had become deathly thin. She suffered constant stomach pains. Swimming in the early morning helped stabilize her mood. It wasn't until the summer after her second year, when she signed on to work at New Haven Legal Services, that her outlook began to improve. She was assigned to the "Hill" office, in a working-class section of New Haven. It was a perfect assignment for her, one where she could use the Spanish she had learned in El Salvador representing the largely Puerto Rican clientele. She liked it so much that she returned after graduation, full of enthusiasm and eager to put her law school days behind her.

Judith Lindahl had no interest in moving up the associate ranks of a large law firm after Harvard Law School either. She wanted to become a public defender, although her choice had nothing to do with wanting to change society or defend poor people. In fact she disparaged lawyers who became public defenders simply to "help the poor." She thought they were misguided. Better to be committed to being an excellent defense lawyer than to the individual clients themselves. "You can choose to be poor, to be a public defender while you're doing it, but just understand, your commitment is to the law and to your role, not to the individuals," Judith explains. "Otherwise you come to a point, and I've seen lawyers do it, where they're affrighted and saying, 'My God. I just got this child rapist off and I don't like him and I don't like myself for doing it!' "

The idea of defending people who might be guilty of committing heinous crimes never seemed to bother her. She had come to terms with such issues early on, and for the most part she never bothered to explain herself. So when she was a young lawyer starting out and relatives approached her at family reunions asking, "When a man comes up to you and tells you that he did it, how do you feel when you get him off?" she would smile and say, "Great! Can I get you another stuffed mushroom, Aunt Agatha?"

"I sincerely believe that we defense lawyers do a very bad job of explaining what it is we do, because it's profoundly personal and very important," says Judith, smoking the first of many Kool cigarettes behind her desk in a small law office on Beacon Street in downtown Boston in 1984, where she is a solo practitioner. "As a defense lawyer, my role is simply to keep the government honest, and it is a high calling," she explains. The small, bespectacled attorney is tired, having been through several grueling months defending one of six accused rapists in the Big Dan's barroom rape trial in Fall River, Massachusetts. The case had been one of the most difficult of her career. She had entered it late, replacing another lawyer who had withdrawn from the case. Coming from Boston, Judith was an outsider among the five Bristol County defense lawyers, and she was also the only woman working on the defense team.

It was going to be an uphill fight. During the trial there were always several different theories of defense operating. The lawyers had to cope with a camera in the courtroom (live coverage was provided on Cable News Network from the gray stone Bristol County Superior Courthouse); translators, because several defendants and many witnesses were Portuguese-speaking; and many different versions of what happened that night at Big Dan's. Initial news stories, based on a police report, contained the explosive detail that bar patrons cheered while a woman was raped on top of a pool table in the tavern.

Among the questions most frequently asked of Judith during the trial was how she felt being a woman defending an accused rapist. She decided if she ever granted interviews after it was all over she would try to explain what she perceived as the idiocy of this question and the importance of her work. And she did—on ABC's "This Week with David Brinkley," on CNN's "Crossfire," and on network morning news shows. "A woman who elected the profession of criminal defense would be well advised to reconsider that election if she hesitated to take a rape case," she told the press. "My defense of Victor Raposo in no way implies my approval of rape, no more than my defense of a murderer would imply my approval of murder."

Judith did not find her niche as a defender right away. She grew up in Melrose, an ethnically mixed community about nine miles north of Boston. Law wasn't in her background. Her grandfather on her father's side was a Swedish merchant mariner who immigrated to Boston in the 1920s to take a job in a Ford plant. Her father had been a salesman and her mother a schoolteacher. Judith and her brother and sister lived comfortably enough in Melrose but she never had, as she puts it, the "problem of choosing between dresses." The family spent summers in rural New Hampshire. Judith, who was a tomboy as a youngster, had been happiest in the woods, barefoot among deer and kerosene lamps, left to her imagination. She excelled in high school and during her junior year won a scholarship to spend six weeks in a special program sponsored by the Telluride Association at Cornell University. Thrown among fifteen other precocious and gifted teenagers in a house on the Cornell campus, Judith was introduced to Beethoven quartets and debated the finer points of Thucydides. It was an intellectual summer camp that inspired her to return to Cornell as an undergraduate on a Telluride scholarship the following year.

Four years at Cornell carried on the excitement of learning for her, but when it was over she didn't know what to do. She knew she didn't want to spend her life in academia. On a whim, she took the law boards. Law school seemed like a good out, a generalist's education. But with no realistic idea of what Harvard Law School was preparing her for, Judith floundered. She cut classes, although not without the best of intentions. She would rise for a 9 A.M. lecture, start reading a chapter of a book and by noon would have missed two classes. Or she would find herself at Cambridge Library, checking out a stack of novels that she would carry back to her room. She knew part of it was avoidance and confusion over what she was doing at law school. Learning about the uniform commercial code could not compare to the excitement of reading literature. And the atmosphere was qualitatively different at Harvard. Judith recalls, "There were many people on what is now crudely called the 'fast track'—people who were absolutely committed to being lawyers and knew exactly what they were going to do. They were going to join Daddy's law firm and consequently they had study groups from 7 P.M. to midnight and nobody had a beer!" Her first November in Cambridge she ran into an old friend from Telluride, Abe Schulsky, at the movies. As they walked out of the theater he turned to her and remarked, "Well, have you figured out law school isn't for you yet?" The question was discomfiting because she shared its premise. "I was almost embarrassed to say I was going to law school," she says.

Her parents had paid thousands of dollars in tuition and she was seriously questioning whether it was all a colossal waste. After completing her second year, she decided to heed the advice of a former boss and mentor, Larry Bernstone, and take a break from school. Bernstone, who had been director of the Center for Criminal Justice at Boston University, had hired her for a research project the summer after her first year at Harvard. "Get out of Harvard Law School," Bernstone advised her. "You can't go there three years in a row." At the time, Bernstone was teaching at the Inter American University in San Juan, Puerto Rico. He convinced her to take a leave of absence and come to San Juan. They would seek a government grant for her to study return migration to Puerto Rico. But when she arrived in San Juan it looked as if the money for the research would not be coming through. Broke and having withdrawn from school, Judith had no place to go. She had sublet her Cambridge apartment and was not thrilled about returning to her family at loose ends. Settling into old San Juan, she decorated her place with books shipped from Cambridge, three mailbags full, and she earned a meager living doing whatever was available,—waitressing, bookkeeping, bartending, even working as a bouncer in a discotheque. After a few months she tired of her bohemian life in San Juan and of ducking law school and returned to Harvard to finish school.

Judith had enjoyed her work at the Harvard Legal Aid Bureau during her second year. The Bureau had given her a taste of the courtroom. In her first trial she represented a soldier stationed in Vietnam in a custody fight with his former girlfriend. Judith became a sleuth and learned from the airline that the girlfriend had sneaked off to Bermuda with a new beau, neglecting her client's child. The opposing counsel was a forty-five-year-old lawyer who underestimated her. She won, but when it took three months for the judge to award custody to the father, Judith realized she wanted to try criminal law, an area that seemed to have an immediacy to it that was lacking in civil matters.

It was Gary Bellow's class in trial advocacy her third year

that persuaded her to become a criminal defense lawyer. Harvard had recruited Bellow from the West Coast, where he had worked in the California Rural Legal Assistance project, a legal aid program for the poor financed by the federal Office of Economic Opportunity. Classes like Bellow's were part of a new movement at the time to teach lawyers practical skills. She was sent out to interview clients charged with misdemeanors like drunk driving and then represented them in court. Something clicked. This kind of lawyering she understood. There was an excitement in the work that was lacking in her corporations and trusts and estates classes. "I could do all that stuff, but it was just boring as hell. And I didn't do very well because I didn't study. And I didn't go to classes. Before exams I would just spend a couple of weeks in sheer agony staying up all night reading books," she recalls.

Years later it would be hard for her to explain the appeal of the defense work. It just seemed to mesh with her personality. It required verbal skills, a certain aggressiveness. Like Judy Berkan, Judith Lindahl had found a niche in the legal profession that meant she would be taking a very different path than most of her classmates.

Judy Berkan knew she was not suited to be a public defender, Judith Lindahl's choice. The notion of plea bargaining bothered her, as did the idea of defending an accused rapist or child abuser who might, in fact, be guilty. Working with the destitute Puerto Rican clients at New Haven Legal Services was challenging enough and she stayed almost two years, helping the clients with housing, welfare and unemployment matters. One afternoon at work she had a surprise visitor—Carlos Julia, the head of the Puerto Rican Socialist Party in New Haven, who dropped by for some legal advice. She had been introduced to Julia at a friend's house six months earlier and found him very attractive. He was dark and mustached, with the compact build of a tennis pro and the big eyes of his cousin Raul, whose good looks and acting ability had made him a star on Broadway. Carlos was from a *buena familia* in Puerto Rico. Although his immediate family was not wealthy, the Julia name was known in the highest social circles on the island. Obviously Carlos had repudiated much of his background. He, too, was an activist, although he seemed very shy. When Judy met him, he had been wearing a button supporting a migrant worker organizing campaign in the tobacco fields of Hartford, Connecticut. Carlos had come to her office because he wanted her advice about a dispute the Party was having with its landlord that had resulted in his being locked out of the office. She told him to simply cut off the lock. "He thought that was the best advice he'd ever heard from a lawyer," Judy recalls. "He was very impressed!" They began seeing each other casually. Carlos would drop by with extra copies of the Party newspaper, *Claridad,* trying to recruit her. When she told him about her plans to vacation in Puerto Rico over the Christmas holidays he invited her over to see slides of the island. Judy was excited about her trip. Through her Puerto Rican contacts in New Haven she had developed an interest in the politics of the island, specifically its relationship to the United States. She wanted to explore the political situation at first hand. Carlos would be there visiting his family at the same time, and he offered to act as a tour guide.

Carlos was waiting for Judy at the San Juan airport when she arrived with two girlfriends in tow. They became a foursome, touring around the entire island together. During a trip out to the countryside Judy began to fall in love with Carlos. She called him by his Puerto Rican nickname, "Kaki." It was wonderful to be welcomed into the Julias' home for the Christmas celebrations.

The relationship continued to develop when they returned to New Haven. Eventually they moved in together. Carlos had a job as a community worker in a public school in their neighborhood, and Judy was winding down at Legal Services. She had already taken a part-time job in Hartford with the Puerto Rican Center for Justice and was helping to form a lawyers' collective in New Haven. "There's something very, very frustrating in legal services practice. The quantity of work was just extreme. You have the sense that you're doing all Band-Aid stuff, and there were restrictions on what you could do when you have to deal with a bureaucracy," she explained. "There were a lot of racial tensions within the office. I think a lot of it had to do with just deciding that I wanted to try the idea of a collective practice, something that was more in keeping with what I thought my politics were at the time."

Judy and her four partners started up the practice with a bank loan and a large donation. Judy herself contributed $2,000 that she had saved while working at Legal Services. After rehabilitating the office space, they opened up the practice, concentrating on representation of battered women. The group attempted to be democratic in the way they ran things. Everyone had his or her say, and they tried to make decisions on philosophical grounds. They refused to take collection cases or represent men in contested divorces. Rather than hire a secretary, the lawyers took turns typing and answering the phones. Judy's back hurt on the days she had to do the typing, and often she didn't get to the legal work she had to do. Money was always tight, which led to personal conflicts. The rule was that each person would take what he or she needed in salary. Judy took the most, $100 a week, and her partners thought even this paltry draw excessive. She felt she needed at least that much because she was saving to go to Puerto Rico.

In the midst of forming the collective, Judy was contacted by the National Lawyers Guild about setting up an office in Puerto Rico to bring civil rights lawsuits in the U.S. District Court in San Juan. Carlos thought the job was a fantastic opportunity; he had been urging her to consider moving to Puerto Rico anyway. She told the Guild to hold off for a year until the collective got off the ground. When the year was up Judy and Carlos decided to pack up and move to Puerto Rico.

While the idea of establishing a new home in San Juan seemed exciting and adventurous, their early months in Puerto Rico were difficult. When she arrived in the fall of 1977 the money for her salary had fallen through. Their furniture and car were left behind on a dock in Elizabeth, New Jersey, caught in a strike. The couple rented a very small, mosquito-infested apartment in a working-class neighborhood of Santurce for $150 a month, which they furnished with a bed and a radio on loan from Carlos' parents. He sold lobsters on the street to pay the rent. Later he found a job in a record warehouse, earning $72 a week for six days of work. For Judy, having a Harvard Law School degree proved worthless in San Juan. She tried the National Labor Relations Board, the federal court, and the local law schools, but without success. Politicians controlled the jobs and she figured since she wasn't in with the statehood party she didn't have the right contacts. *"El que no tiene padrino no se bautiza,"* she was told. "He who doesn't have a godfather doesn't get baptized." They had to borrow money from friends to live; both were too proud to ask their families for help. Three months passed, and just when it seemed she would never find work two job offers came along. The Guild had found money to hire her after all, and the Inter American University wanted her part-time to teach constitutional law. She started both jobs the same day. The combined salary was just over $9,000 a year.

Judy had been at her new job with the Guild barely a month when she was visited by two fishermen and a teacher from Vieques, a small island six miles off the coast of Puerto Rico. Carlos Zenon, a stocky man with a round face who had fished in the waters around Vieques since he was twelve, headed a group called the Vieques Fishermen's Association. Ismael Guadalupe taught school and led the Crusade for the Rescue of Vieques as well as the local chapter of the Puerto Rican Socialist Party. The third man, known as "Mano Santo" (Saintly Brother), was a minister on the island and a fisherman. The trio presented their troubles with the U.S. Navy. Since World War II the United States had been using Vieques and a smaller island nearby, Culebra, to practice military maneuvers. The Navy retreated from Culebra in 1975, and since then the activity on Vieques had increased, with two thirds of the island—the eastern and western sides—under U.S. military control. The maneuvers, the fishermen complained, wreaked havoc with the fishing, especially on the eastern end of the island, where the best lobster, snapper and perch were found. The fishermen also maintained that the 7,000 people who lived on Vieques were driven to distraction by the roar of low-flying aircraft. The island was riddled with shell craters from bombardments. Would the Guild take on their cause?

Judy went with them to visit Vieques. Seeing the white sand beaches, coral reefs and exotic birds, she felt as if she were visiting a tropical paradise. She talked with the local fishermen and was impressed with their knowledge, despite their relative poverty and lack of education. The people referred to their island as a "sandwich" because the Navy owned the land on either side of them. She was shown tattered certificates the government had handed out in 1943 when it bought the land from large sugar companies during the war emergency. The Viequenese had been tenant farmers for the sugar companies and were paid ten, twenty or thirty dollars for their wooden houses. They were given the option of either leaving Vieques or moving to the center of the island. Many of them went to nearby St. Croix.

The situation of the David-like fishermen up against the

Goliath-sized Navy at once struck Judith as a perfect place to put her energies. She began learning all about the lives of the Vieques fishermen, including the minutest details pertaining to traps and endangered species of fish. In March Judy and another lawyer, Pedro Saade, intervened on behalf of the fishermen in a lawsuit brought by the governor of Puerto Rico, Carlos Romero Barcelo. The fishermen sought to stop all military operations and return the land to the residents of Vieques. The governor was also worried about the effect of the bombing on the environment. One of his aides had jokingly suggested that the officers' golf course on Roosevelt Roads Naval Station, the largest U.S. naval base in the world, located at the eastern end of Puerto Rico, would be an ideal replacement site for the Navy's target practice.

The trial began in September 1978 and continued to December. Judy and the lawyers for the Commonwealth called nearly sixty witnesses. U.S. District Court Judge Juan Torruella led lawyers on an undersea expedition to see, at first hand, the damage caused to the coral reefs. They watched while jets dropped 1,000-pound bombs and heard the explosions. But when a decision was handed down, the judge rejected the fishermen's request for an injunction.

When the Navy planned major maneuvers on Vieques, the fishermen often staged protests. They held "fish-ins" to try to disrupt the ship-to-shore and air-to-ground bombardment exercises. Leaving from La Esperanza, a fishing village at the southern end of Vieques, they took their boats out and formed blockades in restricted waters, firing slingshots at Navy destroyers as a symbolic gesture. The boats often returned in a flotilla to cheering demonstrators.

Not everyone on Vieques supported the fishermen; there were many on the island who favored the Navy's presence. Similarly, among those with anti-Navy sentiments could be found a range of political views. Some worried about the fishing, others about the environmental impact of bombing, and some saw the struggle as symbolic of the larger issue of Puerto Rico's status vis a vis the United States. It was Judy's position that the U.S. Navy did not belong in Vieques. She spent about half her time on the island in 1978 and 1979, giving advice about the legal consequences of protest activities and helping with general strategy. The fishermen she was working with had come to trust and love her, even though she was a gringa. Her Spanish was so fluent, they had no trouble communicating. They would greet her at the airport and take her home, where they would prepare a special catch of the day for dinner. She spent her thirtieth birthday picketing outside the naval base, where the other protesters sang "Happy Birthday."

"None of my Harvard Law classmates who went into corporate law are enjoying themselves as much as I am!" she told a local newspaper reporter.

A massive protest was planned for Saturday, May 19. Zenon had gone on television and radio to get people to come. The plan was to protest amphibious landing exercises on a beach within the geographical area controlled by the Navy. Wearing blue jeans and braids, Judy caught the first flight over from San Juan at 6:45 A.M. on Vieques Air Link. She knew all the pilots. Vieques Air Link (VAL) was owned by sympathizers, one of the families who considered themselves to have been expropriated, and they would lend one of their nine-seater planes at all hours if necessary. "It was a very well organized struggle," Judy recalls. "We used to joke about our land, sea and air forces!"

Although there had been no arrests thus far, the situation on Vieques was heating up. Zenon and a reporter from a local paper, *El Nuevo Día*, had been detained with eleven others at a demonstration three days earlier. Judy had a hunch there might be trouble and wanted to stay close to the action. She climbed into one of the small boats and was ferried out to Bahia de la Chiva on the south coast of Vieques, also known as Blue Beach. During the half-hour ride she thought briefly about the fact that she might be arrested. "I didn't like the idea. I sort of remember on the way out thinking, 'Well, Judith, you did it. I mean, if you're going to get arrested, you're going to get arrested.' I sort of realized that was the decision I had made. I wasn't anxious to get arrested but I didn't think very much about the consequences."

By noon, the demonstration had attracted about a hundred and fifty people to the beach. Three clergymen began an ecumenical religious service. As Judy stood near her friend Ismael Guadalupe at the religious service, they were approached by a U.S. Marshall and the Navy's young liaison officer, Lieutenant Alex De la Zerda. De la Zerda was always lurking around at protests. She thought he was there to recruit informants. Once he had come up to her at a huge rally in the plaza in Vieques and told her that he'd noticed she had cut her hair. "I'd cut my hair like two inches and none of my friends had noticed! He did that on purpose . . . he always made you know that he was watching you," she said.

Alex said a few words and departed, walking up the grassy knoll to talk to the admiral. That was when she noticed him—Rear Admiral Arthur K. Knoizen, Chief of Naval Operations in the Caribbean. A tall man with a sturdy build, bushy white hair and a determined gait, the admiral was easy to spot in his starched whites. Judy and Knoizen knew one another; he had shown her and others around Vieques on site visits during the trial. But neither of them was thinking about tours of the island now. Within minutes she saw about thirty military police—some wearing tear gas masks and carrying rifles and bayonets—start to descend on the beach. As the police began struggling with people who were some distance from the service, Judy saw rocks and sand fly in the air and ran toward the skirmish. Figuring she should make herself useful, she began taking notes on a yellow legal pad and told those around her to remain calm. Ismael resisted and was dragged off and

handcuffed by security officers. "The MPs formed a line
down the middle of the beach and arrested everyone on one
side. The people on the other side were allowed to go back
to their boats," she recalled. "It was kind of a frightening
situation." Judy decided to try to get to the departing boats.
But as she moved toward the line the officers crisscrossed
their weapons to prevent her from passing. She was pushed
onto a large landing barge, where she joined twenty-two
other detainees for a two-and-a-half-hour trip to Roosevelt
Roads Naval Station.

The ride back was miserable. The gas fumes from the
barge made her ill. Judy tried to stay calm and play a lawyer-
like role throughout the ordeal. "I was scared but I wasn't
terrorized. I was pretty rational throughout the whole thing.
I took down the names of everybody who was arrested and
took notes throughout. . . ." Among the group were the
Roman Catholic bishop and the two Protestant ministers who
had led the religious service, and four other lawyers. She
noted that four people were handcuffed and one had a cut on
his head. When they arrived at Roosevelt Roads they passed
through columns of heavily armed guards to board buses that
took them to a security building on the base. From there they
were ushered into a small room, where they sat on the floor
for several hours while they were called one by one for fin-
gerprinting and photographing. When she left the room to
make a phone call, Knoizen taunted her by calling, "Oh,
Judy, I thought lawyers were supposed to uphold the law!"
She could not think of a retort, so instead shot him a hostile
look.

The group sang on the way to the courthouse and listened
to the news reports of their arrest on the radio. When they
arrived it was almost midnight. Judy had worked in the federal court, so she knew the marshals and they were friendly
to her. The men and women were taken to separate lockups
on the fourth floor, where they could hear people outside

chanting slogans of support: *"Vieques sí, marina no."* She was one of the first to be called before U.S. magistrate Juan Perez-Gimenez. She had met Perez-Gimenez on the tennis courts of the Caparra Country Club, with Carlos, shortly after they arrived in Puerto Rico. He had been impressed with her Harvard Law School credentials and had offered to help her find a job. Now she was standing before him, being charged with trespassing on military property. The judge agreed to her release on a $1,000 nonsurety bond, which meant she did not have to pay unless she skipped bail. She could not leave the court's jurisdiction without permission until her case was over, and Perez-Gimenez made it clear he did not want her returning to Vieques, either.

By daybreak she was out and walking home to her apartment in old San Juan, exhausted from her ordeal. She had to call a friend to let her into her apartment. Her purse with her keys inside had been left behind on Vieques.

As a young lawyer starting out, Judith Lindahl's career, while somewhat less controversial, had also become the center of her life. Her salary working as a public defender at Massachusetts Defenders Committee, a publicly funded agency set up in 1958 to represent indigents in need of legal counsel, was a mere $12,500 but she loved her job (no year that she worked at Mass Defenders did she ever earn more than the starting salary for first-year associates out of Harvard Law School). She started at the bottom with an assignment to Dorchester District Court.

Dorchester had one of the highest crime rates in the Boston area and its courts were always busy. The lawyers referred to the court as a "community court"—the lawyers, court officers, police, prosecutors and probation officers all knew one another. Dorchester got every kind of case (although the Mass Defenders did not handle murder cases) and it was trial by judge; there were no juries. Misdemeanors were handled on the spot. If a person was charged with a felony the presiding judge would either reduce the charge or hold a probable cause hearing to determine whether there was enough evidence to turn the case over to a grand jury and then, possibly, to Superior Court for a jury trial.

Judith handled everything from petty drunk driving cases to serious felonies like armed robberies. She talked to the cops and got to know the good ones. She would find out what they thought about her client, and if they believed he was a decent sort she would try to talk the DA into a suspended sentence. Sometimes it seemed as if she and the cops were on the same side; the prosecutors didn't always seem to understand what was going on in the streets.

She was especially proud of maintaining her poise in front of Judge Paul King. "Are you Ms., Mrs., Madam or Miss?" he had asked her the first time she appeared in his courtroom, as a student defender. She was arguing a driving infraction with all the seriousness of a first-degree murder. King was amused and started interrupting her with frivolous questions. "Call me whatever you like, your honor, I am not married," she retorted in her no-nonsense baritone, unaware that he was teasing her. "I was so damn serious," she recalls.

King was in fact sympathetic to young lawyers and he understood that the public defenders had a tough job. The saying among defendants had been "Get a PD, go to jail." They had to handle twenty cases a day, one after another, often with only a few minutes to talk to their clients and even less time to investigate their stories. The judge had seen scores of them come into his courtroom like Judith, bogged down with files, running hither and yon all day long without a break. They would be on their own almost from their first day on the job, trying to figure out how to pry the truth from clients and at the same time size up the prosecutors and police officers in order to get the best deal possible.

The public defender's lot had begun to improve by the

time Judith started working in Dorchester, so that she was
handling about eight cases on a typical day. On a bad day she
had ten; if she was lucky, just four or five. The reduced case
load meant she could actually sit down with her client and
visit the scene of the crime. There was time to decide
whether to make a plea or go to trial. The change was the
result of a transition under way at Mass Defenders. The
agency was revamping itself in response to a report written
by the National Legal Aid & Defenders Association that was
highly critical of the case load and the pressures it put on the
staff. Gerard Schaefer, a Mass Defender in his mid-thirties
who had been with the organization since graduating from
Harvard Law School, was installed as chief counsel. With federal money, Mass Defenders was expanding from a small,
low-budget operation into a larger, more structured one.
Training and supervision were formalized. Salaries were
raised. Schaefer required judges to appoint additional lawyers in cases where there were multiple defendants, and he
fought to hire investigators and social workers so the lawyers
did not have to run around finding clients places to live or
drug or psychiatric referrals.

Her office at 120 Boylston Street, across the Boston Common from the State House, bore a greater resemblance to a
welfare office than a law office. She shared a tiny cubicle with
another young graduate of Harvard Law School, Geoffrey
Packard. They were constantly overhearing one another's interviews and talking about cases. Often they would be interviewing at the same time—he'd have an armed robbery, she a
rape. Packard was impressed with her commitment. "I had
never met anyone as dedicated to being a criminal defense
lawyer as Judith," he recalls. "That is what she is and how she
defines herself. I don't think anybody can hold a candle to
her." Judith insisted on doing her own investigations at all
hours of the day and night. Often that meant going down to
the Columbia Point housing project, a place few careful peo-

ple roamed at night. Carrying a .22 caliber revolver in her purse, she knocked on doors and asked questions, trying to reconstruct the crimes. The cops in District 3 were concerned for her safety, even though they were bound to be shaken up by her in court the next day. Once when she visited police headquarters to get a report the cops offered to accompany her on her investigations. They explained that they would rather spend the time covering her than investigating her rape or murder the next day. But she declined the offer. "What if a defendant saw me in a cop car? Great way to establish trust!" she exclaimed to Packard afterward. Most of her clients could not see her anyway. They were locked away in the Charles Street jail, too broke to make bail.

There were other women at the Mass Defenders, but not many, maybe a handful out of fifty lawyers when Judith started. They were looked down upon as window dressing by some of the tough ten-year veterans. At five feet one, Judith was so small that some of the lawyers thought she was misplaced in the operation. "When I walked into the Mass Defenders the attitude was, 'There ain't never been a good broad defense attorney,'" Judith recalls. "I figured if I showed I was committed to becoming a good defense lawyer the 'woman' would take care of itself." The office was not soft on assignments and she took whatever came her way. In spite of whatever provincial attitudes about women that may have been lingering, the men did love practicing law and apparently were willing to teach any young person who was really committed.

After putting in their time in Dorchester, both Judith and Packard were happy to be promoted to Suffolk Superior Court in Boston. Finally they would have jury trials. In court Judith saw few female faces and she thought the prosecution often failed to take her seriously. "Three fourths of them figured they were home free because there was a woman on the other side," she remembers. But she did not mind being the outsider, and she learned to turn the situation to her advantage. "It's always better to be the underdog. You just recognize the odds so well and you learn to be sensitive to every little nuance," she says. "If you think the odds are equal, then you're not so sharp about it." In her first few trials Judith had what she called a "bloom of youth" as a lawyer.

She loved to argue her case to a jury. It was a creative moment. She tried to be authentic and get the jury to see what she called "the human side" of her client's case. Walking back and forth before the jury box, her hands stuffed in her pockets, she looked a bit like the little girl who had walked down the country road kicking pebbles in the New Hampshire sun. Judith knew she had to be herself in front of the jury. "If they think I'm a phony, forget it," she says. It was always a hard moment after she finished arguing. She had done all she could and there was nothing to do but wait for the verdict to be read. "A hundred years pass, and the foreman and all the jurors are looking down, serious and downcast, and you're thinking, 'Oh, my God, fifteen to twenty!' " Every once in a while a juror would wink at her upon reentering the courtroom. Then she knew she had won. "There's no juror in the world who's ever given me a wink when it wasn't a 'not guilty,' " she recalls. But most of the time, she did not know what the outcome would be.

As a defender, she was always on her own in the courtroom. It was her name on the appearance slip, she was the one who was antagonizing the judge or persuading the jury. Being alone in court made the collegiality in the office all the more important. When she came in from court people wanted to know how things had gone. If she had won she would flip a thumbs-up signal. She wore her long brown hair pinned back in a bun, always a piece of it hanging askew, and she wisecracked out of the side of her mouth, usually puffing on a cigarette. She was cocky, her vocabulary salty. "She intentionally talked below her intellect," recalls Bob Banks, her first supervisor at Mass Defenders. It was a style she adopted from the sage elders among the Defenders, like Neil Colicchio.

A short man in his early fifties, with thinning hair and glasses, who sometimes wore rumpled suits, Colicchio was chief trial counsel at the Mass Defenders, and Judith deeply respected him. Three years out, she and Packard were assigned to work under Neil in his Major Violators Counterforce, and they leaped at the chance to work with a mentor. The trio were supposed to be a counterforce to the DA's new Major Violators Unit. Most of the cases they handled were real losers. The clients were usually buried overwhelmingly by the evidence.

Neil was shrewd and his legal advice was usually right on target. "There's your defense," he would say, pointing his finger after Judith had laid out the facts of a case in his office. But she had to be prepared beforehand. If she went in without the police report she'd hear, "What the hell are you wasting my time for?" If she could get past Neil, no judge would be able to get under her skin.

Her social life also revolved around the job. After work the lawyers would walk down to the 1776, a local bar, for a few beers, or occasionally to a club in the "combat zone," the hard-core entertainment area of downtown Boston. "You! Harvard kids! You think this and you think that," Colicchio and some of the other veterans would say, trying to take Judith and Packard down a few notches. The men could be absolutely brutal in their sarcasm.

Although they seemed harsh and their praise was almost nonexistent, it was clear to Judith that beneath the tough exterior Colicchio and the others did care, very much. But they knew that she and Packard did not need coddling. They needed to stand on their own feet, to define their own standards. "Basically what they said was, 'Take your own delight in being a lawyer. We'll show you, but your ups, your downs, they're yours. I don't have time,' " Judith recalls. "It gave you independence."

Judy Berkan had no idea what was in store for her when she was picked up on Blue Beach that Saturday in May 1979 and charged with trespassing. As a college student she had participated in demonstrations at the Pentagon and the U.S. Department of Justice, and she had always known there was a possibility she would be arrested. Indeed, many of her friends had been arrested, but the result had usually been a small fine or dismissal of the charges. Judy couldn't help but be nervous as she prepared to go before Judge Torruella, the same judge who had rejected her argument on behalf of the Vieques fishermen.

Judy was the fifth in the group to be tried. Every week there was another trial, and sympathizers would picket the federal courthouse in old San Juan when court was in session. Nearly all of the defendants insisted they were innocent, but some refused to allow their lawyers to mount a defense. In this way they could renounce the jurisdiction of the U.S. court in Puerto Rico. Their trials were very short. They were found guilty and fined, and many were jailed after refusing to pay their fines.

On September 5, 1979, the first day of her trial, Puerto Rico was in the grip of hurricane Frederick. Judy had been following the weather reports, hoping for another postponement. Her trial had originally been scheduled for the previous week, but that date had been canceled at the last minute because of an earlier hurricane, Elena. If the judge decided to go ahead this time it would be difficult for her supporters to get to court.

But Torruella decided to proceed as planned. "Nothing else in the whole country happened that day except my trial!" she exclaimed. The whole scene struck her as comical, once

the proceedings got under way. The windows in the courtroom rattled and lights blinked on and off during testimony.
Thunder resonated from the darkness outside the courthouse. Some members of the press who ordinarily would
have been there were busy covering the hurricane. The Navy
had to alter its presentation because the weather made it impossible for certain witnesses to fly in from Roosevelt Roads.
There was testimony about whether Judy had been standing
above or below the high tide mark. The Navy needed to
establish she was actually on government property. She
thought they didn't really know exactly where anyone was
standing. When it was all over Torruella asked her if she had
anything to say. "I feel proud to be here as a North American, as a lawyer who has been involved in this fight, and I feel
proud to be here for sentencing today," she told the court.
Then the judge found her guilty and imposed the maximum
sentence—six months in jail and a $500 fine.

She was stunned. None of the previous defendants had
received such stiff prison terms. She thought Torruella had
bought the prosecution's argument that she should be dealt
with more severely because she was a lawyer. She also
thought the judge had taken a special dislike to her. "I don't
think he personally disliked me," she explains. "I think he
didn't like what I represented and I think it was particularly
complicated by my being a woman and a North American
with my credentials. It has to do with a whole colonial mentality. . . ." She would appeal.

Although Judy did not want to go to jail, she did not regret
going to Vieques that day. She did wish, though, that as she
stepped into the boat that took her out to Blue Beach she had
thought more about the consequences of what she was about
to do. "I think I sort of let myself fall into it without realizing, and I think it's partly because I was North American, not
realizing that you really could get sentenced to jail. I think I

would have made the same decision, but it just would have
been a little more knowing decision."

It was not unusual for people to recognize Judy as one of
the "Vieques 21" and to respond to her accordingly. Sometimes they were cold, other times the response was very
friendly. The man who sold her plants would give them to
her at half price, and the restaurant where she bought coffee
would insist on giving her a cut rate. Around the time of her
sentencing she received her routine billing statement from
the San Juan *Star* and written across it was the misspelled
word "curtesy." She was very appreciative but afraid to call
up the newspaper to offer thanks lest it lead to someone's
being fired. At Inter American University her case had cre-
ated a stir, although for the most part the students had been
on her side. The Student Council had passed a solidarity resolution and the dean of the law school, Alberto Ferrer, was
very sympathetic. Faculty reaction had been mixed.

When the trials were over Judy appealed with three others
who had been arrested with her—Bishop Antulio Parrilla
Bonilla, Episcopal priest Andrés Trevathan, and Salvador
Tió, a legal services lawyer in Puerto Rico. The three others
had each received one-year sentences to be served on probation. They settled in to wait for the news from the First Circuit Court of Appeals in Boston.

Meanwhile, things had quieted down on Vieques, and Judy
had left the Lawyers Guild project. Political differences had
developed with people in New York who had been setting
the agenda, and she had left under fire. The only real demand on her time was her part-time teaching. Since she
might want to open her own practice at some point, she decided to take care of another problem that confronted her—
admission to practice.

In order to represent the Vieques fishermen, Judy was admitted to federal court pro hac vice (for the case only). In
January 1979, about the same time she began working for the

fishermen, she had wanted to work on another very controversial case, representing the families of two young Independentistas who had been killed by police on a mountain-
top called Cerro Maravilla the summer of the previous year.
The activists were accompanied to the site by a police under-
cover agent and, according to police, went there to destroy a
television transmission tower. Police maintained the killings
were in self-defense; the two were gunned down when they
ignored an order to surrender. A later inquiry by the Puerto
Rico Senate uncovered evidence that the young men had sur-
rendered to police after an exchange of gunfire and were
later shot, while kneeling, by a police firing squad. The Senate hearings were broadcast on television and the new evidence led to charges of cover-up on the part of the police and
Governor Romero. Everyone was talking about Cerro
Maravilla, and the case became known as Puerto Rico's
"Watergate."

Judy drafted the initial complaints for the families of the
men. In May, Juan Perez-Gimenez, who had been promoted
from magistrate to district court judge, ordered the court
clerk not to accept any documents with Judy's name on them.
She could not work on the civil suit because she had not been
officially admitted to the federal bar and she had lived in
Puerto Rico too long to be admitted pro hac vice. These
were the rules of the court.

Judy viewed the process as a clerical matter. She would first
take the local bar exam, be sworn in at the local bar and then
apply for admission at the federal bar. All she would have to
do would be to pay $18. She set aside twenty-eight days,
studied from 6 A.M. until 10 P.M., and when she took the test
in the middle of March 1980 she was calm. The exam was in
Spanish but by special motion she was allowed to answer in
English. When she walked out she told people, *"lo tale"*—she
aced it. When the results came out Judy received the highest

score of the three hundred lawyers who took the exam. Fewer than half passed it.

But there were complications. Shortly after she passed the exam the federal court put into effect a new set of rules that called for the appointment of a Committee on Admissions that would advise the court whether candidates were qualified to practice. To Judy's lawyer friends, the timing seemed suspiciously close to her filing for admission, causing them to joke about the "the Judith Berkan rules." She put in her application in May and began the wait.

While Judy was concentrating her efforts on the federal court the local court was having its own problems with her admission. She received a phone call from a lawyer who headed the "Reputation Commission" of the local bar association. He wanted her to come to his office. When she arrived he told her there was a minor problem—she would have to rewrite an affidavit before her admission could be completed. Then he told her that the Commission had decided against admitting her but had been overruled by the Supreme Court. This was the first she had heard of any snag and she was furious.

She stormed out of his office and over to the Supreme Court to look up her file. She discovered that the Court, having learned the Commission was investigating her trespass conviction, had issued a special resolution directing the Commission not to consider her federal trespassing case in evaluating her character. While she was angry about her treatment by the Commission, she was impressed that the Supreme Court had defended her, and so fast. After the swearing-in ceremony two days later, Angel Martín, one of the most conservative judges on the Supreme Court, approached Judy from the dais to offer congratulations. She was sitting in the front row wearing a black robe. "I just want to tell you that I thought it was a terrible thing that they tried to do to you, to keep you out," he told her. It was extraordinary for a judge to make such a personal statement. She could not help but smile.

Judy continued to call up the federal court from time to time, only to be told that there was no news on her application. Finally in November she received a single-sentence letter signed by the clerk of the court informing her that her application for admission was denied. No reasons were given. She thought the letter was so outrageous in its brevity that she bought a cheap black frame and hung it up in her apartment. This, too, she would appeal to the First Circuit in Boston.

The bar rejection hit the papers and, she thought, seemed to capture people's imaginations more than her arrest on Vieques had. "It [the Vieques arrest] wasn't seen on a level of, say, stealing from your clients, which people would recognize as a reason not to let somebody be admitted to practice . . . it really looked like they were harassing me," she remembers. Judy received support from very different quarters. The head of the local Federal Bar Association, a conservative, spoke out on her behalf, and the San Juan *Star* ran an editorial criticizing the court for not stating its reasoning.[2]

Although the support was gratifying the attention was beginning to bother her and she was starting to feel like an object. "The cases became my life. That Christmas period, wherever I went I remember joking that I was going to get a daily computer printout about the status of my cases because nobody would ever talk to me about anything else." In addition to feeling a distinct lack of privacy, she did have the real pressure of her appeal on the trespassing conviction coming up soon. If she lost she would be going to jail for six months. Carlos had moved back to Connecticut and, with him gone, she felt very much alone. "I was not in my best shape. I don't know how much it affected my behavior. I know it meant

[2] San Juan *Star*. 11/21/80.

crying a lot by myself. I felt overwhelmed. God, those were lonely years."

She also had to cope with telephone threats. She received a letter nominating her for the "Criminals of America Society." One of her students, whom she suspected of being affiliated with a U.S. intelligence agency, warned her that she was under threat from the right and the left and that she should take on the protection of the U.S. intelligence agencies. "I never knew if he was trying to recruit me or intimidate me," she explains. She became cold to him when he kept up with the offers of protection, and finally she changed her phone number and moved in with friends for lengthy stays. Eventually Judy convinced herself that she was not a likely target. If she, a North American, were to be harmed in Puerto Rico it would be big news in the States—and bad news for her assailants. "I took great comfort from my analysis," she recalls. Carlos phoned from Connecticut during these hard times and offered to marry her if it would make her feel better. It was the only time in their relationship he had proposed marriage. But marriage was not the answer to her problems.

With her cases to worry about, Judy realized she could drive herself crazy if all she did was think about whether or not she was in danger. She tried to prepare herself for jail. The Vieques trespassers who had received jail terms were serving their time in the States and had returned one by one to *recibimientos,* or receivings. Judy assumed she would be sent to the federal women's prison in Alderson, West Virginia, where her friend Emilia Rodriguez, a schoolteacher, had served her three-month sentence. Emilia gave Judy names of sympathetic people inside the prison to contact when she arrived. Although she had a glimmer of hope she would be vindicated, she was prepared to go to jail. "I think that one of the differences between me and most of the people I know in the States is that I'm in a context in which at some point it might be necessary to go to jail or whatever, depending upon what happens here," she says. "If that has to be, it has to be. That's part of living here. The people on the left go to jail. Not everybody, but it's not unusual."

In February 1981 the First Circuit Court of Appeals came to San Juan and heard her appeal. Three months later, two years to the date of her arrest, Judy received a phone call from Andrés Trevathan, her codefendant. "Judy, sit down," the priest told her. "We have been acquitted." Apparently the foursome had got off on a technicality: the Navy had placed them on the wrong spot on the beach. She was so excited she could hardly concentrate on the conversation. She hung up and immediately started dialing the phone, calling Carlos and her parents, among others. She went home and wrote about her feelings. "I wanted to preserve that moment. I remember feeling kind of conflicted because I was very happy not to go to jail but other people had gone to jail. I questioned whether I should have appealed or shouldn't have appealed. The circuit court went way out of its way to acquit us. Was that because we were two lawyers, a priest and a bishop? I felt a little guilty. I think I also recognized that it was stupid to feel guilty, but I felt those tugs and I wanted to write that down . . . I remember it wasn't total unabashed joy."

The next day she called a lawyer in Boston, Michael Avery, who had picked up a copy of the decision over at the First Circuit Courthouse. As Avery started reading to her from the decision the words did not seem to make sense, they did not fit the Vieques case. ". . . insist that a district court in this Circuit do more than play at cat and mouse with a rejected but seemingly qualified bar applicant . . ." He was reading about her application to practice in the federal court. As it turned out, both decisions had been issued the same day. The justices were directing the lower court to tell her why they had denied her application and ordering them to give her a hearing. She was also delighted about the second victory and felt it would only be a matter of time before she would be able to carry on with her work.

During this turbulent period in Judy Berkan's life Judith Lindahl's career had progressed smoothly. In the nine years she spent at Mass Defenders, she blossomed into a confident and competent trial lawyer. In 1983 she decided it was time to break away and try to make it on her own. She was scared but she wanted the challenge of private practice. "I did not want to look back after twenty years in the Defenders office and wonder, 'Could I have made it on my own?'" In February she took with her a few cases that were ripe for trial and opened a solo practice at 11 Beacon Street, just across the Boston Common from her old stomping grounds. Almost immediately she plunged into the most controversial trial of the year. Judith also would soon know the pressures of being at the center of a media fire storm.

Seven months after opening her shop, Superior Court Judge Guy Voltera, before whom she had once appeared as a Mass Defender, appointed her to represent Victor Raposo, twenty-two, one of six men accused of aggravated rape in Big Dan's Tavern in New Bedford. It would not be a lucrative case. Appointed lawyers were paid $35 an hour for court time, $25 for preparation, and the state could take years to pay the bill. Most first-year associates at firms in Boston were charging more than $75 an hour for their time. She would have to set up temporary headquarters nearer to the trial, which would be held in Fall River, sixteen miles from New Bedford and almost two hours from Boston. In spite of these inconveniences she was eager to get to work. "It was the kind of case I had always prepared for," she recalls, "—despised clients, horrendous crimes, with the weight of public opinion against the accused." With the national spotlight that later would be focused on the trial, it might also turn out to be a fantastic break for her career.

Big Dan's was the biggest trial to come to Fall River since Lizzy Borden was tried and acquitted for murdering her mother and father with an ax one morning in August of 1892, and it would be a long time before the old whaling town of New Bedford and its large Portuguese community forgot about Big Dan's. It all began one Sunday evening in March 1983, when twenty-one-year-old Cheryl Ann Araujo left her apartment in the North End of New Bedford and ended up at the tavern, a few blocks from where she lived. Hours later she fled from the bar, practically naked and hysterical. She said she was gang-raped on the pool table at Big Dan's while onlookers cheered.

The lurid story was immediately picked up by the national press, and a week after the incident thousands marched by candlelight in New Bedford to protest the attack. Gloria Steinem sent a telegram: "We will not rest until those men are punished and all women are saved." Six Portuguese immigrants were eventually charged with aggravated rape. They were to be tried under a Massachusetts law of "joint enterprise," meaning that they shared a common intent to rape. The maximum penalty facing them was life in prison. More than half the 100,000 citizens of New Bedford were of Portuguese descent, and after the arrests the city had experienced an outpouring of anti-Portuguese and anti-immigrant sentiment. "Ship them back to Portugal," callers to one radio station had demanded.

Several weeks into the trial, Judith sat at the bar of the Ramada Inn in Seekonk, Massachusetts, a place she came to call her home away from home. Seekonk is only a twenty-minute drive from the century-old Bristol County Superior Courthouse in Fall River. Sandwiched between other customers at the bar, Judith could let her hair down and unwind from the daily strain of the trial. The hours alone would have taken their toll on anyone, and she was putting in her share, rising at 6 A.M. most mornings to prepare to cross-examine witnesses at nine when her trial, the first of the two, resumed. (Judge William Young had divided the case into two trials with separate juries. Four defendants were tried in the morning and two others in the afternoon. The separation was meant to avoid having some of the defendants incriminate one another.)

As a lawyer, she felt frustrated by having to cross-examine through translators. While the witnesses engaged in dialogue with the translator, the testimony lost the spontaneous quality she needed to score points with the jury. Sometimes meaning was lost in the translations. With her limited knowledge of Spanish from her days in Puerto Rico, Judith pointed out to the jury during cross-examination of the bartender that the word for "scream" and the word for "shout" were the same in Portuguese. Every time the bartender had used the word *gritar,* it was being translated as "scream."

Each day seemed to bring new evidence. Witnesses contradicted not merely each other but their own, earlier, statements. The victim, too, kept changing her story. It struck Judith that Araujo's statements in court were edging closer to what actually happened. She admitted that she might have exaggerated her original statements to police because she was nervous and confused. A lot of criticism was being leveled at the defense lawyers for grilling the victim, but there were discrepancies between her testimony and her pretrial statements and the testimony of other eyewitnesses.

For Judith, it was also difficult being second seated to another experienced trial lawyer. She followed Kenneth Sullivan, a courtly Irishman in his sixties. Sullivan represented John Cordiero, who Araujo claimed had tried to force her to perform oral sex. Following Sullivan meant that Judith never had a clean shot at the witness, and there was always the risk of boring the jury by retracking the same territory.

Judith's client, Victor Raposo, was also accused of forcing the victim to perform oral sex. When it came time for Judith to cross-examine Araujo she did not want to appear to be badgering her but she did want to establish what had happened. She took the witness step by step through her memory of events. Even though Araujo could not testify that Raposo had ever touched her, Judith knew she could not rely on the victim's testimony to free her client. That was the problem with trying a case that had a constellation of defense counsel whose clients had conflicting interests.

When the time came to deliver her closing argument she was up like an actor in a play, having tried out versions of the final argument many times to her motel room curtains. She sat waiting for her turn, wearing a brown suit and dark pink blouse. As Sullivan concluded his argument Judith stood up, cleared her throat and wiped the edges of her mouth. "Mr. Foreman and ladies and gentlemen. No witness has fully told you the truth. You don't have to find that Cheryl Araujo is a slut or a whore. . . . Each one of us has done something we regret and very often under the influence of alcohol. . . . A pack of Kools. That, according to Cheryl Araujo, is where it all started," she told the jury of six men and six women, while tossing a pack of cigarettes on top of the model of Big Dan's. Judith painted a picture of a lonely, drunken woman who had gone to the bar not for cigarettes but to have fun. Then, in an effort to explain what had happened to her, she had exaggerated the real story. "Women have a responsibility by their words and by their actions to say no. If men violate the no they should be held responsible," she said.

The jury in the afternoon trial deliberated just over four hours before finding its two defendants guilty of aggravated rape. Judith's morning jury took longer. At midday the jury emerged and asked the judge for more instructions. Judith took this to be a sign that they were considering convicting Cordiero and acquitting her client, Raposo. When the jury came back into the emotionally charged courtroom at 4 P.M. after more than seven hours of deliberation, the foreman, dressed in green for St. Patrick's Day, read the verdict. Raposo and Cordiero—her client and Sullivan's client—were guilty. The other two morning defendants had been found not guilty. Raposo broke down and sobbed and Judith put her hand on his shoulder to calm him. "My first concern was for Victor, how he was going to take it," she recalls. "I was concerned with his being able to control himself. He was in the public eye. I had a lot of sympathy for him."

Although the verdict wasn't a shock, she was profoundly disappointed. She knew she had an uphill fight on her hands, but she also thought that, in looking beyond and beneath the testimony of the various witnesses, the jury could have acquitted Raposo. "I certainly believed it was possible," she said. Afterward court officers congratulated her on her performance. Even Robert Kane, the prosecutor, told her he thought she had been "a pro." But at such a moment the compliments were little consolation.

Judge Young sentenced the convicted men to prison terms at Walpole State Penitentiary, a maximum security prison south of Boston. Raposo received nine to twelve years. Judith, of course, viewed the sentences as very severe. Outside the courthouse after sentencing, an angry crowd cursed the district attorney and cheered the convicted rapists.

It had been an exhausting case. "I tried very hard and put a lot of myself into it," she recalls. "One always wonders what one could have done, should have done, differently—and always more critically on a loss than a win, but I don't regret accepting the case."

During the six-week trial Judith Lindahl's only diversion was a pancake breakfast one morning with a few friends. If she headed home to Boston on weekends, she spent much of her time catching up on other work that had piled up in her office. Whatever she was working on, Judith committed herself totally, often at the expense of doing more pleasurable things. She knew a lot of people in her field who, like herself, seemed driven by insecurities about their self-worth. By being so devoted to their work, proving their worth in at least one area, they didn't have to put themselves on the line socially. If Judith did have a spare moment she was more likely to pick up a novel than call a friend.

Because a lawyer's skills and time were both so desperately needed in the legal services/public defender/public interest sphere of the profession, it was easy for lawyers like Judith Lindahl to let their personal lives become swallowed up by work. There was always so much work left undone, emergencies erupting constantly. Burnout was sometimes the result for those who went into public defender and legal services jobs.

On her second day as a brand-new attorney for the New Hampshire Legal Assistance program in Manchester, Barbara Sard was assigned forty-six cases. Carolyn Daffron, who, after several years of service, left Community Legal Services in Philadelphia, had more than a hundred and fifty cases assigned to her in a single year.

The extremely demanding nature of the work made some women from the Harvard Law School class of 1974 who went into this line of work more conscious of the need to maintain lives outside. Without her husband, a pick-your-own berry farm they run together and outside interests, including yoga, Lois Wood worries that she would have tired of her job as a legal services lawyer in a very poor, predominantly black area of Illinois, particularly following a spate of recent budget cutbacks and layoffs that have made her own job even more demanding. Joyce Miller, who has worked in poverty law programs across New Jersey, relies on the people who live with her in a collective house for diversion and support. Rosemary Williams Hill looks to her born-again religion, her husband and her children to help her deal with the daily strain of working in the Roxbury ghetto near Boston.

During her struggle to practice in federal court and her trespass case, Judy Berkan had also found it hard to have an outside life. She had become so involved with her own cases that she could hardly think about anything else. Her relationship with Carlos had played itself out. Her struggles had not only taken a toll on her personal life, they had put her out of commission as a practicing lawyer for more than a year. She realized it was time to get her career back on track.

After the First Circuit Court of Appeals ruled on her admission to practice, two of the five justices at the U.S. District Court in San Juan voted to admit her immediately to the bar. But a majority of three voted to hold a hearing first. The court sent her another letter outlining its reasons for denying her application: she had been convicted in a criminal case; it appeared that she had violated an injunction against interference with naval exercises on Vieques; and, finally, she had failed to inform the court of her trespass conviction. In light of her acquittal on appeal, the justices agreed they could not consider her trespassing conviction. A hearing on the other points was scheduled for September, and Juan Perez-Gimenez was appointed a "fact finder" in the case by the chief judge.

At her hearing Alberto Ferrer, dean of Inter American University School of Law, appeared as a character witness on her behalf. "If I had to choose a word to describe Professor Berkan's reputation in the community, I would say that it is impeccable," the Dean told the court. Judy argued that she had not violated the injunction and that the government had made no effort to press contempt charges against her. She said she had not reported her trespassing conviction because the court's application had not asked for the information. After all, the entire incident had been front-page news.

Another eight months passed and still no decision. Judy began the research for her appeal to the First Circuit. Finally, in October 1982, two years and five months after she had put in her application, she was admitted to the bar. But in their ruling the court rebuked her for violating the Vieques injunction. "I had never been accused, I had never been tried . . . but they found!" she exclaimed. She immediately turned to Boston but was told that she had no grounds for appeal. Too tired to fight on, she would just have to live with the decision.

Sitting on the porch of her modest home in Cupey Alto in the summer of 1984, Judy Berkan reflects on her life since Harvard Law School. Another two years have passed since her successful fight to gain admission to the bar, and she is still picking up the threads of her career and is facing yet another troublesome situation. The fall semester at Inter American is scheduled to start in three weeks, and the university has not yet renewed her annual contract. The tension always settles in every year at this time as she is left to ponder whether she will be able to continue teaching. The chance of being fired seems remote, and she vows that, if let go, she will sue the school in a flash, charging she has been let go because of her political views. The law school's Personnel Committee has called for her promotion. But the president has not yet seen his way to offering her the plum—a tenured contract. Maybe it will happen this year, but she is not optimistic.

Although it is unusual for a woman to be living alone in the country, Judy cherishes her privacy and is not eager to marry. She has a hard time meeting single men anyway. Someday she would like to have a child. "I would love to be in love and to share raising a kid with somebody," she says, "but I don't think there's a 'right man' for me to fall in love with and the day he comes along we'll fall in love and have a family. Maybe that would have been so ten years ago, but at this point in my life I'm more set in my ways."

To ward off loneliness, Judy relies on the emotional support that is readily available from friends and acquaintances in San Juan. She might take in a concert one evening and then end up at the bars in old San Juan where young Independentistas gather. But she would never be found at Juliana's discotheque or the Condado, the beachfront strip where the North Americans party. Sometimes she wishes that Puerto Rican society had a healthier respect for a woman who is single. But she has learned to be self-reliant, partly because she is so involved in her work.

Although her life in Puerto Rico has not been easy, Judy believes that those who have followed her story on the island have learned an important political lesson about the U.S. courts. She likes the idea of making an example of herself. If she had been living in the United States it is doubtful she would have become the center of so much attention. Also, with her fluent Spanish and federal court experience, Judy feels she fills a special need in Puerto Rico. She is always able to find work researching, writing and translating for other lawyers who need her skills, and she has begun to develop her own practice in the area of constitutional torts—suing for money damages over violations of constitutional rights. She also represents activists in grand jury cases and is bringing sexual harassment cases, never before tried in Puerto Rico. In Boston or New York she would be one of hundreds of young female attorneys. In Puerto Rico she is practically the only North American woman lawyer with such a practice.

Judy knows that because of her political activities her future options are somewhat limited. She jokes that she could never become a judge in Puerto Rico unless the island were granted complete independence. She rarely thinks about Harvard Law School and never sees any of her former classmates, despite occasional trips to New York, where so many of them work as corporate lawyers. She is, of course, keenly aware of how different her life has turned out from the Harvard Law School mold and is content with the choices she has made. "A set of circumstances brought me here and once I was here I really identified. I don't consider this separate from the 'cause' I've had all my life, which is that I want to see social change. It just happens that it seems to make sense to do it here and there's a particular role for me here."

The most controversial episode of her career, the Big Dan's rape trial, has also had a lasting impact on Judith Lindahl. Two weeks after Big Dan's she argued another rape case in Boston. The impact of the loss of Big Dan's was palpable. As she prepared to deliver her closing argument she grumbled to court officers that her impulse was to say to the jury, "Ladies and gentlemen, if you haven't figured this out there's nothing I can say to you!" But she made her presentation and her client was acquitted. The experience of Big Dan's had reaffirmed Lindahl's belief in her work. During the trial she had received hate mail, and the sentiments expressed had reminded her why she was a defense lawyer. "Hang the bastards. Your client and you, too, it should only happen to you!" That was why she had become a defender. It had not been to handle the routine shoplifting case or the easy "not guilty" but to represent those guys who were really in the corner, who did not have anyone.

Immediately after the Big Dan's verdict Judith tried to fulfill what she saw as her obligation to inform the public about what she thought the trial had meant. The fact that she was the only woman lawyer on the defense team in a rape case made her especially attractive as an interview subject. She and Bobby Kane appeared on network morning news shows together, broadcast live from the basement of the courthouse. Judith told the press that, although she thought a reasonable jury could have acquitted her client, she believed the jury had done its best. Nevertheless she would appeal the verdict. When they asked her how a woman graduate of Harvard Law School could defend a rapist, she tried not to fly off the handle. "A Harvard Law School degree means only one thing," she said, "that you have a legal background." She thought a lot of the questions were inane. The interviewers seemed to want to talk about the general topic of rape, not about Big Dan's.

Some of her more widely read critics lambasted her role in the trial. A New York *Times* columnist, Sydney Schanberg, criticized Judith in a column, saying she had been "very aggressive in cross examining the victim, trying to impugn the victim's credibility and reputation, portraying her as a liar and a promiscuous woman . . ."[3] Judith did not feel she had, in fact, attacked the woman's reputation or portrayed her as promiscuous, in keeping with the Massachusetts rape shield law, but she *had* called her credibility into question. "It is part of the new mythology of rape that no woman can lie," Judith counters, "and that flies in the face of both experience and human nature." She was offended by the column but never bothered to respond.

It was a novel experience, being chauffeured by limousines and made up for the television cameras. But there was a point at which she began to question the value of the interviews. During the taping of a late night show in New York, Judith felt she had strayed too far from the subject of Big Dan's. She returned to Cambridge and spent a sleepless night castigating herself for losing sight of why she had been on the program in the first place. "You are not the star," she told herself. "You are Victor Raposo's attorney. That is the persona, that is the authority and that is what counts." She did not want to be a television personality or a media commentator. That role was better left to authorities like Harvard Law School professor Alan Dershowitz. All Judith wanted was to be known as an excellent defense lawyer. When the next invitation came in, one to appear on the David Finnegan show one Sunday morning in Boston, she referred the call to another attorney

[3.] New York *Times* (3/27/84).

involved in the case. "I certainly did not want to be perceived—because I know it was not the truth—as using this case as a springboard to just parade my little bod around and pontificate in areas where I don't have expertise."

Big Dan's was a milestone in her career. Judith is now recognized as a leading criminal defense lawyer in Boston. Her personal life is far less defined. She is thirty-six years old and is aware that the biological clock is running. "Having children is important to me," she says. "They are perhaps more grief than joy, but they are a unique joy and they stretch the soul." But for Judith marriage is a prerequisite to parenthood. "Perhaps I regret that my profession does not involve me with the kind of man I imagine sharing Horace with," she says, launching into Latin, "and it does bring out my contentiousness rather than warmth. My fantasy spouse teaches history at Dartmouth and lives in an old farmhouse in New Hampshire."

Judith's career is her life. Her solo practice is just beginning to take off. She does not envy her former classmates who are earning thousands more than she in prestigious law firms. "What do they do on Wall Street? They don't walk into court and get decisions that allow liberty!" Eventually she hopes to take some good civil cases to round out her experience, but she will go slowly, remembering the words of Bob Banks, at Mass Defenders: "You make your reputation every time you enter the courtroom."

Both Judy Berkan and Judith Lindahl became minor celebrities, although neither sought fame and both were at best ambivalent when they found it visited upon them. Most of the dozen or so other women from their law school class who chose public interest careers have spent the last ten years in relative obscurity, displaying the same fortitude they had to exhibit back in law school when their interest in public sector work was frowned upon. Lois Wood has stayed with Land of

Lincoln Legal Assistance Foundation in East St. Louis, Illinois, where she is directing attorney of an office that services 50,000 poor people in a sixty-five-county area in south central Illinois. "Everybody goes through periods of burnout," says Wood. "I don't try to save the entire city. I try to keep my sights set on short-term goals. There isn't going to be a renaissance in East St. Louis."

In 1978 Barbara Sard became one of four senior attorneys out of a staff of ninety lawyers at Boston Neighborhood Legal Services and the first woman to hold such a senior position. Sard, who now has two children and is working a part-time schedule, has wondered occasionally whether it was a mistake not to have sampled a law firm job, even if only for a summer. "It might have satisfied some questions, though I'm convinced it would not have led me to do anything else." Carolyn Daffron, who spent five years working in legal services says she would sample private practice "if somebody would give me scads of money to go work for a firm and administer some wonderful pro bono program, but I've never been tempted at all to have a general litigation practice in a major business type firm."

In 1983 Bari Schwartz, who decided at age ten she would devote her work life to helping poor people and minorities, left her job as executive director of the Coalition for Legal Services in Washington, D.C. She married law school classmate Barry Hager and moved to North Carolina where she consulted for poverty law programs. "We all go through the need to recharge," said Schwartz, "but I intend to spend the rest of my life doing this. . . ." When we caught up with Bari in 1985 she was moving back to Washington to work for Congressman Howard Berman, a liberal Democrat from Los Angeles, California.

If the sacrifices for the public interest lawyers are many, the financial rewards are few. Even after a decade of service most of the lawyers are paid far less than the going rate for first-year associates at most New York firms (in 1984, $48,000). "It says something about the practices of this country that you earn based on the amount of money your clients have, instead of how good a lawyer you are," observes Daffron, who has left her career in legal services to write a novel and raise her baby. Like Daffron, four other women who spent the early parts of their careers in legal services left to do other work. "I sometimes feel a little uneasy," admits Daffron, "that I still have these skills and, if anything, there is a lot more work to be done that I was taught and groomed to do— to redress injustice in this country, and I'm not doing it."

The women, including Judy Berkan and Judith Lindahl, who have remained working in public-service-type jobs share a passionate commitment to their work that equals, if not surpasses, their counterparts who took the more lucrative route Harvard Law School expected of them. They have found a deeper meaning in their work—the sense of purpose that some of their sisters in corporate law crave.

4

Burning Out and Dropping Out

There was no group of women more determined to "have it all" than those in the Harvard Law School class of 1974. Describing the "superwoman" mind-set of her classmates, Rene Townsend Robinson says, "You want to do everything. It's part of being driven. You've got to be the perfect lawyer, the perfect mother, the perfect woman. That's three perfects and, although we hate to admit it, probably unattainable."

During the first five years of their legal careers the women in the class threw themselves into their work with a single-minded dedication. "I worked my ass off," says one member of the class who spent the first three years of her career at two large New York firms. "To succeed you knew you had to work nights and weekends, that your work had to come first. But you can't get all of your emotional satisfaction from work. It's a rotten life." After three years she left the world of big firms to take a job as a staff attorney at a Fortune 500 corporation with more flexible hours.

Perhaps their expectations were unrealistically high. Many of the 1974 Harvard Law women thought their new roles as lawyers would bring intellectual and professional challenge, as well as emotional satisfaction. Disappointment was an inevitable result, given the toll of hours and the boring nature of the assignments doled out to beginners. Even at the five-year mark the realities of their jobs, coupled with family demands, was very different from their original expectations. The result was that a majority of the women ended up switching out of their original career paths, and many of them spent years trying to find new jobs that better suited their lifestyles. The casualty rate was particularly high (more than 50%) among those who went to private firms.

A legal degree equips young professionals to move in several directions—into private practice, government, business, public interest work, and academia. The women from the Harvard Law School class of 1974 did not enter the profession with preordained notions of having their first job be their "life's work." They were not afraid to try their hands at different types of jobs. If their work was dull they were quick to pull up stakes and quit. The men in the class tended to stay put for longer, most of them trying to stay on partnership track at large firms. Ten years out of law school, 51% of the men in the class are partners at law firms (as opposed to just 23% of the women) and others are working at high levels of government and in the business world. One, Charles Schumer, is a U.S. congressman (D, N.Y.). Because of these differences many more of the women than the men from the class are at the beginning stages of their careers, still trying to establish themselves.

Because the high dropout rate among women associates was manifesting itself at firms everywhere, even women from the class of 1974 who stuck it out noticed a growing perception that women lawyers as a whole were not making the same investment in their careers as men. "There's a perception that women won't tough it out," says one who did, Karen Katzman, now a litigation partner at New York's Kaye, Scholer, Fierman, Hays & Handler. "Women are perceived as being more willing to pick up and leave, more likely not to get locked into job situations they don't like.

There's a feeling women are less permanent fixtures." But those that felt this way rarely stopped to consider *why* so many women were dropping out of firms. Was it because of the individual makeup of the women, or the nature of the firms themselves?

The men in the class were less inclined to give up the security of high-paying law firm jobs. At various junctures in his career, Mickey Mixon, a partner at an Atlanta firm, has considered changing jobs. "Something called inertia," he claims, kept him on partnership track. "The first two years of being at a firm are the worst experience you can have," he says. "You're at the bottom of the totem pole and you get the work that no one else wants." Mixon adds, "My impression of the women in my class is that they were better qualified and smarter and perhaps less willing to put up with scut work." Also, family responsibilities sometimes required that the men hold on to their jobs. Several of the women in the class were married to higher-salaried professionals and, consequently, had more latitude in their career planning.

Many of the men in the class did leave jobs at firms to work in government for a few years. But, whereas the women went into government to build new careers, the men often parlayed their government experience into better jobs back in private practice or industry. William Neff, a tax partner at Washington's Crowell & Moring, has considered working in government to augment his experience as a private practitioner, but instead has followed a straight and narrow path to partnership at his firm. At the critical five-year mark as an associate, Neff calculated that he was not taking that big a risk by sticking around. "At five years," he observes, "I think the women may have judged their chances worse than a man would have." Neff says he sensed "a certain lack of confidence" among the women in his class. And there were reasons for their lack of confidence. In the late 1970s, there were still very few women partners. With dim prospects for promotion, why stay? Like Mixon, Neff attributes his longevity in private practice to "a failure of imagination." The men may have dreamed of picking up and traveling to exotic places but they remained glued to their desks. And, like so many of his fellow classmates, Neff became a partner.

When, in the late 1970s, headhunters in New York and other big cities were suddenly flooded with résumés from young women lawyers, the managing partners at various firms often blamed the high attrition rate among female associates on family conflicts. They said it was an unfortunate fact of life that the partnership track coincided with prime childbearing years. But only women from the class of 1974 who left their original firms cited family conflicts as the reason for their departure. These women were not leaving to have babies but for a host of other reasons, many of which had to do with the law firms themselves.

"I was always questioning, 'Is this it?'" explains Shelley Green, who joined a politically connected Washington, D.C., firm, Sutherland, Asbill & Brennan, after graduation. "I never took for granted what male associates seemed to take for granted—that you entered a firm right after graduation and left it in a box." Since women were still relative newcomers to the law firm scene, even in 1974, Green thinks the women in her class examined their firms more critically. After a few years at Sutherland, Asbill, Green concluded that "partnership did not necessarily bring a more delightful way to spend the day." She is now general counsel of the University of Pennsylvania, a job she finds far more rewarding.

"I wanted to be out saving the world, not businessmen," explains Roberta Baruch, who was uncomfortable with the hired gun status of the private firm lawyer when she worked at a Boston firm for two years after graduation. She also felt uncomfortable in a male-dominated atmosphere in which most of the other lawyers at the firm talked about "sports, sex and stereos," according to Baruch. She left the firm and moved to Washington, where she works for the Federal Trade Commission. Becoming a government lawyer reminded Baruch of coming to Harvard Law School and finding kindred spirits, the Freaked Out Friends. "Government is filled with law firm exiles who didn't fit in," she reports.

Others were simply unwilling to become slaves to their jobs. "It was difficult for me to dedicate myself fully enough to the job to bill the kind of hours I knew would be required if I was going to make a long-term career at the firm," explains Candace Fowler, who left her associate's job at Arent, Fox & Kintner to work in government also.

Bari Boyer, who joined a small Harrisburg, Pennsylvania, firm, became disillusioned early when, in one of her first cases, a divorce matter, the parties ended up arguing over a bag of tennis balls. Although Boyer went on to handle more important matters, she discovered she did not have the personality for trial work. Sheila Bell chose Boston's Hutchins & Wheeler because she was interested in doing hospital work and the firm represented several hospitals in the area, including the Children's Hospital Medical Center in Boston. Although Bell did do some hospital work, she was also assigned lots of trust and estates matters and a steady stream of "drudge work." What Bell disliked, she says, was the "political dynamics of a large firm . . . the presumption of adapting oneself to the mold of the firm. I realized I didn't." Bell moved to Nashville with her husband and became general counsel at Fisk University.

Teresa Arnold got a fast start at Chicago's Keck, Mahin & Cate, but when she received a good offer to join the legal department at Standard Oil she decided to take it. "I wanted to handle more cases on my own," Arnold said. "I'm probably making ten percent less than in private practice, but I'm not putting up with the law firm baloney either . . . the stupidity of working and billing hours whether you've got anything to do or not."

In general the women associates from the class seemed to be more restless, less willing to put up with the daily grind, particularly since the ultimate payoff—partnership—was a much dimmer prospect for the women than for men. Perhaps if their law firms had welcomed these women more enthusiastically, made a genuine effort to integrate them into the institutional fabric, and offered better prospects for promotion, the results would have been very different.

Five years out of Harvard Law School, Rene Townsend Robinson had reached a crisis point in her life as an associate. Anyone passing by her office that morning could tell that she was not herself. The tall, big-boned, forthright black woman was usually one of the warmest and most outgoing associates at Washington's Wilmer, Cutler & Pickering. Her door was always open and, although she was perpetually swamped with tax work, Rene was usually happy to take a break to share a joke or chat about the day's headlines. She also liked to project a tough edge and preferred for her friends at Wilmer, Cutler to call her Townsend. If, as a black woman, she felt out of place at one of the country's most prestigious firms, which, like all its competitors, was predominantly male and white, Rene usually projected only confidence and ease to her coworkers. She had the politician's air about her and made success look easy. For the past five years she had done well at Wilmer, Cutler and she appeared to have a happy marriage and well-rounded life outside the firm, which included serving on the boards of various community organizations in the district.

Everybody liked Townsend, but few people at Wilmer, Cutler knew her well. As a new associate, she had quickly adopted the lawyer's habit of seeming open and candid while keeping most of her real thoughts and feelings to herself. Survival at a firm like Wilmer, Cutler required this kind of discipline. Mulling over her future on this spring morning in

1979, as she sat behind her desk in the firm's sleek and elegant downtown offices, Townsend was indulging in a rare display of emotion. Her depression showed clearly on her face; the shine was gone from her eyes. In the past year she had billed close to three thousand hours and knew that if she was serious about making the push to partnership she would have to work even harder. But working harder seemed inconceivable. Her arduous schedule had already put a strain on her marriage, and the toll of more hours might actually ruin it. But when Rene Townsend Robinson graduated from Harvard Law School in 1974, she had promised herself that she was going to stay on the fast track and become a partner while she was still in her early thirties.

As a fourth-generation Washingtonian, Townsend concentrated her job interviewing after graduation from the law school on just a handful of large, downtown firms in her native city. She wanted financial security but she also wanted to help bring about social change, particularly for blacks, and she felt that the best way for her to be heard was to ensconce herself in a major law firm that served corporate America. "The greatest impact could be felt through the corporate channels," she would say years later, reflecting back on her job choice. "I knew that having not only the credential of the law school but also the credentials that a large law firm could give me would make people listen who might not otherwise be disposed to listen to someone advocating social change."

Wilmer, Cutler & Pickering, she felt confident, was the right choice. As a double minority, she carefully scrutinized the hiring statistics of all the firms where she interviewed, and Wilmer, Cutler hired a larger number of women and blacks as associates. Still, both were a small minority—there were five other black associates and only slightly more women associates when Townsend joined the firm. At some of the firms where she interviewed, the hiring partners were obviously just looking for a token black to hire. Although in

1974 her firm had neither black nor female partners, Townsend believed she would get a fair shake at Wilmer, Cutler. Also, the firm had a liberal, civil-rights-oriented reputation that she found tremendously appealing. Name partner and rainmaker Lloyd Cutler had organized the influential Lawyers Committee for Civil Rights Under Law in 1963. In the violent aftermath of Dr. Martin Luther King's assassination five years later, Cutler had spent all night in the D.C. jail coordinating the defense of those arrested during the rioting and looting that paralyzed the District. Nearly all of the lawyers at Cutler's firm had donated their time to these cases.[1]

Besides being a liberal trailblazer, Cutler was one of Washington's most respected and feared corporate gunslingers. He represented the automobile and pharmaceutical industries, as well as CBS and IBM. He was a legal renaissance man, a generalist in an era of narrow specialization. Cutler had entered law school at age sixteen and had graduated first in his class at Yale Law School in 1939, where he was editor in chief of the prestigious *Yale Law Journal*. The associates Cutler's firm hired usually had law review credentials and several had served as clerks for U. S. Supreme Court justices before joining the firm. Townsend rarely laid eyes on Cutler during her five years at the firm. She did bump into him a few times on the elevator late at night and, although he did not know her, the owlish-looking firm patriarch greeted her with a cordial "Hello, how are you?"[2]

Cutler insisted that all of the lawyers at his firm be trained to handle multiple areas of practice, and Townsend spent her first three years at Wilmer, Cutler in a rigorous rotation program that took her through the firm's corporate/tax, litigation, antitrust and communications departments before she settled into her chosen area of expertise, tax. Townsend en-

[1] Brill, Steven, "Lloyd Cutler Takes Charge," *The American Lawyer*, September 1980, pp. 19–24.
[2] *American Lawyer* magazine, "Lloyd Cutler . . ." on preceding page.

joyed her training and thought the firm had given her just the right amount of responsibility. She especially liked the time she spent in communications, where in-house counsel would call her up and ask her advice when they needed to renew their television or radio licenses. The personal contact with clients made the work more interesting. Some of her friends at other firms never got to see what a client looked like, let alone develop a personal relationship. There were too many layers of lawyers in between.

As a tax specialist, Townsend worked under the supervision of Marshall Hornblower, leader of the firm's corporate group. Hornblower was known to be a stern perfectionist, and she had been trained to double and triple check every citation. Her immediate supervisors were tax partners David Lake and Sam Lanahan, lawyers she found relatively easy to work for as long as she kept her work product flawless. But Townsend was still putting in sixty and seventy hours a week, hours more usual for a litigator than a tax lawyer. "Work harder," she kept driving herself. "You've got to work harder to be among the very best."

The competition among the associates was intense. By 1979, her fifth year, there were not that many of them left from the class of 1974, and everyone was presumed to be in contention for partnership. Although the partners gave her favorable reviews each year, Townsend had no idea whether she was on the "fast track" because Wilmer, Cutler did not "track" its associates the way other firms did, usually placing them in three categories: the clear stars, the maybes and the long shots, who were usually encouraged to look for other jobs. Bonuses, usually one way for associates to compare their performances, were banned by Cutler, who believed in a lockstep salary structure in which all associates were paid strictly by seniority.

Rather than relieve the pressure to outdistance her peers, the salary structure had the opposite effect on Townsend. She felt she had to drive herself even harder in order to match the high hours other associates, who were being paid the same as she was, were billing. She did not want to feel she was getting off easier than anyone else. Oddly enough, Wilmer, Cutler did not have the sweatshop reputation some other firms did, yet if one counted up the hours, they were there. Nobody said the lawyers had to work that hard. But the lights were always on at Wilmer, Cutler.

It was almost impossible for Townsend to gauge what her chances for partnership were. Since her arrival, two women had become partners. No blacks had yet gained enough seniority to even put partnership to the test. Most of the senior black associates who had been at the firm when Townsend joined had left to take jobs in government or industry. "There were so many opportunities for them at the time," says Wilmer, Cutler partner James Robertson, "that it is not surprising that many of them pursued other interests."

Part of Townsend's compulsion to excel stemmed from her belief, as a woman and a black, that she had to overcome certain presumptions about women and minorities. "Every person who graduates from Harvard and comes to a law firm, the presumption is that they are qualified and they can do the work and if they don't do the work it's because they are lazy. I think that in some instances the presumption with a minority or a female, a female with the same credentials, the same situation, is not that they're just lazy, it's that, well, maybe they have tunnel vision or maybe they can't do the work, or maybe they're overachievers," she says. As a double minority, Townsend felt under intense pressure to prove that she was bright, qualified and hardworking. She wanted to leave no doubts about either her motivation or her capacity. She worried that she would have to overcome as well any bad experiences the firm had had with women or blacks who had come before her. "If they ever had a bad experience you could walk on water and it really wouldn't make any difference," she surmised.

But applying pressure on herself and meeting every test was part of Townsend's basic makeup. Although she was nearly thirty, she still described herself as a "pushed child." Her family had always hoped she would do well, and she rarely disappointed them. Her résumé documented a string of successes: top of her class at a prestigious Washington high school for gifted students, a near perfect 4.0 record at American University and first woman president of the Harvard Law School Council.

Lately, however, the pressure of working so hard at Wilmer, Cutler was really getting to her. What was troubling her most was a growing realization that her marriage was under a severe strain. While they were not openly fighting, there were times when she and her husband, Cecil, were finding it difficult to talk to one another. Since they had met as sophomores at American University, she and Cecil had been best friends, totally inseparable. Although they sometimes disagreed—he was more liberal and had participated in the campus unrest of the sixties—their outlook on the world was similar and their values were in harmony. At her Harvard Law School graduation, the mother of one of her best friends had been able to guess immediately that she and Cecil were married. She said that they fit together like two old shoes, and it was true.

Townsend knew Cecil resented the long hours she was working. Other women lawyers she knew were married to lawyers, who were too busy themselves to care who was home. As a photographer, Cecil also set high standards for himself and was understanding to a point, but his wife's driving herself to the brink of exhaustion was crippling their relationship. "Why can't you take a vacation?" he would ask her. "Whenever we take a vacation, you have to turn around and get back!" Part of her problem was having the rotten luck to be assigned projects that would blow up just as she was about to leave town. If she hurried to finish her work and went on vacation as planned, she spent the whole time worrying about whether she had missed something. "Did I check that citation? Oh, my God, I've got to get back!" she would agonize to herself. She had forgotten how to relax and let go.

Cecil was also looking forward to starting a family, although he would never have dreamed of trying to pressure her into having children before she was ready. Besides, he was a very practical man—in the past few years she had barely had time for him, let alone a baby. They both came from large families and planned on having several children, but Townsend did not want to have children before she was a partner. She did not want anything to get in the way of her goal of making partner by the age of thirty-one.

But a combination of fatigue and frustration was finally overwhelming her. A light had gone on in her head that morning that made her realize, "You're probably working as hard as you can and, even if you could work harder, would you really want to work that hard?" Was she really ready to risk irreparable damage to her marriage in order to make partner? She loved her $40,000-a-year salary and managed to spend every penny of it. But there was more to life than material success. Townsend needed a rest. She needed time to think about what she was doing with her life.

As she sat at her desk pondering these questions, she brooded about her partnership chances. Even if she was willing to put in the necessary work, she confronted the harsh reality that partnership was still a very elusive goal. Another event that morning had made this fact painfully clear. Down the hallway from her office, a group of partners and associates were celebrating the end of an important case. Another female associate in Townsend's class at the firm, Carolyn Cox, had had a major hand in resolving the matter. Instead of feeling joyful about her colleague's victory, Townsend was depressed. Although Cox was a litigator and thus not one of Townsend's direct competitors in the corporate/tax area, Townsend convinced herself that the firm was unlikely to elect two women partners from the same class. "Oh, my God, that's all I need," she thought to herself as she listened to the fraternizing down the hall. Besides Cox, none of the other associates had done anything spectacular, she realized. "But it occurred to me that, given the way the world actually works, that, since I share the same sex as this individual, I really had a long road . . ."

Townsend knew that in this dark frame of mind she probably should not make any major decisions. But as the celebrating continued she realized she had let things get out of hand. If she did not remove herself from the highly pressurized environment of the law firm, and let go of the Harvard Law School and Wilmer, Cutler mentality of sacrificing everything to be the best, she knew she might not only seriously damage a wonderful marriage but also break her own spirit.

If Townsend Robinson was a classic overachiever, Dace McCoy was the kind of person who got Cs in high school English but scored a perfect 800 on the verbal portion of the Scholastic Aptitude Test. In 1978, four years after graduating from Harvard Law School, while Townsend and many other women from her law school class were still dedicating themselves to being the perfect law firm associates, Dace was working as a bartender at the Merchant's Café, an old restaurant in Seattle's historic Pioneer Square. After eighteen months of drifting, she was still one of those trying to figure out what she wanted to do with her life, how to make a future for herself in the law. For a year she had dropped out of sight completely and traveled throughout South America with her best friend from Harvard Law School, Carol Schapira. After their trip Dace had considered settling in ultramellow Santa Cruz, California, which she hoped would be a less materialistic, hyper environment than her native Los Angeles. But during a brief stopover she decided Santa Cruz was too laid back for her, and so she followed Carol to Seattle, a city that she had visited on many occasions and one that was becoming filled with young professionals who were searching for a livable and healthy urban environment. Bartending was just one of an odd assortment of jobs she had been trying her hand at, including working as a potter.

Since her graduation from affluent Palisades High School in suburban Los Angeles, Dace had been torn between the straight, professional life and the counterculture. Going to Mount Holyoke College, Harvard Law School and working in the Los Angeles city attorney's office represented the former impulse; getting busted for marijuana possession, dropping out of Harvard Law School to live on a farming collective, and working as a bartender exemplified her nonconformist tendencies. A pattern of dropping out and then pulling herself back on the straight track characterized much of her adult life.

Some of her early escapades were chronicled in the bestseller, *What Really Happened to the Class of '65?*, [3] making her a minor celebrity. The book, published before her trip to South America in 1975, detailed the lives of her high school classmates in the ten years since *Time* [4] magazine had first profiled them in a cover story called "Today's Teenagers." Dace, an attractive redhead with aquiline features, was immortalized by the authors, also 1965 graduates of Pali High, as "the class flirt." She hated to admit it, but she probably earned the title. She had been a spoiled, self-possessed Army brat who drove to school in a Jaguar, dated basketball players and flirted with intellectuals because, she told *Time*, "they are so worthwhile."

[3] Michael Medved and David Wallechinsky, *What Really Happened to the Class of '65?* (New York: Random House, 1976), "Candy McCoy: The Flirt," pp. 148–60.
[4] *Time* (January 29, 1965.)

The book described her transformation from the trivial class flirt known as Candy into a cool and competent Harvard-educated lawyer called Dace, a childhood name that she used in college and law school. (Although her legal name was Margarita, she always went by her middle name, Candace.) "The new name had a tough, competent ring to it," the *Class of '65* authors observed. During the interview for the book she projected the image of the consummate young professional absorbed in her work. She arrived for the interview late, carrying a sheaf of papers from her job at the Los Angeles city attorney's office, and adroitly mixed gin and tonics for her former high school classmates in her house in Beverly Glen, a canyon just east of UCLA and adjacent Beverly Hills. "I've somehow managed to stumble along and get myself to a place where I'm able to make a life that I think is purposeful," she had told the authors confidently. "I feel now that I'm in control of my life." Barely two years later, however, she felt at sea once again.

Dace had not misled the authors of the book. At the time of the interview she was two years out of Harvard Law School and she felt that her life was coming together. After a depressing stint working in the Manchester outpost of New Hampshire Legal Assistance program following graduation from law school, Dace jumped at the opportunity to return to Los Angeles and work for Burt Pines, the city's newly elected city attorney. For the first time in her life she was really enjoying being a lawyer and was sure that her choice of professions was the right one. Her friend Carol had doubted whether Dace was cut out to be a local prosecutor or whether she would enjoy being in the middle of the political fray. But since joining Pines's personal staff in late 1974, Dace had been having a wonderful time.

Pines was an unusual animal—a liberal prosecutor. He had vowed to stop prosecuting certain crimes, such as pornography and sexual acts between consenting adults. As his special assistant, Dace felt as if she was also helping to liberate the city, which, until Mayor Tom Bradley's election in 1974, had a conservative law and order local government. There had not been a genuine change in administration in the city attorney's office in forty years. One reason she loved her job was that it was a generalist's job. She could jump from one interesting project to another, which suited her curious and restless nature. Her first big assignment was to evaluate discrimination cases and recommend which ones ought to be prosecuted and which ones ought to be settled and on what basis. "It was like, welcome to the candy store! It was an assignment I just couldn't believe!" she recalls.

Dace also surveyed marijuana arrests for legislators in Sacramento who wanted to decriminalize marijuana possession. Pines, who felt possession of small amounts of marijuana was a victimless crime, was the first prosecutor in the state to favor decriminalization. Given her own scrape with the drug laws, when she was busted as a Mount Holyoke junior, convicted on misdemeanor charges and kicked out of school, Dace had a special interest in the issue. It turned out that she had an astounding data base to work with; virtually ten percent of all marijuana arrests in the country occurred in the city of Los Angeles. Simply processing these cases cost the state millions of dollars, as Dace's research proved. When a decriminalization law was finally passed, Dace felt she had played an instrumental role in helping the California legislature adopt one of the most liberal drug statutes in the country.

Besides learning her way around a courtroom, prosecuting drunk driving and hit and run cases, Dace served as Pines's personnel coordinator. He wanted to transform the city attorney's office—one of the largest government offices in the country, with more than two hundred lawyers—into a repository for young, ambitious attorneys and he wanted more women and minorities on staff. Under his predecessors the office had become a dumping ground for a lot of lawyers who could not land jobs with firms. Dace was among the first representatives of a local prosecutor's office to go on the road to recruit third-year law students at prestigious national law schools. She traveled to Harvard, Yale, Columbia and top California schools and her pitch to the students was simple: Pines could offer them training and instant trial experience, something law firms could not match. "We didn't want people who didn't question the prosecutor's role," Dace stressed. "We wanted people who thought very seriously about what it meant to be a prosecutor." Also, Pines's lawyers were free to turn down cases they found morally or politically objectionable. Within a year Dace had helped fill the office with idealistic young lawyers like herself.

As Pines's first term wore on, Dace began to feel that the exciting times were over. "The reforming had been done and we had to settle down and run the city," she recalls. As Pines geared up to run for attorney general, the state's top law enforcement job, Dace decided to quit. She did not want to stick around in case the office lapsed back into a hard-line conviction factory. She decided to join Carol on a trip through South America. The adventure would give her time to assess her future. "I wanted to throw myself into the void and see what I would choose," she recalls. "I hadn't ever made a conscious decision to become a lawyer in the first place. Knowing by that time what was involved in being a lawyer, I wanted to step back and make a conscious choice about what I wanted to do." Although working for one of the brightest and most liberal politicians in California had been challenging for a while—the authors of *Class of '65* had caught her at the height of her enthusiasm—she also realized, in retrospect, that it was a mistake to try to build her career around one man. Pines's agenda had become her agenda, and when his political needs changed she had been caught unprepared. While she was away with Carol, Pines had lost the

Democratic primary for attorney general and eventually faded from the political scene.

The trip through South America was a rejuvenating experience. Carol was a good friend and traveling companion, someone with solid values and a clear sense of her own identity. Dace was always fortunate to have long-lasting friendships with women. Some of these friendships bordered on becoming love affairs, but she never had a sexual relationship with a woman. She expected this might happen one day, but somehow it never did. Meanwhile she had had her affairs with men but had not come close to getting married. This was certainly a very different Dace McCoy from the girl who told *Time* in 1965, "You can't marry anyone important without going to college."

Now, thirteen years later, she was trying to build a life in Seattle and still trying to figure out what she wanted to be when she grew up. Bartending, pottery and studying Buddhism were satisfying, but she certainly was not capitalizing on her Harvard Law degree. She knew she did not want to work in a firm. For Dace, being an associate at a big firm represented seven or eight years of indentured servitude. The respectability and intellectual challenge of the profession still appealed to her, but she wanted a job that was socially useful. She was determined to take her time to find a job worthy of her talents.

Meanwhile she was happy learning her way around Seattle and working in the city's historic underground district. Although she was not yet certain what her next job would be, she was confident she would, as always, stumble into something interesting. If the alumnae of Harvard Law School were supposed to emerge from Cambridge, like Rene Townsend Robinson, sure of themselves and their professional goals, Dace McCoy certainly defied the norm. Nearly five years out of law school, she was probably the only member of the class listing bartending as her profession. But long ago she had determined she wanted to live by her own standards, not Harvard's.

Townsend, too, had decided to live her life more freely, to put less pressure on herself to be a superwoman, to devote more of her time to the things that really mattered: her husband and her community. At her fifth law school reunion, which she attended just weeks after deciding to leave Wilmer, Cutler, Townsend was surprised by the strikingly high number of divorces among her former classmates. Also, virtually all of her friends had left, or were on the verge of leaving, the firms where they had launched their careers. Instead of feeling like a failure for not having toughed it out at Wilmer, Cutler, when she began telling her friends about her decision to leave, the response, more often than not, was, "Join the club."

The reunion weekend, filled with nostalgia and familiar faces, gave her a chance to catch her breath, reflect on her life and plan where she was going. All her life Townsend had jumped over every hurdle. Leaving Wilmer, Cutler represented the first time she had decided to turn her back on a challenge instead of vanquishing it. She had always been the shining star, a great success story, a black woman who made winning look easy.

Her parents had instilled in her the drive that propelled her forward. In northeast Washington, the working-class, predominantly black quadrant of the city, her parents had been emphatic that she receive a good education. Her grandfather had often taken her with him to the public library and by the time she was five years old she could write cursively. When she was a little older she was expected to read the newspaper and listen to the evening news every day. "They understood that the only real way for a black person to attain any type of status in America was through education. We went through the whole ritual—if you got an A you got hugged; if you got

a C Grandfather sort of looked at you and shook his head.
. . .''

Besides education, she was firmly taught, family and community were scared. Her father, a salesman at Capital Cadillac, and mother, a nurse, had separated when Townsend was just three and later divorced. Both had remarried—her father twice. But her parents remained on friendly terms and consequently she had a giant extended family. The tradition, on both sides, was for the entire family to gather together at all graduations, birthdays and holidays. On Christmas and the Fourth of July everyone convened—including her two stepmothers, Miss Ruby and Miss Marguerite, a host of half brothers and sisters and all sets of grandparents. "It was the most amiable relationship I've ever seen," Townsend recalls of her parents.

It was her grandmother who first encouraged her to become a lawyer. The black community needed lawyers. In their neighborhood there were already plenty of doctors, most of whom lacked enough paying patients to support a practice. Some of them moonlighted as post office workers, because government salaries far outstripped their medical earnings. There were already many blacks working as teachers, ministers and undertakers. Law, her grandmother believed, was the great uncharted territory. Also, she could make a comfortable living. "I never liked not having enough money to do what I wanted to do when I wanted to do it," recalls Townsend, who held down a part-time job at the post office in addition to a full-time job at American University the summer before college, just so that she would have enough money to live comfortably.

Townsend's academic record virtually guaranteed her choice of professions. She was a star at Western High School, one of the city's "magnet" schools for gifted children. The student body was predominantly white and filled with the children of diplomats who lived in nearby Embassy Row. She could have had her choice of colleges but, as close as she was to her family, she had no desire to leave Washington. So she enrolled at American University and zipped through in three years, earning straight As, except for one slipup in freshman biology.

It was the late 1960s and, except for the area of civil rights, Townsend was more conservative than most of the other blacks on campus. While many of her college friends, including Cecil, were out striking and boycotting, she was tutoring children at one of the local black churches. "We all shared the same goals," she recalls. "It was the tactics I disagreed with." By sheer force of personality Townsend won over even the most ardent revolutionaries. Although she was more conservative, she was just as well informed as her more activist friends and it was fun to argue with her. Plus, when they needed help preparing for exams, Townsend was always available at 3 A.M. to help them study for tests that she would easily ace.

As a political science major, Townsend believed that American institutions were basically sound but needed to be turned in the right direction. If more blacks were admitted to prestigious colleges and professional schools, she argued, black society would eventually be strengthened. She served on the board of an organization that promoted higher black enrollment in elite, private colleges. The other board members were all establishment types, prominent local lawyers and businessmen. One of the lawyers on the board, Russell Weil, took a personal interest in Townsend's future. One day over lunch she told him she was interested in law school and he asked her where she had applied. Thus far she had only put in an application at Yale. Weil, a Harvard Law graduate who also served on one of the university's governing boards, was horrified and urged her to send in an application to Harvard Law immediately, even though her application might be late. When the acceptance letter arrived later in the spring, everyone, from Weil to her family, urged her to go. "Harvard is *the* law school" they echoed.

In September Cecil loaded up the car and drove her to Cambridge. Townsend had never laid eyes on the campus and when they pulled into the shaded courtyard behind her dormitory she was impressed. Her room in Hastings Hall was spacious, with large windows, lovely, wood-paneled walls and a working fireplace. Cecil helped her unpack and then left her to become acquainted with her new world. He left behind a token of his affection, a tiny statue of a lawyer with "Sue the bastards!" emblazoned across the base. "My dearest Rene," Cecil had written, "They may get 33 1/3%," in reference to the typical contingency fee lawyers receive, "but just remember you will always be my 100% windfall love. . . ."

The first week a crushing case of homesickness overcame Townsend. Every night she had two-hour phone conversations with her parents and Cecil, and they had to pile into a car and drive to Cambridge her first weekend just to keep her there. It was the first time she had been away from her family and her native Washington, D.C. Also, like almost everyone else in the class, Townsend was used to being an academic star, and it was disconcerting to be suddenly plunged into an environment where everyone was vying to be number one. But despite her homesickness Townsend maintained her characteristic self-confidence. If she could not be number one, a reality to which she conceded, she would still fight to be near the top of her class, and she would not lose her humanity or her sense of humor in the process.

Townsend also refused to be intimidated by her professors. In her property class she was the very first student called on by Professor A. James Casner. He was tough, and he would keep asking a student question after question until the student got one wrong. "Everyone was terrified," Townsend recalls of the first class meeting. "We were all first-year people, and at that point I don't think anybody had any friends unless they brought them with them." The professor caught her unprepared. But, rather than pass, Townsend decided to turn the tables on Casner, so she simply asked him a different question. The professor started to laugh. "That's not what I asked you," he said. "I know," she coolly responded, "but mine is a more interesting question." This kind of bold move was typical of Townsend. "From that day on I had a lot of fun," she says. "At law school, I'm probably the only person who did. I didn't take it as seriously as some people, who took it as life or death. Some people take everything as life or death. Certain things are not. So you bomb out, so what?"

As the first semester wore on her homesickness ebbed. It helped that Cecil was willing to make the nine-hour drive from Washington to visit her. At the time he was trying to finish his bachelor's degree while working as a clerk at *U.S. News and World Report.* She and Cecil were still a bit old-fashioned, so on his weekend visits he stayed with two of Townsend's closest friends, Maurice White and Ollie Ligon, who also lived in Hastings Hall. In April, however, the couple drove down to Virginia and were secretly married. Townsend did not want her parents to know about the marriage because she knew she would receive the typical lecture about the risks of pregnancy and warning that her expensive legal education would go down the drain. Townsend had every intention of finishing law school and decided to tell her parents about the marriage on graduation day, when they would be too proud to be angry.

With her friendly and open manner, she made friends at the law school easily. For someone in her early twenties, she had an unusual amount of charisma and by the end of the first semester she was one of the most popular members of the class. She was also a natural choice of her section to serve on the Law School Council, a relatively new student government organization. It was one of the reform institutions that arose in the wake of the student strikes of 1969 and 1970.

Female and minority enrollment were among the issues with which the council grappled. Although Harvard maintained it had a sex- and color-blind admissions policy, Townsend argued with the faculty that the school's method of rating each student's past academic performance worked against women and minorities, who had not, historically, attended the colleges that were prime feeders to Harvard Law School. Some members of the faculty were openly hostile to the idea of opening the school's enrollment to more women and blacks. She tried, at the weekly faculty lunches, to use a combination of diplomacy and charm to convince them otherwise. By her third year on the council she felt she knew every single member of the faculty and what made them tick. She won a school-wide election to become the first woman president of the council, a position of real influence on campus.

Although the council took up a lot of her study time, Townsend was a naturally gifted student and excelled in several subjects, including tax. But to be an academic star at Harvard Law School, one had to be a single-focus person. With her interest in student government and her relationship with Cecil, Townsend had many diversions. She had little envy for the students who sat in Langdell Library, glued to their seats, rarely looking up from their books, even if they were earning straight As. She never forgot the determination of one of her classmates, Isaac Pachulski. It seemed to Townsend that Pachulski must have read every *Law Review* article ever written. His only outlet from studying was working on the prestigious *Harvard Law Review*. But Pachulski had even resigned from the *Law Review* his third year, some speculated in order to devote all of his time to studying. He was bent on winning the Faye Diploma, which went to the student with the highest third year grade point average, even though he had won the Sears Prize, an equally prestigious award, two years in a row. To almost no one's surprise, on graduation day Pachulski had walked off with the coveted Faye Diploma. As much as people claimed to love the well-rounded person, Townsend knew it was single-focused achievers like Isaac who finished on top at law school and at firms.

At Harvard it had dawned on Townsend that, given a big enough pool, there would always be someone brighter and harder working than she was, and she just had to accept it. She would tease fellow students if they cited an obscure court opinion to show off, or bragged about staying up until all hours of the morning. "Really?" she would exclaim. "I didn't see your light on!" Townsend knew that part of surviving Harvard Law meant keeping her sense of humor and perspective on things. "I realized there was no way in the world that I could work as hard as they could work and do nothing else," she says. Similarly, at her fifth reunion, Townsend realized that at Wilmer, Cutler, too, people were not so much separated by their natural abilities as by their capacity for work. To succeed, one had to center one's entire life around work. She had not been able to match the Isaac Pachulskis in law school and no matter how late she worked at Wilmer, Cutler there was always another associate working later. There were young lawyers at the firm who were willing to sacrifice their outside interests, their family lives and anything else in order to succeed. Right before the April 1979 reunion Townsend finally realized again that she was not one of them.

There was another question weighing on her mind, one that she kept to herself. Was the firm really ready to elect a black partner? "First they had to agree that they were going to make a black partner, and unless they had agreed upon that, it didn't matter how great you were, it wouldn't make any difference," she says. Although a black did make it several years after her departure, the statistics for black partnership at most firms remained dismal. In government, where

Townsend hoped to find a job, opportunities seemed to be wider.

"I've got to get out of here!" she had told Robertson, the head of the firm's Associates Committee. The two talked long and hard about Townsend's goals. She still wanted to make a lot of money, but she also wanted work that was more satisfying, more socially beneficial. "Nothing I'm doing here is any good except I'm making a lot of money and I contribute to a lot of causes and I'm on some boards," she complained.

When she gave her notice at Wilmer, Cutler all of the partners were understanding and supportive. None of them tried to change her mind, not even Lake and Lanahan. They understood the pressures that associates worked under and realized life at Wilmer, Cutler was not for everyone.

Her former classmates at the reunion and her coworkers could not yet detect it, but soon she would have other news to share with them besides her impending job change. She was pregnant. Immediately after she gave her notice at Wilmer, Cutler she found out, to her astonishment, that she was going to have a baby. Although she had missed several periods, Townsend had just assumed that her body had stopped functioning because she was working too hard and under such stress. But she was wrong, as she learned at a long-overdue visit to her doctor. Although the pregnancy was unplanned, both she and Cecil were thrilled.

Townsend had stayed at a firm longer than any of her close friends from law school with whom she eagerly traded war stories. Still the fact that Townsend, the ambitious and articulate Law School Council president, had failed to cut it at a law firm surprised some of her classmates, who questioned whether this bright, energetic woman would be happy in a routine government job.

If Townsend's drive and competitiveness were traceable to her childhood, so were the seeds of Dace McCoy's problem of figuring out what she wanted in life. She remembered being in junior high school and gazing into a mirror, wondering what she would look like when she was older. That was the extent of her thinking about the future. Harvard Law School did little to channel her energies in any particular direction and, as Dace herself so elegantly put it, she had "blobbed" her way through law school just as she had college.

Her father had badly wanted her to attend a top college and she went to Mount Holyoke, where she seemed to be the answer to every preppie's dream of the California girl. By the early seventies the drug culture had already permeated the prim and protective world of the Seven Sisters. During one of her vacations junior year, she had been driving down to New York with a friend and they had been smoking dope mixed with sherry in a water pipe. The roads were slick, and they crashed into a railing while driving over a bridge. Dazed but unhurt, Dace had tried to cram all the dope paraphernalia into a paper bag, which she threw over the edge of the bridge just as the police arrived. Unfortunately a bystander had seen her and the police recovered the incriminating bag. They got off with a light fine, but Mount Holyoke was determined to make an example of them and expelled both students.

At twenty, she already had a record. Feeling dejected, she went home to Los Angeles and worked as a telephone operator, the only job she could find. During this depressing period of her life her father died. But in spite of her problems Dace was determined to finish college, so she enrolled at UCLA for her senior year and took the LSAT to keep all of her future options open. As usual her test scores were extremely high, and she applied to Harvard and a few other top law schools.

After graduation from UCLA Dace went off to travel through Europe, northern Africa and the Middle East, promptly forgetting about her law school applications. She spent nine months roaming with a Parisienne who smuggled dope from Morocco to England, and traveling with a new boyfriend. She learned of her admittance to Harvard Law School when a letter from her mother arrived at the American Express office at the Istanbul Hilton. "You've gotten into Harvard and UCLA. Yale turned you down. I sent money to Harvard and UCLA. Tell me quick what should I do?" her mother had written. Although law school had been far from her thoughts, she realized immediately that she wanted to leave Istanbul and return home to start law school. With her respectable admittance to Harvard, Mount Holyoke put her back on its alumni list.

Harvard Law School was a positive experience for Dace. She worked very hard her first year. Toward the end of spring semester she decided she needed to reread the first-year material all over again, and the tortuous process of reviewing every case kept her in the library from 9 A.M. to midnight six days a week. She did not even bother to take her books home overnight, leaving them instead piled up on a table until she returned the following day. Unlike some of her classmates, Dace did not find the atmosphere at the law school unduly competitive or cutthroat. She made friends and participated in study groups and on the whole enjoyed her time at Harvard. Never hesitant to speak up in class, she was still caught a little off guard the first day in contracts when Professor Dawson asked her to recite a case. "Ms. McCoy, would you please give us *Groves* v. *Wonder?*" the professor asked. " 'Give us'? What does that mean?" she wondered, before finally realizing he wanted her to recite the case.

Besides Carol, Dace developed close friendships with Alice Ballard and Molly Munger. Alice, who was a leader in the Women's Law Association, was a serious feminist who introduced Dace to the women's movement. It was hard not to have one's consciousness raised in an atmosphere like Har-

vard Law School, where sexist confrontations were not unusual. Dace was living off campus and had a dog who followed her to class. Sometimes the dog even made it to class
when Dace overslept. One morning the dog actually came
into the classroom and the professor demanded that Dace
remove him. "We have got to draw the line *somewhere,*" he
said as she was trying to pull the dog out the door.

Dace joined Alice in trying to organize the Women in the
Law course. They set up a meeting between the WLA and
then law school dean Derek Bok. But at the appointed hour
they caught Bok trying to escape down the back stairs of the
administration building with his rubber boots on. When their
request for a credited course was rejected Dace worked with
Alice and Molly to organize and teach a student-sponsored
not-for-credit course (which was approved for credit by the
new dean, Albert Sacks, the following year). Alice, whose
mother had founded the Philadelphia chapter of the National
Organization for Women, was a bit more radical politically
than Dace and Molly, the two California girls. Dace sometimes joked that she was not so ardent a feminist that she was
ready to do her own vaginal examinations, a practice being
advocated by some of the Boston feminist groups.

"Her politics may have been less radical, but not her personality," recalls Alice. "She wasn't so much a political activist but a provocateur. Dace had a wild approach to life. She
appeared to be more of a free spirit."

Both Dace and Molly were pursued by men from the law
school. Molly, with her shiny blond hair and perfect features,
was the one almost all the men in the class fantasized about.
She was so beautiful that her looks were distracting. At a
party after first-year exams some of the men got drunk and
said nasty things to her. It was obvious to Dace that they had
been dreaming about Molly while they were cooped up,
studying for exams twenty hours a day, and that they were
probably just feeling frustrated. Dace realized that Molly's

looks could be a burden. Dace's father had once told her
when she was a teenager that she was pretty enough so that if
a man were to fall in love with her he would think her beautiful, but no one would be after her strictly for her looks.

Molly was more all-American and straitlaced than Dace,
who was intrigued by all aspects of the counterculture. She
was especially captivated by the back-to-the-earth movement.
During her second year at Harvard Law she began going out
to a farm in western Massachusetts where old friends from
Mount Holyoke were living. "I was there for political reasons as opposed to wanting to grow corn," she explains. "It
was a kind of back-to-the-land movement. I was real interested in it and I'd never done anything like that before.
. . ." She spent a year commuting to the farm and eventually
moved there, dropping out of law school. While living on the
farm Dace decided she wanted to write an organizing handbook for women on labor law, and arranged to meet with an
editor at Harper & Row. But as she sat in the editor's office in
New York discussing the idea, she realized if she were going
to leave the farm to research a book she might as well return
to Cambridge and finish what she had started. "If I wanted to
live on a farm I should have lived on a farm. I realized that if
I didn't want to live on the farm I should get my act together
and go back to law school." She apologized to the editor for
taking up her time and returned to Harvard to finish her JD.

Exactly what she would do after graduation was unclear.
Dace was oblivious to the fact that she had put herself on a
track to Wall Street just by enrolling at Harvard Law School.
"I was aware that Ed Cox (former President Nixon's son-in-
law) was still wearing a tie to class. I mean, there was something else going on there as well as what I was doing, but I
was pursuing what I was pursuing. I never took corporations
in law school, it didn't exist as far as I was concerned . . .
that whole path." She was interested in federal litigation,
constitutional law. She wanted to do something that was so-

cially useful but exactly what she had no idea. A friend from the class of '72 was working at legal aid in Manchester, New Hampshire, and when he told her they were short staffed she decided to accept a position there.

But Manchester was a gray, dismal experience. Dace grew extremely depressed by the plight of her clients, each of whom was mired in a hopeless situation for which legal aid could provide only the smallest relief. With one client, it was a constant battle just to keep him out of a state mental hospital. Another woman had bought an entire freezer of beef on credit and had refinanced the purchase so many times that she was in considerable debt. Although Dace was able to prove that the practices of the finance company went somewhat over the line, she knew there was nothing to keep her client from getting into a similar scrape in the future.

She also found it difficult being virtually the only woman practicing in the Manchester courthouse. She always wore pantsuits to work because, as she said, she had "the world's homeliest ankles." In Pines's office she would be sent into the courtrooms of the most conservative judges dressed like a man, wearing pleated glen plaid suits, to make sure they were not hassling women lawyers about their attire. But in Manchester even fellow lawyers came to gawk at her while Dace relaxed in a lounge between cases. Women lawyers, let alone women lawyers in pants, were rare and curious sights.

Dace admired lawyers from her class who stuck it out at legal aid, but she realized she was just not thick-skinned or dedicated enough. "It's like people who work with handicapped children," she would say. "I'm so glad that people do that but I know that I couldn't keep my spirits up. . . ." The dreariness of New Hampshire and the hopeless circumstances of the New England poor got to her, and at the end of the long winter she quit the job, packed up her blue Citroën and headed to California. Shortly after her arrival home an old friend from law school, Andy Shephard, contacted her. He had begun working for Burt Pines and wanted to recruit Dace for the city attorney's office.

Although her tour of duty with Pines represented one of her longest commitments to a job, being a prosecutor didn't really suit her either. At this point in her life, five years out of law school, Dace was not sure where the answers lay. None of the things she had tried completely satisfied her. She was a restless soul who was trying to find herself in a city filled with other young pioneers, many of whom had also tried and failed to establish themselves elsewhere. Perhaps she would get lucky in Seattle.

If Dace McCoy was a free spirit, she was not alone among the women from the Harvard Law class of 1974. Others wanted to view their careers as open-ended and were willing to try different jobs, even if it meant drifting for a while. "I've never wanted to settle on anything for the rest of my life," declares Jane Eng, who worked at a Chinatown health clinic and taught English in mainland China before taking a job as an associate at a small New York firm. "I have a variety of interests and I've always wanted to stay flexible and open. It is more common for women to feel this way."

"I'm always looking for new challenges," agrees Mary Gallagher, a litigator who has held several different jobs. "You knock something down and you look for something bigger."

Long partnership tracks in law firms were incompatible with such free-spirited notions. "Seven years, the time for consideration, seemed like an inconceivably long time to me," says Elisse Walter, who left Washington, D.C.'s Arent, Fox & Kintner after three years to work for the Securities and Exchange Commission. "I woke up with this frightening thought. I realized that I'd been in the same place for three years and that if I didn't watch out I'd be in the same place for twenty years and would never have done anything else at all with my life, or at least my career." After ten years Mary

Kathleen Hite decided to take a leave from Washington's Amram & Hahn, unsure what she wanted to do with her future. "I had always said I wouldn't practice law forever," she says.

Even one who made the partnership cut at her firm, Sandra Froman of Los Angeles' Loeb & Loeb, was not content to stand pat. Sandy, who says her goal at Harvard was "in ten years to be a partner at a major firm in a major city in the country," achieved that goal just six years after graduation. But in 1984 she resigned from the Loeb & Loeb partnership to begin a new teaching career at the University of Santa Clara Law School. Despite taking a sixty percent pay cut, she says she is happier teaching and that "happiness is more important than security."

Sandy was the first woman partner elected at Loeb & Loeb, and she had fought hard to earn the distinction. By her second year at the firm she was handling cases on her own, spending any free minutes she had downtown at the courthouse, watching veteran litigators from all the big Los Angeles firms try their cases, hoping to pick up tips on style and strategy. After six years of litigation experience Sandra Froman was herself a seasoned, tough trial lawyer and it came as no surprise when Loeb & Loeb decided to make her a partner. "I had times when I really felt I was working too hard," she admits. "There were times I felt I had no life outside the firm. But these were things that were not imposed by someone else on me. These were choices I made for myself."

By 1983, however, Sandy yearned for more time away from the grind of litigation. Her marriage had ended in divorce one year earlier and she was dissatisfied with her career and wanted to pursue new challenges. Almost as a lark, she decided to ask for a one-year sabbatical from Loeb & Loeb to teach at the University of Santa Clara. She loved teaching almost immediately, and the freedom to pursue ideas without having to worry about billing her time to a client. She returned to Loeb & Loeb for monthly partnership meetings and found, as time passed, that she was less interested in what was going on at the firm and even more enthusiastic about teaching. When the dean of the law school offered her another yearlong contract she faced a real dilemma. She would have to make a choice between her new passion, teaching, and the secure partnership for which she had worked so hard. Realizing that she was taking a tremendous risk, she resigned from the Loeb & Loeb partnership. "And I've never regretted the decision," she adds.

Although she hadn't had the satisfaction of being anointed partner, Rene Townsend Robinson also had left without regrets. Finding a new job wasn't difficult. A close friend of hers worked at the General Services Administration and she knew about choice government job openings as they occurred. She tipped off Townsend that the general counsel of the Administrative Office of the U. S. Courts, the agency that administers the federal judicial system, was looking for another assistant. Townsend applied and was promptly hired. If the Administrative Office was a little-known agency, its work was still important. The AO, as insiders call it, is the paymaster of the federal judiciary. Although she was not handling landmark litigation, Townsend enjoyed the process of learning about the courts.

One of the best aspects of the job was that it gave her time for her family. In the fall of 1979 her daughter was born. She was named Mary Elizabeth, after Townsend's grandmother. Two years later she gave birth to a son, Christopher. Townsend was convinced that at Wilmer, Cutler it would have been impossible for her to have had two children and remain a full-time lawyer. Even at the AO, with a basic nine-to-five workday, Townsend sometimes had a hard time juggling. On days when one of her children had a doctor's appointment she made a point of getting to the office by 7 A.M. so that she could take a break later in the day to be present for her child's examination. She would arrange to have a taxi pick her up, ferry her home to her house in the Tacoma Park section of Washington, where she would pick up her youngster and proceed to the doctor. The process was repeated, in reverse, with a taxi dropping Townsend back downtown after the visit was over.

Each day she tried to spend about three hours with her children and weekends were devoted almost exclusively to them. Townsend was absolutely determined to put as much energy into mothering as she had into her career, and she worried that too many professional women were cheating their children out of love and care. If a generation of maladjusted and unhappy children resulted, she believed, society would never improve. But the consequences for women like herself, who pushed themselves to the limit, were also serious. Townsend expects to be a physical wreck by the time she hits fifty.

After leaving Wilmer, Cutler, Townsend plunged back into community activities. She served on the board of the Black Student Fund, a group that promoted black enrollment in the private schools around Washington. Townsend also served as a neighborhood advisory commissioner for the 16th Street area, an elected position in local government. At home she managed to find the time to see that Mary Elizabeth arrived at the National Child Research Center, one of the city's high-powered private nursery schools, every afternoon. Townsend mused that sending Mary Elizabeth to the NCRC cost her more than a year's tuition at American University. "All of that so she can play with children who are as nice as she is!" she exclaimed. When the car pool broke down Townsend had to leave work and take her daughter herself. "I do it all happily. I'm proud of myself that I can do it. Makes me feel good, part of this superwoman image that I like, I must like, because I continue to do it. I wouldn't do it if I didn't have to, though! But since I have to do it I might as

well like it and I might as well brag about it!" If she had
stayed in private practice she might have been able to hire a
housekeeper to drive her children around town. But she
jokes that she would have checked on the housekeeper constantly to make sure she was tending to the children properly,
so this luxury would probably have ended up being just another burden on her time.

It has been five years since Townsend left Wilmer, Cutler,
and she says the main thing she misses about private practice
is the money. The initial $4,000 pay cut Townsend took to
work in government has grown wider. As a partner, she
could be making triple her government salary. But she and
Cecil still lead comfortable lives. He is happy in his job as a
photographer for a government agency. Their marriage has
been thriving since she left Wilmer, Cutler and the birth of
their children. Townsend believes her marriage to Cecil
would have survived even if she had stayed at the firm, but
something between them would have been lost forever.

Her work also has important social content, another reason
she switched into government. In 1983 Townsend was promoted to become director of equal opportunity for the
agency, a policy job that took her out of the general counsel's
office and placed her directly under the head of the AO. She
believes passionately in Title VII, the provision of the law
that prohibits job discrimination. With sixty-three percent of
the judiciary's 14,000-member work force female, mostly in
clerical positions, it is critical for the agency to have a meaningful career development program. She helped to write a
model affirmative action program for the agency and leaned
on managers to promote from within when a senior staff position became vacant.

The job requires her to negotiate with managers across the
country about their hiring and promotion practices in court-
houses in tiny rural counties and large cities. Her job, as she
views it, is to convince other lawyers that EEO is smart pol-

icy. She was startled when one of the male managers of the
agency told her that she would make a good EEO director
because, if he were female or black, he would feel comfortable talking to her. "He told me as a white male he really
could not understand the issues but that I would be able to
understand them. You were not supposed to *do* anything
about them, but I would at least be a sympathetic ear."
Rather than being a passive listening board, Townsend sometimes launched a meeting by challenging, "I'm going to take
your head off and I hope there is someone standing behind
you to catch it!"

Whether government work will be a long-term career for
Townsend remains to be seen. With complete immodesty,
she claims she is a world class teacher and hopes to work in a
classroom one day. Back at Harvard Law School she was also
bitten by the political bug, and local politics is another avenue she may explore. It does not disturb her that her career
now looks more like an unfinished landscape than the defined
portrait she had painted when she graduated from Harvard
Law School, so sure that she was going to become a partner.
Townsend is content with her job and her life. She is doing
the kind of work she imagined herself doing when her grandmother first planted the idea of entering law into her head.
And, strong and self-aware, she is holding true to the family
and community values that have nurtured her.

By 1984 Dace McCoy had also reached some measure of
contentment. The Seattle move proved to be the right one
and she rooted her life there. After spending six months
working at odd jobs at the beginning of her stay, Dace finally
began a job hunt for a permanent position where she could
apply some of her legal background. She was drawn again to
local government. In the Los Angeles city attorney's office
she had enjoyed politics, although she never again wanted to
work for a single politician. Some of her friends recom-

mended trying to find work with the Seattle City Council, which governed the progressive and spotless city in a manner that won outside praise for efficiency and professionalism.

She did not know it at the time, but when she applied to the city to fill an opening for a policy analyst, the council was looking to hire a minority. With a first name like Margarita, it was no problem for Dace to get an interview. She carefully prepared for the encounter, talking to everyone who dealt with the city in order to find out how the council was perceived and what the issues were. She so impressed her interviewer that he recommended she be hired, despite her Anglo-Saxon heritage. But rather than follow his advice, the council insisted on looking further, for a qualified minority. "They were taking an ungodly amount of time," she recalls, estimating she had a three-month wait before being offered the job. Although she had no idea what was holding up the works, Dace wanted the job and was willing to wait however long it took for the council to decide on a candidate. "It's sort of exactly the opposite of what was the malaise before," she reflects. "I knew what I wanted and I know now why I wanted it and I love it."

Once hired, her first important task was to review the city's criminal code and make recommendations on how to amend it. From there she moved on to housing policy. She also helped to write the city's strict noise ordinance. Since 1980 she has been working on the same project—helping to formulate a new physical plan for the city of Seattle. The massive task involves going over the entire city chunk by chunk and rezoning all of the land. She has met with people from every sector of the city—including architects and neighborhood groups and some of Seattle's most influential businessmen and real estate developers. In 1984 she became the manager of the five-person team that has responsibility for legislative review of the new land use policies.

Being a policy analyst means being a generalist, which is

what Dace considers herself to be. She moves from subject to subject, immersing herself in one issue and then moving on to something else. The pace of the work suits her personality. She also works with all of the council members and is not at the mercy of any one politician's agenda, as she was in Pines's office.

The caliber of the staff is high. Although Dace is the only lawyer, her office is filled with PhDs, and includes a Rhodes scholar. Even in this high-toned group Dace still finds herself talking the most at meetings. She is often the one volunteering to write the first draft of a proposal, the person with the guts to say the wrong thing in order to get a tricky issue onto the table right away. She enjoys the challenge of trying to figure out how to tackle a problem. To the public, sometimes she is a hero and other times a villain. At first it was hard for her when unhappy constituents blamed their problems on the council's staff, but Dace learned not to take their criticisms personally. "I sort of made myself understand that there are no friends or enemies in this work, there are just advocates and adversaries. That was a professional lesson I had to learn and I learned it and I am much more detached," she says. Ironically, the fact that she is one of a sizable number of women in the office has made it impossible for Dace to move up a career ladder and she has remained an analyst for the past five years. The current staff director is a woman, and even if the number two position opened, the assistant director's job, it would be awkward for the director to appoint another woman. Dace understands the situation; it is just affirmative action reality.

Although she is content with her present job, with no real prospect of promotion she knows that, from an abstract perspective, it is time to move on. This knowledge propelled her to seek job counseling a couple of years ago. But as she talked with the counselor about how much she enjoyed her work, both of them concluded that for the present she should stay where she is. "What is this pressure to move?" she wonders. "I make good money. I love going to work in the morning. I'm challenged by my work. It's frustrating and difficult and depressing and exhausting and all that other stuff but I really care about it. I feel like I'm in a position where what I do really matters to this city, so I feel like it's real important, what I do, and I feel like I've only gotten good at it in the last couple of years." Dace does not want to settle for something less stimulating or meaningful, even if the change brings a more impressive title and more money.

The hours at the council are also good. She rarely works more than a fifty-hour week, which leaves plenty of time for outside interests. Her latest passion is diving, and she is planning a diving expedition to Australia with a friend. Dace and Carol, who remains one of the mainstays in Dace's personal life, are very much part of the young, professional class that is so influential in Seattle. Carol works for the federal government, at the Equal Employment Opportunity Commission.

Dace's personal goals have come into better focus, too. In 1982 she actually thought she might marry. She was living with a man, Paul, who shared custody of his two sons from a previous marriage. Dace was particularly close to the oldest boy, and the relationship gave her some sense of what having a child of her own might be like. She loved the sense of completeness that living as a family brought to her life. It recalled the happier times of her own childhood, when her parents were still happily married and busy raising their children. But Dace's relationship with Paul had its own set of problems and they broke up. Although the relationship didn't work out, Dace learned she wanted someday to be married and have a child of her own. "I think during my twenties I was changing so much and experimenting so much that the idea of a permanent relationship was impossible because there was no way to predict what I was going to want in three months," she observes.

Dace has renounced the fancy cars she used to drive in favor of a fuel-efficient Honda Civic. She owns the spacious, comfortable house she shares with a roommate on the outskirts of downtown Seattle. As she unwinds from a long day at work, followed by a party for one of the city's weekly newspapers, where she has rubbed elbows with some of the city's movers and shakers, the earthy tones of Billie Holiday emanate from the living room, which is filled with comfy furniture and plants. Although her roommate is out for the evening, three dogs are scampering about. The house seems to recapture the warm 1960s feelings of some of the collective houses where Dace once lived. A bulletin board in the kitchen displays her student identification card from Pali High. Dressed in an attractive, dark green linen shirt and stylish khaki skirt with matching green heels, Dace looks professional and serious, completely different from the long-haired prom queen of 1965. Relaxing at home, she feels tired but content, and in control of her life. "Growing up is a maturing process that I am quite conscious of and it's a real pleasurable thing to me. I feel more and more like I'm the person who decides who I'm going to be, and I sort of have a sense that it may be here or it's coming."

Perhaps her old friends from Harvard Law School would have a hard time understanding her present happiness. Professionally, she has little desire for advancement on its face and, personally, her life is still in transition. But Dace McCoy has a community of close friends, and she believes she has an impact on the city where she has finally settled down. "For the first time in my life," she says with apparent satisfaction, "I can say that I expect to be in the same place for the next twenty years and really mean it."

Government work has provided a haven for Rene Townsend Robinson, Dace McCoy and nine other women from the class who, at the midpoint in their first decade in the profes-

sion, needed to switch career tracks. Working in policy areas
provides intellectual stimulation, and the social content of the
work is also important. The lower pay of most of these jobs,
particularly compared to jobs in law firms, does not seem to
bother many of the women who switched into government
work from private practice or those who, like Dace McCoy,
cannot picture themselves fitting into the stuffier, more constrained world of private practice.

Other women from the class have had a much more difficult time finding a foothold in the profession and seven
women have left law for good. After spending almost five
years at a New York firm, Mary Ann McGunigle, who was
never entirely happy practicing law, enrolled in architecture
school. Bari Boyer, who practiced three years at a small Harrisburg, Pennsylvania, firm, also became disillusioned with
law. In 1980 she formed a real estate brokerage and management company in Worcester, Massachusetts. "I never got
back into practicing law. I discovered I didn't have the personality for it," says Boyer, who is also busy raising two children. "I like the flexibility of being self-employed, taking
vacations when I want, setting my own hours." Four others
are staying home full time to raise children.

Hitting the age of thirty, many women from the class
turned their attention to family planning and began adjusting
their career goals to accommodate children. While many still
clung to the superwoman ideal, others quickly came to grips
with the difficulty of balancing families with full-tilt careers.
Although she loved her job as an investment banker for Salomon Brothers (which she joined after training in Sullivan &
Cromwell's high-powered corporate department) Janine
Wolf Hill left for a less pressurized existence as assistant trea-
surer at Time, Inc. The demands of her home life and raising
two children helped her make the switch. "I had so much
responsibility, I was living my job," she explains. "Even if I
were somewhere else, I'd still be thinking about my clients,

worrying. I had already proven myself and knew I needed more time for my family."

Yet child-rearing considerations were only part of a complex web of factors which led so many women from Harvard Law School class of 1974 to abandon high-powered jobs and sometimes, with them, their dreams of having it all.

5

Managing Motherhood

They were the postwar baby boom generation who brought an abrupt end to the baby boom, often waiting until they were well into their thirties to have children, some deciding not to have children at all. For almost all the women in the Harvard Law School class of 1974—especially during their first five years in the profession—their careers came first. Although a few were married during law school, and a handful of others had entered it later in life, after having children, most of the seventy subscribed to the theory that it was best for a woman to establish herself professionally before taking on family responsibilities.

"I think I would have gone crazy if I had tried to do both," says Sandra Froman, who spent her first six years out of Harvard Law trying to reach her goal of making partner at Los Angeles' Loeb & Loeb. "It would have been like having two bosses compete for your time and your energy and I think a lot of women who have tried to do both haven't succeeded at either, or at least they felt they hadn't. I never thought about it as something I wanted until after I'd become a partner. It was like, okay, that was number one on my list and let's think about number two." But by then Froman was divorced. She says she worries that she may regret not having children (although she is still considering it), and the rigid priorities of her early career.

For those who went into private practice, the eight- and nine-year partnership tracks at most firms made having children a risky proposition (for long maternity leaves and part-time work options, when available, inevitably delayed partnership decisions even longer) and postponement equally risky (for, at age thirty-five and up, some women in the class were having problems conceiving). Given both problems, it is not altogether surprising that half of the women who have stayed in private practice since graduation were still childless ten years after graduation. "It would be difficult to manage having my kind of position in law and my lifestyle and also having children," observes Ellen Marshall, a partner at Los Angeles' McKenna, Conner & Cuneo, echoing the sentiments of several of her classmates who have decided not to take on the twin burdens of a law firm career and child care. In 1984 Marshall billed more than nineteen hundred hours, so it is hard to imagine how children would fit into her life. "Maybe I'm too selfish to be willing to devote the time, energy, resources and attention that would be involved in raising a child," she admits. Her career, like that of so many women from her class, comes first.

But 51% of the women in the class have opted to have children during the past ten years, including six who are partners in large law firms and scaled that hurdle while they were raising babies. For those working full time in private practice, government and other spheres of the profession, the juggle has been one requiring near perfect hand-eye (or rather home-job) coordination. "I've found it emotionally and physically very tough," admits Elisse Walter, who works as a government lawyer and has one son. "I learned not to be a workaholic and that's basically the way it's been manageable. I learned that I'm never going to be able to meet my own standards." Eight women from the class are working part-time, as a way of keeping the dual roles of mother and lawyer in balance, in one of the most hour-intensive of professions. But while schedules can be adjusted, psychological pressures and the perfectionist expectations of many of these seventy women are harder to grapple with. The desire to raise children and devote time to their families runs exactly counter to the driven, workaholic behavior that many of these women developed, sometimes long before they arrived at Harvard Law School. Even for those with less rigid lifestyles and expectations, the balancing act has been awkward. For the nurturing personality of the mother clashes blatantly with the tough, hard qualities of the respected negotiator and litigator. And in the profession examples of women who have managed to succeed at both are scarce.

The demands of raising small children have caused four women in the class to leave the profession or to interrupt their careers indefinitely and have led many others to make radical adjustments in their professional lives. The choices that confronted Renee Chotiner, who waited to have her children until her career as a trial lawyer was well established, and Susan Roosevelt Weld, who started her family much earlier and tried to combine motherhood with private practice, are ones that many women from the Harvard Law School class of 1974 have faced or will face.

Sitting in the cozy living room of her suburban home in New Haven, far removed from the tensions of trial practice, which had been the center of her world since law school, Renee Chotiner knew she might be sabotaging her career. It was a chilly, gray afternoon in February 1984 and Renee was spending the day as she had for the past eighteen months, at home with her daughter Hannah. And, with another baby on the way, there was no telling when she might return to work. In the 1980s it was rare for a woman with such substantial training, a BA from Radcliffe and a JD from Harvard, to stay out of the job force for so long. Renee Chotiner was part of a new breed of professional women who, discovering the joys of motherhood in their thirties, had lost their desire to make work the core of their existence.

It was almost two years since Renee had been inside a courtroom and it could easily be much longer than that before she picked up the threads of what had been a very exciting career. If she had had children earlier in life, Renee believed, she would have felt compelled to go back to work. "If I had made the choice earlier," she reflects, "I would have gone back because of self-doubt about my professional ability." Instead, she had given birth to Hannah when she was thirty-four, after eight years of experience as a litigator. "I had the composure and freedom to really make a choice," she says. And in 1982 Renee's choice to put her career on hold to become a full-time mother was an unconventional one, at least for the seventy women who were in her law school class, many of whom had also started their families in the ten years since their 1974 graduation.

Renee Chotiner is one of six women from her law school class staying home full-time to raise children. One of their group, Anne Geldon, has not worked outside her home since 1977 (although she does trusts and estates work from her home), when the first of her two children was born. "You're either a lawyer or a mother," Geldon says. Some of her friends and former classmates, Geldon reports, had "an extreme reaction," disapproving of her decision to leave a Washington firm to become a stay-at-home mother. While most women from the class have avoided taking this radical step—withdrawing from the profession altogether—many have rearranged their professional lives to accommodate the needs of their children. A few have left their law firm jobs, unable to manage the long hours, and looked for slower-paced jobs. Working part- or full-time, they have all made different sacrifices to do both. Renee thought it was possible for a woman to have a career and a family, but at this stage of her life she found she wanted to concentrate her energies on her family. "I'm intrigued by those who do both—and are happy," she admits, "but most of my friends are pretty torn. I'm about the happiest person I know."

She had not precisely planned on staying home. Before Hannah was born Renee assumed she would return to work after taking a maternity leave. "Six months went by and I was just having such a good time," she says. "I just didn't want to go back. . . . I thought six to twelve months would be my limit, and that was longer than anyone else I knew. . . . But I really felt I wanted to raise her. I didn't want to turn her over to somebody else. . . . Here it is, nearly eighteen months later, and I'm still sitting here. I could never have predicted it."

In 1974, if Renee had been able to see herself ten years later, totally devoted to nurturing a child, she would have been incredulous. Although she looked similar, with the same shiny, dark hair, pretty face with open, inquiring features, and denim wardrobe, she was very different from the brash, idealistic woman who left Harvard Law School in 1974 as a committed feminist and Marxist. "I've simmered down a lot since then," she says. There were a few vestiges of past commitments in the sprawling house she has shared and restored with her husband, Stuart, a pediatric resident, including a framed poster of Che Guevara hanging on the living-room wall outside the entrance to Hannah's playroom.

At Harvard Law School Renee was burning to begin her career in poverty or public interest law. As a law student, she was deeply involved in Gary Bellow's clinical program and spent most of her time volunteering at the Boston Legal Assistance Project. Most of the students who worked with Bellow were kindred spirits, out to change the structure and fiber of society by helping the poor find justice. But even she felt obliged to see what corporate practice was like. She went through an elaborate process, choosing a summer job after her second year at Harvard, hoping to find a firm that wasn't too objectionable on political grounds. She picked Latham & Watkins, a huge, WASP firm that was a pillar of the Los Angeles legal establishment. Latham was also known for its pro bono program, assigning its associates to work on cases alongside the American Civil Liberties Union, the NAACP Legal Defense Fund and other activist groups.

She told Latham's hiring partner up front that she didn't think she would like working at a corporate firm but wanted to satisfy her curiosity and the harping critics who kept telling her she shouldn't knock firm practice unless she tried it. All summer the same partner kept ribbing her when they met in the hallway, telling Renee, "We'll convert you yet." Most of the work was devoid of the sticky moral issues that might bother her conscience. One matter made her slightly uncomfortable—a labor negotiation in which the firm represented management's side—but all in all she liked the work. Still, at the end of the summer, when the firm invited her to return as a permanent associate, she politely declined. Getting the offer was flattering nonetheless. "It helped my self-confidence," Renee says, "knowing that I chose a different path not because I wasn't competent in that path [corporate law]. In the recesses, I wanted to reassure myself that I could succeed in that sphere." But she saw herself as a civil rights trailblazer, activist trial lawyer or a public defender, not as counselor to the corporate elite. She often referred to her summer at Latham & Watkins as her journey "into the belly of the monster."

At Harvard Law School many of her classmates were under the mistaken impression that she was the daughter of Murray Chotiner, one of President Nixon's top political advisers, and thought that her radicalism was a predictable rebellion against growing up in a conservative, Republican home. Actually Chotiner was a distant cousin of her father's but had no

influence on her leanings. Her antiwar sentiments were
clearly formed by the time she left high school, a large Los
Angeles public school called University High. At Radcliffe
she supported the strike that shut down the university in
1969. Her passions had also been stirred by the women's
movement, and she began attending a consciousness-raising
group in 1970, right after college graduation.

Her goal following Radcliffe was to become a muckraking
journalist. Toward the end of her senior year Ben Bradlee,
the editor of the Washington *Post*, came to Harvard to recruit
summer interns for his newspaper. Renee had not even written for the *Crimson*, Harvard's daily, but Bradlee was impressed by this cocksure young woman. Despite her lack of
experience, she was hired and spent most of the summer covering local stories in suburban Virginia. As her grand finale
Renee planned an exposé of the women's state prison in Roa-
noke. She spent a week roaming through the grim cell
blocks, interviewing inmates and taking pictures. But when
she sat down to write the piece her story read more like a
sociology term paper than a newspaper article. It was
"killed" by the editors at the *Post*.

If she wasn't suited to be a journalist, Renee could still be a
social reformer, and law school provided her vehicle. At Harvard Law the next year she hated the competitive atmosphere
and the ten-to-one sex ratio. As an undergraduate she had
been used to a more civilized four-to-one ratio. Without the
Women's Law Association, where Renee spent much of her
time, she would have felt isolated. "Without the WLA," she
maintains, "you would always be the purple thumb, completely sticking out in class. I remember worrying about what
I wore to class, knowing that my clothes would get noticed."

The men in her class looked as though they were fresh out
of Midwestern accounting schools, with their short hair,
hornrims and briefcases. The women wore neatly pressed
slacks, while Renee donned her uniform of jeans, boots and

work shirts. For the most part people behaved politely and sat quietly in class. Some of the other students in her section were obviously annoyed when Renee spent fifteen minutes debating the fairness of prostitution laws with their criminal law professor, James Vorenberg.

Although Renee always had high grades she was contemptuous of the *Law Review* competition and when January arrived she and three other women from the class received permission from Dean Sacks to do an alternative project to the Ames Moot Court Competition. Working with Diane Lund, a local lawyer who later became a junior member of the law school faculty, they wrote a challenge to the jury selection method used in Massachusetts, which disqualified all women with children under sixteen. They drafted a sex discrimination complaint, researching Fourteenth Amendment law inside out. Relying on some of their arguments, the state attorney general later lobbied for a bill to change the jury selection method. Instead of arguing some arcane appeal before a Moot Court panel, Renee felt they had accomplished something important with their feminist law project. The next year she helped like-minded One Ls find their own alternative Ames topics. Ames had taken on an importance that far outweighed its true worth, just like *Law Review*. "It had become a mania, something people were compelled to do," she says.

If she disapproved of the cutthroat competition, Renee was still hooked by the intellectual aspects of her legal studies. "I was excited by the intellectual process, by the Socratic method, by the legal method of thinking," she recalls. "I found it very stimulating. I found the sharpening of your logical skills very pleasant. I didn't like the machoness of the school. I didn't like the political orientation. I didn't like the aggressiveness. But I could see something important was going on." At the end of three years Renee couldn't wait to break into the real world of lawyering. As a young woman of twenty-four, children were about the last thing on her mind.

Susan Roosevelt was an undergraduate at Radcliffe and a student at Harvard Law School at exactly the same time as Renee Chotiner, but the two women hardly knew each other and couldn't have been more different. Susan, the great-granddaughter of President Theodore Roosevelt, was shy and retiring, uninvolved in the political and feminist groups that Renee so eagerly joined at Harvard. Yet, as a young woman, Susan, too, became intrigued by the idea of having a career and despite her nature, which was probably more suited to the quieter life of academia, she also chose law as her field. Susan and Renee arrived at Radcliffe during a time of rapid change when, as their classmate Molly Munger observed, "most women entered college with the traditional view that they were there to find a man," and left, four years later, more interested in finding a job than a husband. As she progressed in her career as a lawyer, Susan Roosevelt, like many of the seventy women in her law school class, found that blending a career with a traditional family life was a lot more difficult than she had anticipated.

Ten years after graduation from Harvard Law School, Susan's life was also centered at home, meeting the demands of raising five children, aged eight months to eight years. In 1979 Susan had given up her career as an associate at an old-line Boston firm, Gaston Snow & Ely Bartlett, right before she gave birth to her third child. For a variety of reasons, the most important being her family, she had decided to give up legal practice to earn her PhD in East Asian legal studies, a lifelong interest. In the spring of 1984 she was still hard at work on her doctoral thesis.

From the comfortable study in her sprawling, nine-bedroom house in Cambridge, just a few blocks away from the Harvard campus, Susan could watch her son Quentin, age three, playing in his sandbox. It was difficult for Susan to set aside the four hours she needed each day to complete the research for her thesis. After earning her doctorate, Susan hoped to get a job teaching at a law school. Despite the fact that she was considering having a sixth child, she viewed academics as a full-time career. "I couldn't be happy without it," she says. She saw herself as someone who was "doing both" successfully. Nevertheless she had given up her associate's job because of her growing family demands. And sometimes, watching her husband, William Weld, who was U.S. attorney for Massachusetts, she missed the excitement of practice.

Blending career and family was probably the most difficult problem for Harvard Law alumnae of all generations. But Susan made her decision to leave practice under very different circumstances than the women of an earlier generation. When she had her first child in 1976 she was one of the first lawyers at her firm ever to take a maternity leave. By the late 1970s, as more women like Susan Roosevelt Weld began climbing up the ranks of the profession, making themselves valuable to their clients and employers, firms began making concessions to working mothers, offering maternity leaves and part-time work arrangements. During her third pregnancy Susan worked part time, but she didn't find this option satisfying.

Before the 1970s the choices were much narrower. Women either stayed single and single-mindedly devoted to their careers, or they left their careers behind to raise families. Women of the former mold also, for lack of role models, emulated their male coworkers and bosses. As a young assistant U.S. attorney, Sylvia Bacon, Harvard Law 1953, recalls making a self-conscious effort to be one of the boys. "You approached your work like they did," she explains. "You also had to enjoy their activities. You would go to the baseball game with the group from the office even if you did not like baseball very much. You would eat at Hodges, the roast beef place, rather than the art gallery. You did not take time off to do household things. Their wives bought their socks. I never pretended I did anything their wives did."

In order to succeed Bacon remained single, working her way up the criminal justice system and becoming a judge in 1970. "I was career bent and I was of the view that it would be very difficult to do both," she says. "I liked the trial scene and I could not imagine myself having to be concerned about whether another person had clean shirts or clean diapers. All I needed to be well prepared in court was a clean handkerchief for myself." Bacon is fascinated by women of the 1970s and 1980s who can handle careers and families but says, even if she were young again, she would not "take on both a career and a family, lightly."

It took superhuman effort for women with families to achieve partnership at major firms. Rita Hauser, Harvard Law 1958, is one who made it. A loyal, live-in housekeeper gets some of the credit from Hauser, whose international practice took her abroad frequently. In order to raise two children and handle a growing practice, Hauser became a "super organizer" and left little notes pinned around her house reminding her children about lessons and school responsibilities. Without supportive partners at Wall Street's Stroock & Stroock & Lavan, who were understanding if Hauser had to miss firm functions or client meetings when one of her children was ill, Hauser says she might not have been able to bring it off. (Part of the reason her partners may have been so understanding is that Hauser, representing a host of European and Israeli clients, is one of the highest billers at Stroock.) Without endless stores of energy and drive, being a partner and a mother would have been, according to Hauser, almost impossible. Although she stands barely over five feet tall, she is one of those dynamos who keeps, as she puts it, "pushing, pushing, pushing."

Pregnant women, even those with Harvard Law degrees, feared job loss if their condition was detected. In the early 1960s Ruth Bader Ginsburg, class of 1959, was pregnant with her second child while she was teaching. "I held an untenured post at Rutgers Law School," Ginsburg explains, "and feared my contract might not be renewed if my colleagues suspected my pregnancy. I got through the spring semester without detection, with the help of a wardrobe one size larger than mine, borrowed from my mother-in-law. My son arrived conveniently in early September. Classes started three weeks later and I was able to show up on time." Ginsburg was eventually offered tenure.

During the 1950s and 1960s, however, it was far more usual for women to break away from their careers to have children, and some never returned to practice. Frederica Brenneman, who was among the very first group of women to graduate from Harvard Law School in 1953, says, "If you asked any one of us where our priorities lay it would have been family first." Brenneman married a fellow classmate and did not work while she raised her three children. She resumed her career when she was much older and is now a superior court judge in Hartford, Connecticut.

Eve Plotkin, Harvard Law class of 1954, stayed home for twelve years to raise her children. "The idea in 1954 that I would stay home was applauded. The attitude was, 'Isn't it nice you have a nice little Harvard Law degree, but now you're a nice mother.'" Plotkin managed to land a job in legal services after her long absence but believes she would have been "permanently derailed" if she had wanted a job in private practice.

Twenty years later, as a young associate fresh out of law school, Susan Roosevelt Weld had also worried that having children, particularly in such rapid succession, would derail her law firm career. For women in private practice one thing had not changed over the years—the simple reality that the partnership track coincided with a woman's prime childbearing years. Despite being able to take maternity leaves and work part time, Susan decided it would be impossible for her to obtain partnership if she kept interrupting her career to have children. And so she switched into East Asian studies, a natural alternative given her background.

Susan was born in Shanghai in 1948. Her father had been in China at the end of World War II and stayed in the Far East to run an outpost for Pan American World Airways. In 1949 the Communists came, and just as the family was making its plans to return to the United States her father died in a plane crash. Her mother brought Susan and her sisters back to Oyster Bay, the wealthy Long Island preserve where many members of the Teddy Roosevelt clan, whom Susan described as "the disreputable Dutch" side of the Roosevelt line, resided. Susan's mother had once told her that she and her father had dreamed of having nine children and the remark had stuck in the young girl's mind. Friends from their China days were frequent visitors in Oyster Bay. They were China's "running dogs," the capitalist class that fled after the takeover by the People's Republic of China. Susan was utterly enthralled by their stories and culture, so much so that she pursued a major in Chinese studies as a student at Radcliffe.

Susan Roosevelt was very different from the activists like Renee Chotiner who surrounded her at Radcliffe in the late 1960s. Her passions were stirred neither by Students for a Democratic Society nor by the various feminist groups on campus. The SDSers, she thought, were misguided and patronizing. They tried to organize the kitchen staff in Susan's dorm. "The ladies in the house we lived in really didn't take to that," Susan recalls. "They thought of the students in a different way. Many of the ladies had worked for twenty or thirty years and they thought of the students as children, whom they could protect and take care of and make sure they ate enough food. And here the children were coming to them and saying, 'We can help save you from your miserable life.' "

Instead of attending political meetings Susan was usually holed up in her room, studying Chinese or playing a complicated game of solitaire called pine orchard poison. "I would sit in my room," she remembers, "and drink a lot of coffee, and think deep thoughts and play pine orchard poison. I was very, very happy." Quiet and intellectual, Susan seriously considered going to graduate school in Chinese studies and won a fellowship to study in Taiwan after graduation. But she had heard that all the good jobs in the academic field were drying up and decided to apply to law school, not wanting to risk a dead-end career.

Over ten percent of the women in Susan's graduating class from Radcliffe[1] also went to law school. Law was becoming the "in" profession for bright, ambitious women. Susan, however, was not as driven as many of her classmates at Harvard Law School. "I didn't really work that hard," she says. "I think part of the reason was that I was afraid if I worked hard I wouldn't get on *Law Review* anyway, so I thought to myself, 'If I don't work hard I won't have to put that question to myself.' "

She spent most of her time at the East Asian Legal Studies Center, located on the fourth floor of Pound Hall. There Professor Jerome Cohen had his command post. There was also a library and a lunchroom where everyone involved in the program congregated for luncheons on different scholarly topics. Having a smaller base of operations at the Center, where Susan had her own carrel, helped make law school a less impersonal experience. She grew friendly with the other women there, including Phebe Miller, whom Susan had known at Concord Academy, Mary Faith Higgins and Alice Young. They could each detect when one of their group was

[1] According to a survey of alumnae conducted in 1984–85 by the Radcliffe College Alumnae Association.

in a bad mood or needed some extra encouragement and
support. Certainly the EALS library was a more comfortable
environment than Langdell, the law school's main library.
"In Langdell," Susan recalls, "people would come by to you
to say hello and then somehow work into the conversation.
'Have you read this or that case?' And, of course, you
wouldn't have and would feel anxious and worried, and they
would have won a point. But that didn't happen at EALS
because we were all friends."

But EALS could not insulate her from all the bruising experiences of first-year life. She hated the Ames Competition,
too, though for very different reasons than Renee Chotiner.
She was not opposed to the exercise on philosophical
grounds—she just hated having to perform publicly. And
when she and her partner, Barbara Parker, argued their case
they were even more nervous than Susan had anticipated.
When they finished, one of the Ames judges, trying to con-
sole them, had said, "Maybe next time you won't be so nervous." It was a patronizing, humiliating experience.

Susan hated being called on in class and disliked the aggressiveness displayed by her classmates. The other women
who lived near Susan in Wyeth Hall remember her as being
unusually calm and kind but hard to get to know. But she
wasn't a snob, despite her impressive ancestry. When she was
invited to join one of the law school's secret societies, which
was very social and had almost no women members, she had
declined.

Sometimes she questioned whether she was cut out for the
profession. Often, when she was supposed to be studying for
an exam, she read bits of Chinese and French literature instead. Professor Cohen was encouraging her to take a teaching job in Singapore after graduation, but Susan wanted to
give practice a try. She had always been curious about Wall
Street. If she didn't like it she could always leave. It made

more sense to go the law firm route first, when she had easy access. The research and teaching could always come later.

By the time she began interviewing for law firm jobs Susan Roosevelt Weld was pretty sure she didn't want to be a litigator. She just wasn't brash or aggressive enough to stand up in court. Renee Chotiner, on the other hand, was confident that the courtroom would be a natural environment for her. After graduation she took a one-year clerkship with Judge Herbert Wilkins, then the youngest judge on the Massachusetts Supreme Court. After sitting in on appellate arguments and doing the research for Wilkins' opinions, Renee knew she wanted trial work—a job that would take her into court all the time, not at a big firm where she'd be stuck in the library researching briefs or carrying somebody else's bags to court, but where she would be representing her own clients.

Finding that kind of job as a young woman practically fresh out of law school was difficult. She enlisted the help of Harvey Silverglate, one of Boston's top criminal defense lawyers. During law school Silverglate had been in the news defending Senator Mike Gravel of Alaska, who was facing contempt charges for reading into the Senate record the text of the Pentagon Papers, the "secret" Vietnam documents leaked to the press by Daniel Ellsberg. Silverglate claimed that Gravel's conduct was protected by the speech and debate clause of the Constitution, and Renee had done some research for him. She went into the bowels of Langdell to search through a stack of dusty documents from the seventeenth century for the British antecedents to the clause.

Silverglate told her to contact Norman Zalkind, one of his former law partners. Zalkind had just hired an associate, but he told Renee if she would work for $100 a week he had plenty of cases to keep her busy. Zalkind's wife was also a partner and there were always more women lawyers than men at his firm. Although the firm handled malpractice, divorce and personal injury cases to bring in money, the bulk of Zalkind's practice was criminal defense work. He defended accused murderers, rapists and drug dealers. Zalkind charged these clients on a sliding scale according to their ability to pay. He tried to pick cases that turned on major legal issues. He was consumed by his work and his dedication and idealism were immensely appealing. She signed on at $100 a week.

All of her friends were living on similar pittances. Renee settled into an apartment in Somerville, a poor, working-class neighborhood abutting Cambridge. Many of her friends from college and law school days had stayed in the Boston area, which had become a magnet for progressive-minded young people, those searching for an alternative to the faster-paced and more materialistic lifestyle of New York. She and her friends often joked that they were working to support their cars.

Soon she, too, was totally consumed by work. Everything at Zalkind & Zalkind seemed to happen in dramatic spurts. Her telephone would ring at two in the morning and her answering service would relay a message: "So-and-so is in Concord jail. The charge is manslaughter. Get over there." She would hop in the car and go. Her life was completely unpredictable; a new case, or a new crisis in an old one, could erupt at any time. Working at least fifty hours a week, dealing with cops, DAs and all varieties of criminals, she worked on several high-publicity murder cases in which the firm won acquittals. She didn't find it hard to relate to her clients, most of whom she believed were innocent. Even the ones who were guilty usually had such difficult circumstances surrounding their lives that it was easy to be sympathetic. Her job, at any rate, was not to determine guilt or innocence but to give her clients the best defense possible.

While some of her friends burned out in their jobs as public defenders, becoming disillusioned about the criminal justice system and the "scum," as they began to call their clients, Renee only became more and more wrapped up in her job. "It was a thrilling, totally unpredictable life," she says.

Renee's near total dedication to her work impressed her boss too. "She was extraordinary," Norman Zalkind remembers. "Every major case I tried with her we won. She was very tough, very fast." With Renee's help Zalkind won acquittals in two high-visibility cases. The first involved a Cambridge woman who had killed her psychologist husband and two children. They successfully used the insanity defense on her behalf, winning a not guilty verdict. They had also successfully defended James Tam, a Chinese man who had been accused of killing a sixteen-year-old girl in the white, working-class section of Boston called Charlestown.

The work didn't leave much room for a personal life. When she met Stuart Gardner, a sociologist who was in the process of switching careers and going into medicine, it was hard to throw herself into a relationship. The job made her so tough that she sometimes felt as if she were encased in iron. It was difficult for her to have a warm, really human relationship. Stuart had just started medical school at Yale, so they saw each other on weekends, either in Boston or in New Haven. But the shuttle romance wasn't very satisfying, and they talked about living together. Stuart couldn't transfer to school in Boston at so early a point in his studies, so she had to consider leaving her job.

It was a big risk. She was challenged and fulfilled at Zalkind & Zalkind. She had learned how to handle herself in court, how to bargain with DAs and how to present herself to judges. Whenever possible, Zalkind allowed her to pick and choose her cases. Renee refused to defend rapists because she felt the defense strategies in most rape cases involved picking apart the victim's reputation. But after five years of trial work she also wanted to lead a more balanced life. The hours and pressure had begun to exhaust her. She didn't want her hide to become so tough that she couldn't feel anything, and she loved Stuart. She hoped she could reassemble her life in New Haven and find socially meaningful work. After hunting for a house to purchase with Stuart she landed a job at Yale Law School, staffing the volunteer-run prisoners' rights clinic. In the summer of 1979 she moved to New Haven for good. Despite her value to his firm, Zalkind didn't try to dissuade her. "Back then," he explains, "it was common for the woman to follow the man. Actually, it still is."

Susan Roosevelt's love life would also complicate her career plans. Although she had been dating someone in Boston, Susan had still wanted to give Wall Street and the New York business world a try. She hoped, somehow, to make use of her Chinese, perhaps with a firm with an international practice. In Boston there were no such animals. In New York there were a variety of well-known international firms, including Coudert Brothers and Cleary, Gottlieb, Steen & Hamilton.

But first she had to land a job, and Susan found she wasn't very good at interviewing. "I think it's true that if you're what's called a 'live wire' your chance of getting a job is much better and I have never been a live wire," she admits. Nevertheless she interviewed at several New York and Washington firms and whether she liked a place usually depended on whether she liked the hiring partner. She knew this was a silly basis on which to judge an entire firm. But seemingly insignificant details like this could influence her thinking. At Willkie Farr & Gallagher, the firm where she had worked the summer after her second year at Harvard, the paging system had irritated her. Each lawyer was given a code with a certain number of pings. You could even hear them in the bathrooms. She didn't like being summoned by pings. They reminded her of a department store.

So, instead of returning to Willkie, she accepted an offer

from Cleary, Gottlieb, Steen & Hamilton, a mainstream Wall Street firm. For Susan, one of the allures of Wall Street was that it was so male dominated. The women in her family were groundbreakers and pioneers, and Susan liked the idea of carrying on this tradition. She remembered a dinner conversation in Oyster Bay when she was younger, about one of her cousins who had been the only woman in her law school class. The rest of the family was so admiring of her.

At Cleary there were a number of ambitious, capable women in her group of new associates, including Wendy Singer and Deborah Fiedler, both classmates from Harvard Law. But Susan barely had time to meet all of the other associates before she became engaged and decided to move back to Boston. She left Cleary after only nine months, still feeling very much the incompetent young associate. During law school she had begun dating her fiancé William Weld, a lanky, red-haired associate from Hill & Barlow, one of Boston's most respected firms. Weld also came from an old Long Island family. He had occasionally taken one of Susan's sisters to local dances, and Susan had admired him from afar. When she learned he was in Boston she asked him to dinner and a romance blossomed between the shy, attractive law student and the self-confident associate.

If Susan Roosevelt was retiring and reserved, William Weld was very much the live wire. At Harvard College he had been elected to Phi Beta Kappa as a junior and graduated summa cum laude in classics.[2] He was chosen to deliver the Latin oration at his Harvard commencement in 1966 and wrote a witty, tongue-in-cheek treatise called *"De Puellis Radcliffiensibus,"* which warned about the dire effects of letting Radcliffe women study in Lamont Library on the Harvard campus. He then studied at Oxford on a Knox fellowship and

[2.] *"What Next, William Weld?" Boston Globe Magazine,* Sunday, July 31, 1983.

came back to Harvard to get his law degree, graduating in
1970, four years ahead of Susan.

When she became involved with William Weld he was a
young lawyer on the fast track. He had just been plucked
from Hill & Barlow to serve on the legal staff of the House
Judiciary Committee investigating the Watergate break-in.
He had been hired by the Republican counsel to the committee to research the historical background on impeachment
proceedings. Many of the young lawyers who went to Washington to work on the Watergate committees were destined
to go back to their old jobs as recognized superstars. Bill
Weld was one of them.

It seemed nonsensical to interrupt Bill's career, which was
already so well established. He was on partnership track at
Hill & Barlow, and Susan had barely established her presence
at Cleary. So when they decided to marry Susan had left Wall
Street without a second thought and, like Renee Chotiner,
she willingly uprooted herself to follow her man.

Finding a job in Boston similar to the one she had at Cleary
would not prove that difficult for Susan Roosevelt. Although
there were no international firms, there were a number of
very well regarded corporate firms similar in style and practice to Wall Street. Trying to duplicate her job at Zalkind &
Zalkind was a much more difficult proposition for Renee
Chotiner. When she began looking for work she found that
New Haven, being a much smaller community than Boston,
had few criminal defense firms. And the lawyers who had any
kind of criminal practice thought she was a big-city slicker
and said they couldn't afford to hire her. When she described
her job at Zalkind & Zalkind, many of the New Haven lawyers with whom she interviewed told her she had been crazy
to leave. After exhausting the possibility of finding something
similar, she accepted the teaching offer from Yale. Clinical
law courses were in vogue at all the major law schools, and

Yale needed someone to staff its prisoners' rights clinic. She would be teaching one or two courses each semester, but the classroom aspect of the job was secondary. Handling the clinic's case load and teaching the student volunteers the basics of motion and trial practice were the core of the job.

Even with two hundred active cases on the clinic's docket, joining the program was a period of decompression for Renee. The hours were more regular and the pressure was much less intense. An individual's fate was no longer resting on her shoulders. Most of her new clients were already in prison and were bringing suits to get better living and working conditions, or were trying to get their verdicts overturned. She was no longer standing in front of a jury making an impassioned plea for justice. While she liked having more time to herself, she missed the rush of blood to her head, the excitement of making a closing argument. But she enjoyed supervising her volunteers. "The students were great," she says. "They had so much nerve. They'd say anything to a judge." She didn't remember being quite so bold as a law student, although Stuart assured her that she probably had been. She and Stuart got married in 1981. They sometimes laughed about the old days, when Renee was supertough, the iron lady. She still had to adopt that tough, litigator's mentality when she traveled to the state correctional institute at Cheshire or to the federal prison in Danbury where her students represented clients with parole applications, prison-condition and medical-care complaints, misconduct proceedings against guards, and habeas corpus appeals.

These gray, concrete institutions contrasted sharply with the large, sunny house she and Stuart were restoring in Hamden. It had a big backyard, perfect for children. They both wanted to have a family, even though Stuart's hours as an intern would be worse than Renee's had been as a new trial lawyer. The time seemed right to become pregnant. After three years at Yale she really missed the stimulation of trial practice and was ready to leave. It seemed silly to look for a new job while she was pregnant, and better to wait until after she took a maternity leave. Then she would be ready to start looking for a new job. Or so she thought.

Renee Chotiner had eight years of experience as a lawyer under her belt before she had a child. Susan Roosevelt Weld took on the responsibility of motherhood much earlier in her career, less than a year after she resettled in Boston. Again, just as she was learning the cast of characters at her new firm, Boston's Gaston Snow (which was not so affectionately known around the Boston legal community as Ghastly Slow), her career was interrupted.

Gaston Snow was one of the oldest firms in Boston and had been a mainstay of the city's conservative financial community since the mid-1850s. The firm represented a number of banks and mutual funds. Susan was assigned to work for partner Tom Chase and, like other women from her Harvard class who went the law firm route, Susan was assigned to do ERISA work. The pension work was peaceful if not thrilling. She didn't really mind sitting in her office going over pages and pages of pension plans, making sure the firm's clients were in compliance with the new tax laws. Her menu was varied with some mainstream corporate work and she wrote a few briefs and argued some small motions for a partner who handled malpractice and products liability cases.

If Susan was more of a back-room type, Gaston Snow was not holding it against her. Her work was dependable and competent. She noticed that some of the more aggressive male associates—the young lawyers whom Susan viewed as the real stars—were leaving the firm. Actually, they displayed more style than substance and their work product was not all that terrific. With her husband busy with his own trial practice, Susan was willing to put in long hours in the library, researching cases into the night. She might sit there for hours, enjoying the peace and quiet, reading odd bits out of casebooks before she sat down to research and write the assigned memo. "I think I'm not the world's most efficient researcher," she admits. But her work was reviewed favorably by the Gaston Snow partners.

She became pregnant a year after she joined the firm. Gaston Snow did not have a maternity leave policy, and Susan was one of the first lawyers at the firm to take time off to have a child and then return to work. After the birth of her son David, Susan hired a full-time housekeeper, hoping this would ease the difficulty of having a two-career family. After taking four months off, only partially paid, she returned to work full-time. But soon she was pregnant again and took another four-month leave after the birth of her daughter Ethel. She was told that the leaves would delay her partnership but that having children would not sideline her completely. Susan was concerned because there was another woman associate at the firm, in the tax department, who had become a permanent associate after she had had a child. If she was going to continue to work so hard, Susan wanted the status of being a partner.

She thought it best not to decorate her office with pictures of the children. "I remember being careful not to talk about them too much," she recalls, "feeling, maybe, unprofessional. . . . It still seems to me unfair that men don't have this problem even though the children are theirs too." She had returned to Gaston Snow full-time after the births of David and Ethel but, going on her third pregnancy in almost as many years, Susan began to be concerned about the constant interruptions of her practice. Gaston Snow did not seem to mind her repeated maternity leaves. In fact her fertility became something of a joke and Susan heard that the firm's new maternity leave policy had been christened the Susan Weld Memorial Maternity Leave Policy.

Reintegrating herself into practice grew more difficult with each child. "You come back and you have to develop your own work again," she explains. "You have to get into contact with clients again and it's arduous each time and you kind of feel bad for the first few weeks because you don't have enough work and then you try to get more and have too much." But she and Bill wanted their children to be born close together, so that they could eventually move on to a new stage in life that wasn't centered around parenting. In terms of career advancement, Susan knew she would have been wiser to make partner first and then have her children. But she had heard about too many women who had waited so long that they had a hard time conceiving.

Even with a full-time housekeeper it was difficult to balance her responsibilities. If a child was ill and she had a court appearance she felt terrible, no matter where she chose to be. She didn't want her children growing up and becoming more attached to a baby-sitter than they were to her. William pitched in with child care and changed his fair share of diapers, but with his practice, and a burgeoning political career, there were severe limits on his time too. "It's the woman who gets overtired," Susan observes, "by having the house and the children." And she realized that being a partner would only mean she would have to work even harder to pull her weight at the firm.

Juggling high-powered careers with child care was a constant source of exhaustion for other members of Susan's class. Like Susan, Anne Redman, who stuck it out to become a partner at Seattle's Foster, Pepper & Riviera, employed household help. But while baby-sitters might solve her practical needs, they didn't help resolve her internal worries, the guilt feelings she had over having to leave her son while she was working. "You take the baby to day care," Redman says, describing her routine, "and then you kind of dash out of your meeting to pick him up and take him home and park him with a baby-sitter and run back to your meeting. And

he's asleep when you get home at three in the morning. Then
you get him up the next day before he's awake to bring him
to day care again. You know, after a few days like that you
begin to think you can't continue to try to have everything."

When she learned she was pregnant for the third time,
Susan decided to try working part-time. Officially, she was
working three days a week, but when the firm needed a project completed she was working as hard as always, only getting paid less. For Susan, part-time work wasn't a solution. It
didn't really give her that much more time at home, and at
work she knew that she needed to make a full-time commitment in order to make partner. Other women in the class also
had a hard time working part-time as associates. Carol Schepp
returned full-time to her job in the corporate department at
New York's Debevoise & Plimpton, but after a year of commuting, working a full day and trying to raise her son Adam
she was exhausted. The firm granted her request to work
part-time. But as a senior associate Schepp was working on
major transactions, and when there was a closing or a big
financing she was in the office working just as hard as before.
In 1984 she left the firm and took a real part-time position at
an investment banking firm.

Part-time work was a salvation for others. Mary Nelson of
Hill & Barlow, the firm where Susan's husband worked, says,
"The firm wanted me to succeed in arranging my life in such
a way that I could continue to practice law." Nelson believes
her firm's unusually positive attitude about part-time work
made the difference in her situation. "There is no doubt in
my mind that if the firm had been uncooperative and had
said, 'No, we're not going to let you work part-time,' or if
they had said, 'We're not going to give you a maternity leave
longer than a few weeks'—I would not have continued to
practice there." Nelson had her first child while she was an
associate and the time she took off (ten months) pushed her
partnership election back a year. Since the birth of her first

child she has worked part-time, from about 8:30 A.M. to 2:30
P.M. each day. She admits that her corporate practice has not
developed as quickly on account of taking two long maternity
leaves and working part-time. She also gave up most of her
litigation practice when she began working part-time, partly
because she anticipated that the hours of trial work would be
incompatible with her schedule. The trade-off, of course, is
having more time for her family. Trying to become a rainmaker at Hill & Barlow or playing a role in its management
will have to come later. Nelson is content. "I'm probably not
as ambitious as I ought to be," she says.

Susan was also not driven in the same way that some of the
other associates were. Practicing and gunning for partnership
were not the center of her life. Her family was her top priority, and when her doctor told her she needed more rest she
didn't hesitate to take his advice to quit working altogether
until her third child was born. Gaston Snow would probably
have given her another leave, but Susan had grown more and
more convinced that the law firm lifestyle wasn't working in
her case. Instead of keeping the firm dangling, she gave her
final notice.

Shortly after she left Gaston Snow in 1979 she went to see
Professor Cohen at the law school. He wrote her a recommendation for Harvard's PhD program in East Asian legal
studies. She was confident that academic life would make a
better blend with her large brood and felt relieved about her
choice to leave practice.

"Here we are in all these liberated marriages," Renee
Chotiner observes ten years after her graduation from Harvard Law School, "but it still isn't an issue for men. It's a
much bigger sticking point for women, how to have a family
and have a job." Stuart would have liked to have more time
at home with Hannah but as a resident he didn't have a
choice about anything. And he had never really seriously

considered giving up his career to raise her. It was Renee, however willingly, who made that sacrifice.

This was a common pattern among women from her law school class. Most of them married during a time of unconventional morality but they had settled into traditional marriages in which the husband's career took precedence. Candy Fowler, who left a law firm to work as a government lawyer, is married to a partner at a well-known firm, Washington's Howrey & Simon. Fowler worked part-time following the birth of their child. Her husband never really considered adjusting his schedule because of the baby. "While he is very involved with our daughter," Fowler explains, "he was raised with traditional expectations. It would take a very unusual circumstance for him to think the best thing for him to do was work part-time. He is much more established in his career and earns more than I do. Looking at the status of my career as opposed to his, it seemed as if I had a lot less to lose." But Fowler also worries about stalling her own climb up the government hierarchy.

The men in the class who married professional women are also aware that the "equal partnership" marriages they may have envisioned in law school didn't materialize. To raise three children, Mark Mazo, a partner at Washington's Crowell & Moring, says he has had to sacrifice some of his interests outside the firm. But compared to the sacrifices of his wife, a doctor, Mazo knows his don't amount to much. "Her sacrifices are more significant in terms of professional development than mine," he admits. "I see that as a common pattern in two-profession families."

The difficulty of delegating child-care responsibilities equally led to the breakup of Roscoe Trimmier's marriage. During Harvard Law Trimmier spent most of his time outside of school caring for his daughter while his wife worked. After law school Trimmier became the breadwinner as an associate, and later partner, at Boston's Ropes & Gray. When his wife decided to apply for her MBA and took a job with a Boston bank there were repeated clashes between husband and wife. Trimmier says he couldn't stop himself from having the "selfish" attitude that his career was more important. "We simply couldn't work out the compromise," he says. "I had a higher income potential. Her career was marginal in terms of producing anything other than satisfaction to her. I became a very selfish person in that respect and that's why we are no longer married." Trimmier and his ex-wife, who is now an assistant bank vice-president, share joint custody of their daughter.

Renee and Stuart have none of these tensions in their marriage. They make no economic calculations about whose career is more important. If Renee had wanted to return to work Stuart would have fully supported her decision and helped arrange a child-care arrangement. But when Hannah was born Renee found that taking care of her child was more wonderful than she had thought possible. As the months passed she began to think that to do both—be a mother and a trial lawyer—would require a dual personality. "I can't imagine putting on those clothes," she says, "and with them that suit of armor."

While Stuart has one of his rare afternoons off and sits in the kitchen reading to Hannah, Renee has time to reflect on the many changes in her life since Hannah's birth. "It isn't until about six months are over that you start thinking, 'Am I a lawyer?'" she explains. "I know I'm trained to be a lawyer. But people say 'What do you do?' And I say, 'I'm at home with my baby.' I used to say, 'I'm a lawyer but I'm not working.' Now I almost never say I'm a lawyer, because I wonder, 'What is it that makes me a lawyer?' I don't do it. I don't think about it in the same way anymore. I just kind of dropped out of the whole culture of lawyering.

"I still enjoy hearing some war stories about cases that are really interesting, but a lot of the technical stuff that I used to really enjoy talking about with my friends—it doesn't interest me anymore. I don't identify with it in the same way. I really wonder what's going to happen when or if I go back to work."

She does miss the challenges of having a career. "I have the memory of the excitement and reward of doing a job well —the collegiality. And I miss the sense of accomplishment. Because the kinds of tasks I do now, there's no 'well' about them. Okay, so you do the laundry or clean the house or bathe the baby. I really miss testing myself and meeting the test. Because I don't find raising Hannah difficult at all. I just love doing it. It's like coming out of some visceral, primordial instinct, some incredible subconscious memory I have. And I guess I'm masochistic enough that I miss having hard tasks."

Staying at home has also changed her outlook on the world. "I'm the same person but the texture of my life is completely different than ten years ago," she says. "I care about different things. Now I feel I'm somewhat more removed from the real world. I have less daily contact with it. I read about stuff in the paper and occasionally I react the way my non-criminal law friends have always reacted. I say, 'God, what a grizzly crime. That person should be put away for the rest of his life.' "

It seems like several lives ago instead of several years that she was defending the accused perpetrators of grizzly crimes. "I miss focusing out on the world," she says. "What I do with my daughter is meaningful, but there is something very self-centered about it." She still gets angry over politics and fumes over the Reagan administration's policies in Central America. But instead of attending protest marches she sends a letter to her congressman or some money to peace groups. The fight has gone out of her.

Renee is intrigued by women who are working while raising children and realizes that others react very differently to the role of mothering. Molly Munger, one of Renee's class-mates, is determined not to let her two children slow her down and finds she needs an outward focus to her life. She returned to work as a litigator within five weeks after the births of each of her two sons. She had intended to take three months off after her first son was born but ended up calling her boss and begging to return earlier. "All babies do is eat and sleep," she says. "It was uninteresting to be around them. Their needs were easily met by others." Munger and her husband, also a lawyer, now employ two au pairs to care for their children in their Pasadena home. During the week Munger spends two hours each morning with the children. When she and her husband arrive home from work in Los Angeles their children are already asleep. For Munger, a "hands-off" child-care arrangement works. "People define child care differently," she says. "To be with them all day long and read the book about the little engine that went over the hill eighteen times . . . I don't like to be with them that much." Munger's philosophy has also allowed her to pro-gress professionally. In 1984 she opened a litigation firm with two other women with whom she had worked at the U.S. Attorney's office in Los Angeles.

Renee Chotiner does not feel moralistic about her decision to stay home with Hannah. She doesn't feel she is necessarily doing "the right thing" by being a full-time mother. She admires women who are doing both, but she knows at the moment that she is doing what is right for her by staying home. In a few years, when her children are older, it is very possible she may want to return to court. She knows a long absence will make her job hunt more difficult but she is will-ing to take the risk. Although she did not attend her tenth-year law school class reunion in April 1984, she did write something for the class report. Her short entry reads, "I left full-time law practice sixteen months ago to have a baby and never went back. This is much more fun. Someday . . .''

Although she lives just a few blocks away from the law school, Susan Roosevelt Weld also missed her tenth reunion. "I don't really like reunions," she explains. "And I didn't really enjoy law school all that much." Besides, having been away from practice for five years, she probably has little in common with her former classmates, the vast majority of whom—particularly the men—are working in firms. And on weekends Susan and William are usually on their own with the children and plan family outings.

Susan has never regretted giving up practice. As soon as she began intensive Japanese- and Chinese-language classes as part of her doctoral program she knew she was back in her true element—academia. "I just had so much fun," she says of her return to East Asian legal studies. "I realized that it had been a long time since I had been having fun."

The past few years have brought their share of difficulties. For Susan, there was a broken leg that refused to heal and a miscarriage. And, finally, the birth of two more children. Her life has also been changed by William Weld's foray into state Republican politics, which included a disastrous run for attorney general against a popular incumbent. Susan did not relish campaigning for her husband—all the speeches and glad-handing—but she was more than willing to pitch in. There are persistent rumors in Massachusetts that William Weld will soon run again for statewide office, perhaps governor. Susan has mixed emotions about being in the political spotlight herself but supports her husband's political career.

Books and children are now her main companions. So that she can help supervise the five children she has assembled a library of Chinese texts and a computer in a small room off the circular staircase that leads up to the second floor of her imposing house. Working at home is often difficult. If the children are fighting she often has to break away from her work to be the mediator. Even with two shifts of housekeepers who do almost all of the cooking, there are constant chores. Little friends come to visit her children and need to be driven home. Sometimes her day is a never ending chain of car-pool assignments. Susan doesn't really mind and always makes sure to take a book along.

If studying and children leave her isolated from her peers, William's job as U.S. attorney snaps her back into the real world. Since his appointment by President Reagan, Weld's name has rarely been out of the headlines. After Weld became U.S. Attorney, his office indicted eleven members of the administration of former Boston Mayor Kevin White in an anticorruption campaign that has shaken the entire city. When William was in the middle of an investigation, FBI agents and officers of the Drug Enforcement Agency were frequent guests at Susan's dinner table. Their conversations, Susan had to admit, were a lot spicier than her Chinese texts.

Susan realizes that the fabric of her life has been dramatically altered by her decision to have so many children so early in her career. But she is not aware of how different her life is. When she is informed that she has far more children than any other woman from the class of 1974, Susan responds, incredulous, "Really? But we've been out for ten years!" Having a large family and wanting even more children seem so natural to Susan.

But she is very different. Many of the women from her class put off having children until they were in their late twenties or early thirties and just as many were childless in 1984. "It really does bother you, the old biological clock ticking away, but it doesn't bother me on a regular basis," says Mary Faith Higgins, who has spent most of the past ten years traveling around East Asia for Graham & James and living, as she puts it, "like a gypsy." "I have a niece and a nephew so I spoil them hopelessly."

Susan doesn't regret having her children for a moment, even when the noise level inside her house becomes unbearable. If appearance is any guide, the children have helped keep Susan young. She still looks like a student, with her short, straight blond hair, plaid skirt, matching red socks and book bag dangling beside her. The only giveaway to her age —thirty-six—are a few flecks of gray hair. In fact, riding around Cambridge on her bicycle, Susan Roosevelt Weld can easily pass for a first-year law student.

And in the past ten years she hasn't really changed that much. Some of her happiest moments are still spent alone in her study, with her nose in a book. Being able to give up practicing and retire to her study to work on a PhD is, she realizes, a luxury, since she is not earning a salary. For professional women working to support their children, she knows, the choices are harder and the pressures to capitalize on having a Harvard Law degree are greater. Susan is grateful that her choices were, by comparison, relatively simple and clear-cut.

While most of them entered the profession full of drive and single-minded ambition, many women from the class of 1974 have reexamined their priorities over the past decade, trying to hit on the magic formula that leaves room for both professional success and a family life. A few have found it. Others, like Renee Chotiner and Susan Roosevelt Weld, have had to make choices; these women and fourteen others in their class have molded their careers (or given them up) to accommodate children. The "career first" ethos seems to have waned as the years have progressed. "The practice of law should not be an impediment to a good family life," says Rosemary Williams Hill, mother of three, who works as a public defender in Boston. "I'm not going to let it interfere, even if it means not working for a while. Have a family, have your children. That's the enduring thing."

Ten years ago, Hill's statement would have sounded quite reactionary to many of her classmates, although ten years later many of them were voicing similar views. Though maternity leaves and part-time work options have made it easier for some women to remain in practice, the law remains one of the most competitive and demanding professions. If you are trained to be the best, as were the seventy women in the Harvard Law School class of 1974, it is hard to shift to a slower track. But to stay on the fast track—and have children —is often impossible. In subtle, often unspoken ways, the profession still penalizes working mothers. If they continue working, they sometimes face the wrongheaded assumption that their commitment to work will not be the same once they have children. Such assumptions make partnership an even more elusive goal. "When I came back after the birth of my son," says one woman from the class, "I never considered not working. To prove that my commitment was the same, I worked harder than ever before." After a year, she became exhausted and asked to work part-time. Ultimately, she left her firm, knowing that partnership was out of the question unless she was willing to resume a backbreaking schedule.

The sacrifices and self-discipline required of those women who tackled families alongside their legal careers, without lowering their sights, are considerable. But equally great are the pressures felt by those women who have chosen, for a variety of reasons, to not have children and to put most of their energies into their careers. Some of them expressed worries that their childlessness and availability to work longer hours lead other lawyers to take advantage of them, to expect too much because their time is undivided. Karen Katzman, a partner at New York's Kaye, Scholer, Fierman, Hays & Handler, pursues several outside interests, including the ballet and opera. "I have an important part of my life outside the office," she says. "Not being married shouldn't be an excuse to take advantage of my time."

"There is almost a supposition that those of us without children will have all of our time available for the job," adds Bari Schwartz, who has spent much of the past decade working in the legal services area. "I haven't complained because I'm driven by my commitment to the work I've been doing. Nobody has made me do this work. But there is a notion that you will be available round the clock to do this work where, with someone who has a family, it's more readily understood that they won't be available. That does irk me sometimes."

The nature of the ultra-demanding legal profession is such that, when it comes to the issue of lawyering and having children, it can be a "damned if you do, damned if you don't" conundrum.

6

Pushing
for Partnership

"Up or out" are the three words that haunt associates
throughout their early careers. The twenty-four women from
the Harvard Law School class of 1974 who stayed on partnership track at their firms, displaying near slavish devotion to
their jobs, each arrived at a moment of truth: the partnership
decision. After eight or nine years (sometimes more, sometimes less depending on a firm's location and tradition) of
billing eighteen hundred to two thousand hours each year, a
single vote of their firm's partners would determine their
fate. "Up" meant promotion to partnership and the lifetime
career security it represented, akin to receiving tenure at a
prestigious university. "Out" meant leaving their firms as
soon as possible following the partnership vote and starting
from scratch somewhere else.

The "up or out" system is a foundation of big-firm practice. The philosophy behind it was formulated by Paul
Cravath, who ruled Cravath, Swaine & Moore, the epitome
of the elite corporate Wall Street firm, until his death in
1940. Explaining "the Cravath system," which was emulated
by all the blue chip firms, Robert Swaine, Cravath's partner,
wrote, "Ten years is too long for a man to remain a Cravath
associate under normal conditions unless he has been told

that the chances of his being made a partner are still good. A man who is not growing professionally creates a barrier to the progress of the younger men within the organization and, himself, tends to sink into a mental rut—to lose ambition; and loss of ambition induces carelessness. It is much better for the man, for the office, and for the clients that he leave while he still has the self-confidence and determination to advance."[1] Although Swaine's argument had its points, "up or out" was a brutal system, psychologically. For many of the women from the Harvard Law School class of 1974 who faced it, the partnership decision represented the first cut they didn't make. After years of compiling successes and credentials, there was a sudden, precipitous fall.

Although a majority of the roughly fifty women who began their careers at law firms left long before putting partnership to the test, twenty-four women from the class remain at law firms ten years after graduation. Of these, sixteen made the final cut and are partners. Five were formally passed over or strongly encouraged to find jobs elsewhere. Two remain on a delayed timetable because of taking time off from their jobs and are still waiting to learn their fates. In the most competitive marketplace of all, New York, where so many women from the Harvard Law School class of 1974 began their careers as associates, only three women from the class are partners. And, looking at the class in broad terms, only twenty-three percent of the women are partners ten years after graduation, as opposed to fifty-one percent of the men.[2] Carol Goodman and Julia Bonsal were among those most determined to become part of this select group.

[1] The text of "The Cravath Firm" by Robert Swaine is printed in its entirety in James B. Stewart, *The Partners* (New York: Simon and Schuster, 1983), pp. 367–75.
[2] Figure compiled from Tenth Year Class Report, Harvard Law School Class of 1974, April, 1974.

On a Friday evening in the fall of 1983, Carol Goodman was sitting in the kitchen of her home in Brookline, Massachusetts, perched by the phone, waiting nervously. She had only been home for an hour but the wait was already excruciating. Carol, a short, somewhat plump woman of thirty-six with a pleasant face and chin-length brown hair, knew that on this same evening the partners of LeBoeuf, Lamb, Leiby & MacRae were huddled in a conference room in the firm's brand-new headquarters in midtown Manhattan deciding which associates to elevate to the partnership. Carol was on the list of names being voted on. Paul Connolly, the LeBoeuf partner in charge of the firm's Boston office, where Carol had practiced as a litigation associate since 1981, had promised that he would call her the moment he knew the outcome of the vote.

She had considered waiting for the news in her office, a cozy nook with exposed brick walls and an antique desk in a restored building in the heart of Boston's old financial district. But by midafternoon, following Connolly's departure for New York, she had grown restless, tired of staring at the heaps of papers piled high on her desk and at file drawers packed far beyond capacity with pending cases awaiting her attention. Come Monday, whatever the outcome of the vote, she was due in court to argue a motion for one of her clients. Knowing she already had a reputation for being a workaholic, Carol thought the other lawyers and paralegals who were still in the office would think her ridiculously compulsive if she kept up the pretense of working while her fate hung in the balance. So she headed home to Brookline.

Her husband, John, a special education teacher and administrator, was already home, ready to sweat out the decision with her. As he darted in and out of the kitchen it was obvious that he was as nervous as she was. Because there were a large number of associates—six altogether—being considered for partnership, Connolly had told her to expect a long wait. Hoping for the best, John had brought home a bottle of good champagne. There was harder stuff in the house already if the news was bad.

The telephone rang and her heart jumped. Although the call was from New York, it wasn't Connolly. "Congratulations," one of the New York associates at LeBoeuf was saying. Although the vote hadn't happened yet, this associate was calling to let her know that word was out around the firm that she had made it, that she would be elevated to the rank of partner. "Listen," she told the associate firmly. "It's not in the bag until the vote comes down." She'd been through this excruciating ritual before. At her previous firm, Boston's "white shoe" Goodwin, Procter & Hoar, her colleagues in the litigation department had told her repeatedly that she looked like a shoo-in for partner, that she should just relax and wait for the good news. But when the recommendations for new partners were made her name didn't appear on the list. Because she had been completely unprepared, emotionally, for the defeat it had been a totally crushing experience. She just couldn't stand to go through it all over again. In the weeks leading up to the partnership vote at LeBoeuf, Carol tried to stay on an even keel, steeling herself for a negative outcome. While all the signals and scuttlebutt were good, she had refused to let herself become complacent. She certainly wasn't going to allow herself to get into a celebratory frame of mind before Connolly himself called with the news. She would stay in the kitchen until his call came through.

Actually Carol Goodman had every reason to be confident. She had had a spectacular first year at LeBoeuf, billing close to $250,000. As a lateral transfer into the firm's litigation department, she had brought with her twelve active cases that she had been handling at Goodwin, Procter & Hoar. Every client for whom she worked, except one, had kept their cases with her when she moved to LeBoeuf, even Chas. T. Main, the engineering company that was one of Goodwin, Procter's

biggest clients. She had been handling an important case for
Main involving the freeze of Iranian assets as a result of the
hostage crisis and had made quite a name for herself during
the protracted litigation. Since her arrival at LeBoeuf other
clients, including United Technologies Corporation, had
come to her to handle their disputes with the Iranian government. She had been shuttling back and forth between New
York and The Hague to argue these cases before the Iran-
U.S. Claims Tribunal, working shoulder to shoulder with
partners from leading firms, including Los Angeles' Gibson,
Dunn & Crutcher, Washington's Wald, Harkrader & Ross,
and several Wall Street firms. She had been chosen to serve
on a select committee of plaintiffs' attorneys from these elite
firms, a real honor for an associate.

Anybody who had ever seen her argue in a courtroom, or
who had worked with her on a case, would have to agree that
Carol Goodman was as tough as any litigator. The professors
in law school who had warned her that women weren't cut
out to be litigators, that they were too soft, that stern federal
judges would make them cry, need not have worried about
Carol Goodman. One former Goodwin, Procter partner calls
her "ferocious" in the courtroom. "She is brilliant and can
stand up to anyone," he says. She was also a perfectionist,
very demanding, and sometimes tough on the associates and
support staff who worked with her. If she was sometimes too
hard on them, she brought the same drive and aggressiveness
into court for her clients and the results were usually outstanding.

The partners at Goodwin, Procter had had few quarrels
with her courtroom performance and had always reviewed
her work favorably, giving Carol generous bonuses. But
when two senior partners came into her office to explain why
she would not be nominated for partnership they had complained that she was too aggressive, that too many lawyers at
the firm just didn't enjoy working with her. Law partnerships,

after all, were almost like marriages in some ways. Doing top work was not enough to win acceptance—an associate also needed to be well liked to fit in. It was on this nebulous, subjective criterion that Carol Goodman had been rejected. Too aggressive. She wondered if these same words were being uttered about her as her name came up for consideration by the LeBoeuf partners in New York. "Come on, Connolly, please call."

Almost a year later, in the spring of 1984, Julia Bonsal was part of a similar ritual. The tall, thin and reserved thirty-four-year-old corporate lawyer was methodically going over the last details on a closing for one of her clients at White & Case's midtown office in the Bankers Trust Building, a skyscraper on Park Avenue. Downtown at the firm's main office on Wall Street, White & Case's seventy partners were meeting to elect new partners. Julia Bonsal had been with White & Case since graduating from Harvard Law School in 1974, longer than any associate being considered for partnership. In the weeks leading up to the meeting that would decide her fate she thought that partnership was a possibility but by no means a probability. She knew the vote could easily swing either way and had tried to put herself in a philosophical frame of mind. "I kept hearing, 'It looks possible,' so I could not be overly confident," she recalls. "I tried to keep myself mentally prepared to move in either direction very quickly."

At White & Case, a firm that has grown rich with blue chip clients that include Bankers Trust Company and United States Steel Corporation, there was a set tradition for electing new partners. In the weeks leading up to the vote the partners met in small caucuses to discuss the candidates. Individual partners lobbied heavily for their own protégés. Julia was sure that Casimir Patrick, the partner under whom she had worked for most of her career at White & Case, and who had trained her in the difficult area of leveraged lease financing, had gone to bat for her with the rest of his partners, as had other members of the corporate department.

The White & Case partnership met every Wednesday morning except one each month, and on the Wednesday morning designated for the partnership vote almost every partner was present. No decision, not even the division of partnership shares, was considered more important than the selection of new partners. Although the firm's four-man Management Committee made its recommendation on the candidates, the full partnership, on a one-partner-one-vote basis, had to ratify the committee's choices. After the vote was taken the partners shuttled off to a luncheon, while the firm's managing partner called the successful candidates and invited them to come down for lunch.

Julia had had ample time to learn about the process. She had been part of the ritual on three occasions. The partnership vote usually came in October, and in October of 1982, when the rest of the associates who were left at White & Case from the "class" of 1974 were under consideration she had been deferred. Deferral meant her name would not be brought before the partnership for a vote. It meant the partners felt she wasn't quite ready for partnership, that she might benefit from another year of seasoning, during which time more of the partners could scrutinize her work and get to know her better.

Being deferred was not the same thing as being passed over, the polite term used by most firms to mean rejected for partner. If Julia had been passed over she would have been expected to make a graceful and immediate exit from White & Case. Sometimes passed-over associates found jobs in the legal departments of White & Case's clients. But these in-house jobs were growing scarcer as larger classes of associates came up for partnership, and there were more rejected associates in search of jobs. Younger lawyers, fed up with the law firm grind and the long wait for partnership, had already gobbled up many of these jobs, and more and more corporations were promoting their promising stars from within.

Being passed over usually meant being flung into the hands of headhunters, professional job hunters who specialized in helping displaced lawyers find new niches. But even with a headhunter the competition was tough. It was easier for the headhunters to place more junior-level associates, who could still be used in large numbers by other firms as cannon fodder and whose associate careers still showed promise. At Julia's level the salaries that senior associates commanded—often $70,000–$90,000—made it more difficult to place them. Few firms were anxious to hire laterally. It hurt morale among younger associates moving up through the ranks. And many headhunters were complaining about having a surfeit of female résumés.

Deferral meant hanging in limbo, remaining a White & Case associate, postponing her fate. But at least she hadn't been passed over in October. "I think I did expect to be deferred," she recalls. "It still is a bit of a wrenching feeling when you see other people your year making partner and you don't." Another corporate associate had made the cut in 1982. Meanwhile Julia was invited to stay at White & Case and told that there was still a chance she would make partner the following October, her ninth year at the firm. It was a hard choice for her—whether to face an ego-bruising "extra" year as an associate or find another job. Julia decided to stay. "It got to the point where I'd waited so long," she says, "I thought I should continue to wait and see if it would work out." If the partners had major doubts about her abilities, surely she would have been weeded out long before now. Law-firm economics dictated that only a small number of twenty or so new associates hired each year would be elected partners. So most of the associates who were clearly not partnership material were encouraged to find other jobs by the midpoint of their associate careers. White & Case tried to give its associates a fair appraisal, without making any promises, as early on as possible.

Although she hadn't contacted any headhunters, Julia had begun quietly exploring some other job possibilities. She couldn't afford to be complacent. But it was difficult to put out feelers as long as she was committed to staying at White & Case until her name was voted on, up or down. Some of her clients had told her that they might be interested in talking to her about a job if she didn't make it, but it was impossible to have any really serious discussions as long as her fate hung in the balance. Another New York law firm had also been interested in acquiring her corporate expertise. With no promise of partnership, however, it seemed more sensible to hold fast at White & Case.

But when October 1983 rolled around the White & Case partners could not agree to make any of the candidates partners, including Julia and a group of lawyers from the class of 1975. The Wednesday morning meeting had extended into the afternoon and suddenly, as Julia recalls, "My supporters were running into the office saying, 'Quick! Do something brilliant! Go impress So-and-so.'" She felt like responding, "I've been smiling for ten years." What more could she do to impress people? The deferral the year before had not been unexpected and she had been prepared for it. But this sudden crisis came out of the blue. The partners met longer but the wrangling continued. Finally there was an announcement: the partners were unable to decide and the partnership vote had been tabled altogether. There would be no new partners elected in 1983.

With everyone else in the same boat, she couldn't take the outcome personally. But she was in a difficult position. When the deferral came the previous October she had steeled herself for a final push toward partnership. She had continued to plug away, working late into the night on many occasions and on weekends. When she had to cancel plans with a friend for the opera or, worse, call off a dinner planned with a casual date, she could reassure herself that in another year she would be able to plan her life more easily. She would have more control over her hours if she was a partner or if she was installed in a new job somewhere. Now the partners weren't saying when a decision might come. Her final push had begun to look like Moses' march out of the desert.

Finally in March the word went out that the partnership vote had been rescheduled. While her nerves were frayed on that Wednesday morning of the partners' meeting, she was glad there was going to be a decision at last. Not knowing had become almost worse than having the decision go against her, although she had become fairly philosophical about it. "I just figured if I made it, that's great; if I didn't make it, I'd invested enough time and would just move on. There were plenty of good opportunities out there."

Julia Bonsal and Carol Goodman were part of an unusual group of survivors from the class of 1974, those who had stuck it out long enough at their firms to put partnership to the test. Julia and Carol were not only determined to stick it out, they had both waited much longer than most of the members of their class to find out whether they would receive the ultimate reward. This was actually one of the few things they had in common.

And in 1983–84, while both of them were sweating out the partnership decision, an important case was waiting to be decided by the U.S. Supreme Court,[3] a case that, while not involving their firms directly, was being debated from Wall Street to Boston's State Street and concerned all lawyers, particularly women. In 1979 Elizabeth Anderson Hishon, a

---

[3.] The best accounts of the Hishon case are Connie Bruck, "The Case No One Will Win," *American Lawyer.* Nov. 1983, p. 101, and James B. Stewart, "Are Women Lawyers Discriminated Against at Large Law Firms?" *Wall Street Journal.* Dec. 20, 1983, p.1.

1972 honors graduate of Columbia Law School, had filed a
sex discrimination suit against her firm, Atlanta's King &
Spalding. Hishon had spent more than six years at the firm
before being passed over for partnership. Although located
in Atlanta, King & Spalding was the equal of Wall Street firms
like LeBoeuf, Lamb and White & Case, an elite establishment
that counted among its clients Coca-Cola and General Motors
Corporation, and whose partners included former Attorney
General Griffin Bell. The media attention focused on the
Hishon case had underscored the poor chances of women becoming partners at the nation's leading firms.

When Julia Bonsal came up for partnership at White &
Case only three of the firm's sixty-seven partners were female, and at LeBoeuf, Carol Goodman was looking to join
two women partners out of seventy-one. At the nation's hundred biggest firms fewer than 5% of the partnership ranks
were female, while women accounted for 30% of the associate ranks at these same firms. Three of the hundred largest
firms had no women partners. At King & Spalding, Betsy
Hishon was the first woman ever considered for partnership.
Since her departure King & Spalding had elevated two
women to its sixty-four-member partnership ranks.

The Wall Street partners who were quoted in the press
about the *Hishon* case usually argued that these statistics did
not amount to sex discrimination. They stressed the fact that
associate classes with large numbers of women had joined
their firms only in recent years and that these women had not
had enough time to filter up through the ranks. When Julia
Bonsal joined White & Case back in 1974 there were five
women in a group of nineteen new associates, and none of
the other women had stayed long enough to become a partner. In the classes ahead of her there were even fewer
women. After 1974 there was a steady upward drift and,
besides Julia, there were at least three other women from the
class of 1975 being considered for partnership at White &

Case in March. By 1984, like many Wall Street firms, White & Case was hiring large numbers of women. Half of the entering class of new associates in 1984 was female, a huge jump in the ten years since Julia had arrived. Maybe it was true that you couldn't judge the firms until these big classes started coming up for partnership. Maybe you had to accept the partners' assurances that their ranks would soon reflect these burgeoning numbers of women. But, with the *Hishon* case hanging over their heads, the firms were under pressure to get rolling. And Carol Goodman and Julia Bonsal were certainly putting them to the test.

That Carol Goodman had even arrived at the point of becoming a partner in an elite New York firm was itself a fluke. She began her legal career in a way that shouldn't have delivered her to Wall Street. In 1971 she had enrolled at the University of Maine Law School, where virtually none of the big-name firms ever recruited. She had decided to go to law school relatively late, at twenty-six, and had chosen Maine because it was the cheapest school she could find. Tuition for New England residents was only $500 a year, and her parents were living in Connecticut.

Since graduating from Barnard College in 1966 Carol had worked as a film editor, had ghostwritten some children's programs and had landed where many left-leaning liberal arts graduates of the 1960s had landed, as a case worker at the New York City Department of Welfare. There she had been exposed to some activist lawyers who seemed to be movers and shakers and she had decided to go to law school. Her boyfriend John, who worked for the American Arbitration Association, followed her to Portland.

Women were a tiny minority at the University of Maine Law School. At Barnard she had been used to speaking up in class, being nurtured by her professors. In law school she was one of seven women out of the seventy students in her class. Some professors rarely called on women and the placement service was usually less than helpful in finding them jobs. "There were all sorts of inhibitions on women being recommended for summer jobs," she recalls, "because you might be taking one away from a man who really needed one." While there were some stimulating professors and bright students, she had risen to the very top of the class with little effort.

She and John were married on the night before her final exam in criminal law. During their time in Maine John worked in a local antipoverty program and hoped to enroll in graduate school to get a degree in special education. Carol had just one year remaining at the University of Maine, but John was lobbying for a move to Boston, where several universities had strong special education programs. One of the secretaries at Pine Tree Legal Services, in Portland, where Carol worked while she was a law student, mentioned that she thought Harvard Law School had a special program for students who had started their legal education at other law schools. She had once worked for an assistant dean at the law school and gave Carol the name of someone to call.

Harvard did indeed have a "special students" program. The law school invited a substantial number of "special students" onto campus to take courses at Harvard to broaden their legal education. These students had to have top grades at their own law schools, and undergraduate records and LSAT scores high enough to have qualified them for admission to Harvard Law in the first place. The only catch was that the "special students" couldn't receive a Harvard Law diploma unless they stayed at the law school for two years. That was out of the question for Carol, who could not afford to shell out thousands of dollars for a largely superfluous fourth year of law school. But the chance to go to Harvard even for a year seemed like the answer to their problems, so Carol applied to the program, was promptly accepted, and she and John moved to Cambridge.

At Harvard she was amazed at how scared and silent most of her classmates were—men and women. They almost never participated in class and usually passed if called on. At the University of Maine, where classes were so much smaller, her hand had been raised constantly and she had loved nothing more than to spar with her teachers over the meaning of the legal puzzles in their casebooks. At Harvard she eagerly engaged some of the most celebrated professors, like Vern Countryman and Archibald Cox, in debate over issues raised in class. While the other Harvard students lived in fear of "stern Vern," Carol Goodman loved to be called on by Countryman. After one of her verbal contests with the bankruptcy law scholar another third-year student came up to her after class and told Carol he was afraid that Countryman was going to yell at her during class. "They didn't see that they had paid for the privilege of being able to spar with Vern Countryman," she says. While others back-benched their way through classes or skipped them altogether Carol was busy visiting her professors during office hours, trying to tap into their experience and intellects.

One of the main advantages of being at Harvard her third year was an unanticipated one. Harvard's high-powered placement office was like a separate cottage industry, churning full time to make sure Harvard Law students were getting the best law firm jobs. She hadn't really considered working at a big firm, and she and John expected to return to Maine when he received his master's degree from Boston University and she finished her year at Harvard. Her goal, when she arrived at Harvard, was to go back and get a permanent job at Pine Tree Legal Services or to join one of the rural public interest firms that were sprouting up around New England. But these big firms were offering to fly the students to New York and Washington for job interviews, and even if she didn't think she was interested in working for one of them, interviewing was a good way to see what the law firm world was like and to get some free trips to New York, where John's family lived, and to Washington.

But as she began interviewing her attitude toward the firms softened. She was taking a full load of corporate law courses at Harvard, even a course on Japanese corporate law taught by Jerome Cohen. The material was surprisingly interesting to her. It was possible that one of these large corporate firms might be more exciting than she had thought. Also, she and John were pretty deeply in debt, and the $19,000 starting salaries being dangled before her classmates sounded awfully tempting.

One of her first interviews was at Cravath, Swaine & Moore. Carol had never been inside a large law firm before and she was amazed by what she saw. Growing up in rural Massachusetts and then going to public school in Syosset, Long Island, the WASP, preppy elitism of Harvard was something she had never before encountered. But Cravath carried its blue-blooded heritage much further. "It was culture shock," she remembers. "It was so stuffy. It was like a museum."

Among her classmates, Cravath, Swaine & Moore was viewed as the preeminent Wall Street firm. In one year Cravath had dramatically raised its salaries for first-year associates and was traditionally viewed as the pacesetter for associate compensation. Its client roster was unparalleled.[4] Cravath represented IBM, Chemical Bank, Time, Inc., and several large investment banking firms, including First Boston and Paine Webber. The firm dated back to 1819, making it one of the oldest in the country. The offices were strewn with antiques and covered in dark paneling, including a "treasure room" that contained the desk and papers of William Seward, an early Cravath partner and President Lincoln's Secretary of State.

4. *The American Lawyer Guide to Leading Law Firms* (New York: AM-Law Publishing Company 1983).

At Cravath Carol was interviewed by a partner named Royall Victor. He looked just like his name sounded—imperious, superior, royal. Victor was pleasant enough but she was taken aback when he asked her if she was interested in joining the firm's real estate or trusts and estates departments. Carol was counting on becoming a litigator, a specialty in which the presence of women lawyers was particularly thin. She told Victor that she had been interested in oil and gas leasing as an aspect of real estate. He shot her a strange look, making it clear that this was not exactly what he had in mind. She left the interview knowing that Cravath was probably even less interested in her than she was in Cravath.

She also interviewed at a few other old-line Wall Street firms, including Davis Polk & Wardwell; at several prestigious firms in Washington, including Arnold & Porter; and at some predominantly Jewish firms in midtown Manhattan, including Weil, Gotshal & Manges. As a Jew, although a nonobservant one, Carol was not particularly concerned about whether she went to a predominantly Jewish or WASP firm. She wanted to go where she would have the best chance to be trained as a top litigator. When she arrived for an interview at New York's Paul, Weiss, Rifkind, Wharton & Garrison she knew she had found the kind of firm that she was looking for.

Paul, Weiss was not only the premier Jewish firm in New York but arguably the top litigation firm in the country. It was an intense powerhouse built by talented trial lawyers. The firm's spiritual leader was Simon Rifkind, a former federal judge who, although in his seventies, was practicing actively. A few years earlier Rifkind had represented Supreme Court Justice William O. Douglas in the impeachment investigation instigated by the House of Representatives. In the late 1950s Rifkind had brought Adlai Stevenson into the firm.

Paul, Weiss had a liberal, trailblazing reputation that also appealed to Carol. It was one of the first New York firms to have a woman partner, Carolyn Agger, the wife of former Supreme Court Justice Abe Fortas. Its clients included Warner Communications, Revlon and the estate of Cole Porter. Most important, the firm's litigators attracted big, complex, headline-making cases.

She was instantly captivated when she met one of the firm's star litigation partners, Jay Topkis. His brilliance was immediately apparent. Topkis had successfully argued several landmark antitrust cases before the Supreme Court and was part of the defense team defending Vice-President Spiro Agnew against charges of taking bribes and tax evasion while he was governor of Maryland. While Carol had no particular sympathy for Agnew, it was the biggest criminal case going on at the time. That was the kind of firm Paul, Weiss seemed to be. If a client was in big trouble or had a very complex legal problem and had the money to pay for the best, he turned to Paul, Weiss.

The firm had a reputation at Harvard for being a sweatshop for young associates, but everyone Carol met that day seemed to be totally captivated by their work. "Paul, Weiss was electric," she says, "a really alive place." The lawyers might be working outrageously long hours but the cases were exciting. At some of the other firms she visited the lawyers didn't seem nearly as excited by their work. By lunchtime she knew that if she decided to go the law firm route she wanted to work at Paul, Weiss. Her enthusiasm increased when she went to lunch with an associate at an excellent French restaurant, La Toque Blanche, on East Fiftieth Street near the firm's Park Avenue headquarters. When an official offer from the firm came three weeks later she agonized briefly about turning her back on a legal services career and then accepted.

She and John moved from Cambridge to a pleasant enough apartment in the East Thirties, in Manhattan's Murray Hill section. They were more than $10,000 in debt by the time she finished her third year of law school, so Carol decided to begin working that June, even before she took the bar exam. Most new associates would be starting work in the fall, after taking a review course and the bar. Studying for the bar could easily become a full-time occupation, but she felt she couldn't afford that luxury. She was the first new associate to report for work.

No sooner had she found her desk than she was summoned to report to Arthur Liman, one of the senior partners at Paul, Weiss. Carol was not completely aware of Liman's tremendous reputation but, judging from his spacious corner office, he was obviously someone important. He needed another associate to work on a giant securities and takeover battle that had been consuming his time since 1971, a struggle between Chris-Craft, Paul, Weiss's client, and a company called Bangor Punta for control of Piper Aircraft. It was one of the largest and most fiercely contested takeovers in history. Liman was readying Chris-Craft's appeal to the Second Circuit Court of Appeals. Another securities case needing associate manpower involved some disgruntled shareholders and homeowners at Co-op City, a giant housing development in the Bronx, who had sued the firm's client, United Housing Foundation, in a class action. This was Judge Rifkind's case, but most of the work was being handled by George Felleman, a senior associate, who needed some backup urgently.

Carol knew almost nothing about the securities laws, so Liman sat her down with the 1933 Securities Act to teach her the basics of his practice. She was thankful to have arrived when she did. The summer months were usually a bit slower, and Liman was obviously in the mood to teach. Since she was studying for the bar exam, he was sensitive not to overfill her plate. It seemed to Carol that Liman was actually enjoying the process of imparting his wisdom to a brand-new associate, and she was thrilled to be in the company of such an eminent partner. In a way, it was luck of the draw. The most powerful partners usually had first call on getting associates assigned to their cases. And, apart from Rifkind, there was no one more influential at Paul, Weiss than Arthur Liman.

Liman, a distinguished-looking though rather rumpled man in his early forties, already was being hailed as the finest civil litigator of his generation. He had graduated first in his class from Yale Law School in 1957 and, as a young Paul, Weiss litigator, had become Rifkind's protégé. He had served as chief counsel to the special New York commission investigating the uprising at Attica prison and had supervised the disbarment proceedings against Richard Nixon in New York. His corporate clients, which included Warner Communications and Becton, Dickinson & Company, considered Liman to be a trusted business adviser as well as a lawyer. Chris-Craft's president Herbert Siegel had once said, "Arthur is as close to me as a brother and better than most brothers are."[5] His services did not come cheaply. His billing rate was over $200 an hour. With his tremendous reputation, it was natural that some of the younger lawyers at Paul, Weiss were in awe of Liman and a bit scared of him.

Besides Liman, Carol learned the nuts and bolts of litigation from Edward Costikyan, a veteran trial lawyer who had learned how to fight as a leader of Tammany Hall. He was peppery, energetic, and his trial technique was excellent. She worked with Costikyan on an employment discrimination case. After she took the bar exam Carol worked intensively with Felleman on the United Housing case. It took them four months to write the appellate case brief. Carol rarely made it home before 10 P.M. Most of the other lawyers at the firm laughed at their argument in the case, thinking their legal reasoning on what defined a share of stock to be completely misguided. But they stopped sneering when the court granted *cert,* agreeing to hear their appeal.

[5] David Margolick, "Arthur Liman: Winner Without Flash," *American Lawyer,* March 1981, pp. 34–36.

Judge Rifkind was slated to argue the case and he had asked for the necessary background material. Carol sent cartons of documents to his office. Another partner working on the case told her to be more selective, to attach as few documents as possible to Rifkind's draft of the brief. But Carol had worked like a slave on the case for nearly a year and she wanted to make sure Rifkind was prepared for any question from the bench. She continued shipping documents to him.

Carol and Felleman traveled to Washington to hear Rifkind's argument before the Supreme Court. One of the more senior lawyers on the case nervously asked him which documents he had read and Rifkind responded, "All of them. I read all of them. Carol told me I needed to read all of them and I did." Rifkind challenged them, "Quiz me." After she and Felleman shot a few questions his way it was obvious that Rifkind was totally prepared. His recall was extraordinary. During his oral argument Rifkind had only been unsteady for one question from the justices. It was a brilliant performance. The opposing argument had been presented by Louis Nizer, a litigator equally famous and just as cogent as Rifkind. She had no idea what the outcome would be but it had been exciting to be inside the Supreme Court listening to these brilliant lawyers go head to head.

A few months later, when a favorable ruling was handed down by the court, Liman stopped by her office to congratulate her. He said, "Here you are. You're a first-year associate. Where do you go from here?"

Julia Bonsal had a completely different style and background. At Emma Willard boarding school, from where she progressed to Wellesley College, Julia was voted "most reserved" in the class. She didn't like to admit it but the title, even at a school that was filled with cool, aristocratic prep school girls, was probably deserved. Her calm and aloof exterior did not mean, however, that she lacked backbone or

opinions. In fact her political views were just as well formulated as the SDSers who surrounded her in the Wellesley
dorms, noisily debating U.S. policy in Vietnam. Julia's politics were not only more quietly articulated but diametrically
opposed to theirs.

She had been brought up by Republican parents in Upper
Montclair, New Jersey, and at Wellesley she had been president of the college GOP Club. During the late 1960s, when
radical politics were de rigueur even at the Seven Sisters,
Julia was a supporter of the Nixon administration. Although
she wasn't completely sold on the administration's Vietnam
policy, she was more opposed to the way college students
were expressing their outrage over the war. Out of curiosity,
Julia used to attend all the SDS meetings at Wellesley, just to
hear the current line.

During her junior year, when opposition to the invasion of
Cambodia turned into strike fever, spreading from Harvard
to Wellesley, Julia was one of the handful of students to speak
up against the strike. She continued going to whatever classes
were meeting. The students in her dorm were constantly
working her over, trying to change her mind. "Given the
climate of the time," she recalls, "merely saying one sentence
to the effect that you did not think the strike was advisable
was enough to gain you the attention of five hundred people
around you who wanted to strike."

Although there seemed to be less political fervor among
the law school student body, she did meet a student who
claimed to have helped bomb a bank. Her first week in Cambridge was difficult altogether. As she approached the door to
her room in Wyeth Hall she saw a sign with a jolting message: PLEASE BEAR WITH US WHILE WE GET RID OF THE
RATS. There certainly hadn't been rats at Wellesley.

In a few weeks the rats were gone but dorm life was getting on her nerves. The surroundings were bleak, the pressure to study all the time was intense and having other stu-

dents constantly talking about studying only made it worse. She moved into an apartment with two classmates, Gail Sticker and Enid Hochstein. Two weeks before exams she holed up in her room, studying straight through until the early hours of the next morning, allowing herself only a half-hour walk as a break. In class she participated only when called on, but her grasp of the material was thorough nevertheless. She emerged from law school with honors.

In the yearbook her picture appeared with the law school's Republican Club. Her shoulder-length hair and print blouse stand in sharp contrast to the pinstripes, club ties and horn-rims surrounding her. The club had been one of her only outlets from studying. She was the only woman on the GOP Club's Executive Committee. Politically, there were more kindred spirits at Harvard Law. A few of the conservative students had jokingly formed a Rehnquist Club, a lampoon of the law school's more serious-minded Learned Hand, Harlan and Marshall clubs, named for eminent judges. The Rehnquistians proclaimed themselves in favor of the "New Mc-Kinleyism" and described their ranks as being "devoid of intellectual merit." They often poked fun at the Women's Law Association and once posted a fake agenda on the bulletin board outside the WLA's office announcing a bake sale. Julia stayed away from the WLA.

The first time Julia encountered sexism was at a job interview during college. She was asking about one of the major departments of a big corporation and the interviewer informed her that women weren't hired for that department. If Julia was hired she'd have to work in one of the back rooms. She left the interview without confronting him and it wasn't until she was in her first year at Harvard Law that she realized she could have sued. "I suddenly realized maybe there were things people didn't want me to do because I was a woman. I had not been raised that way. I did not know that there was any difference and it came as a big surprise to me," she recalls. But that wasn't her style anyway. It never really occurred to her that Wall Street might be a difficult place for a woman. Although she had heard some of the stories about how hard it had been for the women of the previous generation, Julia was hopeful that a strong performance would find its reward.

She had offers from several top firms, including Shearman & Sterling, Wall Street's premier banking firm, and White & Case. Along with Shearman & Sterling and Sullivan & Cromwell, White & Case had always been considered one of the great, gray gentlemen of Wall Street. One of its founders, George B. Case, was not only an excellent lawyer but the inventor of the squeeze play while a member of the Yale baseball team in the 1890s. Two years after the firm was founded, in 1901, White & Case partners had helped organize Bankers Trust, the firm's largest (representing about ten percent of total billings) and oldest client.

Despite its pedigree White & Case was operating under somewhat of a cloud when it came to Harvard to recruit Julia and three other women from the class. In 1972 the SEC had filed a 46-page complaint against one of White & Case's clients, National Student Marketing, charging securities fraud. In the complaint, which soon became the most widely read document on Wall Street,[6] the SEC also charged that White & Case had failed to exercise "due diligence" to prevent the fraud. Even more unusual, the SEC was contending that *all* the partners at the firm, not only the partner handling the National Student Marketing account, should be held liable for the securities law violations. The firm was forced to hire Washington counsel, Arnold & Porter, to defend its reputation. Although the case was eventually settled three years after Julia's arrival, White & Case's "white shoe" image had been considerably scuffed.

[6] Paul Hoffman, *Lions in the Street* (New York: Saturday Review Press, 1973), pp. 167–71.

Still, Julia had liked all the partners with whom she had interviewed and figured that a Wall Street institution like White & Case could not be toppled so easily. As one of the five women in a starting class of nineteen new associates she began a rotation through the firm's two corporate departments (one on Wall Street and one in the midtown office that largely serviced Bankers Trust), the litigation department and trusts and estates. She was fairly sure that she wanted to land in the corporate department and there seemed to be no real impediments to a woman joining that practice. There was never a suggestion from any of the firm's partners that she should choose trusts and estates.

She had only one encounter with sexism, while she was training in the corporate department. One of the senior officers of a White & Case client asked her casually during a meeting where she had gone to law school. "Harvard Law School?" he had murmured in an incredulous tone. "I didn't know they let women in there." She quietly let him know that women had been at the law school since the 1950s, but he was no less appalled. He ignored her for the remainder of the meeting. As the junior person on the deal, it would have been bad form for her to talk back to the client. Anyway, she wasn't that angry. She just thought he was "off the wall," out of touch with the times. His attitude certainly wasn't typical of the other lawyers at the meeting.

Any associate serious about making partner, she realized, had to find the right niche, a specialty necessary to the firm's practice. The corporate department needed someone to specialize in leveraged leasing, a complex method of financing large pieces of equipment such as ships and airplanes. Leveraged leasing required a firm grasp of corporate as well as tax law. Some lawyers found leveraged leasing to be intolerably dry, slogging through pages and pages in order to draft a closing document, every deal similar to the last. Many of the documents that Julia drafted were several inches thick. Her office had quickly become overgrown with leveraged leasing documents, subleases and contracts. There were deals on her shelf that dated back to the late 1960s about which few White & Case lawyers, besides Julia, could remember the details. She often worked with the leasing group at Bankers Trust and she got along well with Casimir Patrick, the White & Case partner who led the leasing practice.

For Julia, leveraged leasing was not a boring, back-room specialty. Many of the deals involved new ideas and very complex methods of financing. You couldn't, as some lawyers believed, just take out last year's deals and copy them over. She spent one entire summer working on the closing of a gas storage facility in Texas, representing the insurance companies that were lending the money for the project, called Valero Energy. There were lawyers from Paul, Weiss; Shearman & Sterling; and several big Texas firms working with her on the deal. Their meetings lasted until 11 P.M. almost every night. The drafting alone was a giant task. The basic contracts sat in a huge pile on her desk, growing larger each day. After the deal closed she and the other New York lawyers joked about forming an alumni club. For Julia's development as a lawyer the deal was an important one. She played an up-front role and, as Patrick later recalled, her work was noticed by other partners at White & Case.

Some of the deals she handled with Patrick involved several hundred million dollars. They financed 747s and oil rigs. She once went on board one of the ships they had financed at the Bath Shipyards in Maine. The work didn't have the glamor of litigation but it suited Julia's quieter, more methodical style. Her main strength as a lawyer was the ability to handle complex, extremely detailed financings.

What leveraged leasing shared with litigation was the toll of hours. When she was in the middle of a closing Julia worked a punishing schedule, working late into the night, working weekends. It didn't leave her much time to develop a social life. She often went out to dinner with other associates but her outside friends had to be tolerant of her practice of breaking dates at the last minute. Gail Sticker, one of her roommates from Harvard who was also working as a lawyer in New York, tried to introduce her to some available men. "But Julie's always working," Sticker complained. Although a few relationships seemed promising, she never came close to getting married. Men just didn't accept hearing, "Honey, I have to work tonight," the way generations of women always had. "I think women tend to be much more understanding if a male lawyer says, 'Sorry. I just can't do it tonight because I have to work.' I think there's always a suspicion in the man's mind that maybe it's just an excuse. Why does a woman have to work?" Julia observes. Without much extra time, it was hard to meet men. Work and staying on track were her top priorities.

Setting priorities was also becoming difficult for Carol Goodman. She and John wanted to start a family and she had become pregnant in 1976. She was in the middle of preparing Liman's brief for the Chris-Craft case, working crazy hours. When she asked for a maternity leave she was stunned that Paul, Weiss, the beacon of liberal thinking, did not have a maternity leave policy for its women lawyers. She talked to several partners on the Legal Personnel Committee and was shocked to hear their reasons for not having one. She was told that women didn't come back to the firm after they had babies and, if they did, their commitment to the practice was never as strong. She explained that she was sure she would be returning to work on the same basis as before. Still, no maternity leave.

She was deeply annoyed but continued slaving away on Chris-Craft. As she grew bigger and bigger on into her ninth month Liman, worried about her health, kept urging her to go home earlier at night but she wanted to make sure everything was letter perfect. Finally Liman insisted that she go to her obstetrician to get his advice on working so intensely at the end of her pregnancy. The doctor had assured her that the baby wasn't coming for several more weeks and that it was fine to continue working. That same evening the Chris-Craft brief was finished at last. The next day she was supposed to proofread it and take it to the printer.

She got home early enough on Friday to have dinner with John. Then, without any warning, she went into labor. Their daughter Lizzy was born the next morning. Carol had been so exhausted from work that she actually fell asleep during the painful labor. Liman, who was impressed with her effort on the final brief, called her in the hospital. "Okay, Carol," he said after offering congratulations. "You've made your point. You can have your maternity leave." Although the firm established a fairly generous maternity leave policy shortly thereafter, Carol Goodman's example of working until the moment of giving birth had become a small legend at Paul, Weiss, setting a tough example for the other women associates to follow.

Carol went back to work after two months, leaving John, who decided to take a one-year paternity leave from his job at the New York City Board of Education, in charge of Lizzy. They had moved into a giant estate in Westchester, which they were renting at bargain rates in a caretaking arrangement. It was a vast and beautiful expanse of trees and walkways, but it was also very isolated. While she was at work John was secluded with an infant. He wasn't getting out enough, seeing people. Meanwhile she was working even longer hours and traveling on cases. Sometimes she took the baby with her, because she was breast-feeding, and hired a baby-sitter to watch Lizzy in the hotel.

John felt alone and isolated during his year as a stay-at-home parent in Westchester. Liman knew John through Carol and sensed his unhappiness. Carol began discussing with Li-

man the possibility of a move. John wanted to move back to
Boston, where they could buy their own house, raise Lizzy
and find jobs with hours that, at least for Carol, might be a bit
less brutal. Although she loved Paul, Weiss, the maternity
leave episode left a slightly bitter aftertaste. And though he
hated to lose her, Liman steered her toward a few top Boston
firms.

At Goodwin, Procter & Hoar, Liman knew a young hot-
shot corporate partner named Joshua Berman. She went up to
Boston to interview with Berman and they hit it off. Berman,
too, was Jewish, brilliant and extremely aggressive. He handled big-time securities matters for several large New England companies, including Tyco Laboratories. He had a na-
tional-style practice—big deals for big clients. He was very
much in the Paul, Weiss mold. Carol also met Rya Zobel, the
firm's only woman partner, and several senior women associates. They all had high praise for the firm.

John had sold her on the idea of a move and she accepted
the offer when it came from Goodwin, Procter. Remembering her encounter with Cravath, she was a little uneasy about
joining an old-line, WASP, "white shoe" firm, but there were
few firms in Boston that didn't fit this description. Anyway,
GPH, as it was called within the firm, did not have nearly as
stuffy a reputation as Boston's venerable Ropes & Gray.

Like most of Boston's top corporate firms, Goodwin,
Procter & Hoar represented a large bank, New England
Merchants National Bank, and occupied a suite of offices in
the skyscraper the bank had built in the heart of the old
financial district near State Street. The offices were elegant, in
an understated way, with beige carpeting and old paintings
with hunting scenes and landscapes of New England.

Berman, in his early forties, had built his corporate practice
into a major profit center at the firm. Although he lacked
seniority, he was already one of the firm's highest billers. But
he was cut from a very different cloth than his partners—he

wasn't a clubman and he didn't have the same aristocratic, craggy New England features. He was a relentless workaholic who often skipped firm social functions and was never seen at the exclusive Somerset Club, where some of his partners socialized after work. He was also outspoken and unpopular with some of the Goodwin, Procter elders. But they put up with Berman because of his hefty contribution to the firm's profits.

Three-fourths of the work Carol was doing was for Berman. She was also working on some cases for a litigation partner who despised Berman. There was a lot of tension, as she was tugged in both directions. Berman would tell her to concentrate on his cases and the other partner would advise her to do less for Berman. With his excellent skills and important clients, Carol liked working for Josh and didn't mind being identified as a Berman protégée.

Like Berman, she was not really involved in the firm's social life. When other lawyers rounded up groups of people to go to lunch she was almost never asked. She wasn't a drinker, which made her even more of an outsider at firm social functions. At the annual firm dance, which was usually held at an exclusive country club, she and John felt out of place. Carol wasn't impeccably groomed like the wives of Goodwin partners and felt far more comfortable in her suit and tie than a cocktail dress. John, with his frizzy dark hair, just wasn't Brooks Brothers material. Neither of them was any good at making small talk about golf handicaps, tennis and other subjects that seemed to enthrall most of the other GPH lawyers.

Carol had a reputation among the junior associates for being a workaholic and difficult to work with. As soon as a first draft was done she wanted immediate revisions and a second one. One partner remembers her as a veritable "paper mill." She felt close to Zobel but no particular camaraderie with other women at the firm. (Zobel had good-naturedly advised Carol to wear only suits and ties to work.) One of Carol's clients had added his two cents, warning her not to walk around without a jacket. "It's hard enough for women lawyers without being mistaken for a secretary," he had chided. When Zobel left the firm to become a federal judge, Carol became one of the most senior women at Goodwin, Procter and she felt even more isolated. The younger women seemed to fit more easily into the social fabric of the firm. They happily chatted about the Boston Red Sox and to Carol it seemed as if they were almost being flirtatious with the male lawyers at GPH. Carol, on the other hand, wore her suits and ties like protective armor.

Her style and demeanor were sometimes criticized in her salary and bonus reviews, which came at six-month intervals. But she always received high grades, usually an eight or nine out of a possible ten, and she was well compensated. She knew that collegiality was part of the mix of qualities used to measure partnership potential. But at Paul, Weiss many brilliant lawyers who were not necessarily popular had been elevated to the partnership and Berman's presence at GPH seemed to signal the same tolerance. Besides, she could not really change her personality.

Berman, meanwhile, was making secret plans with some of the other lawyers at GPH to form his own firm. Berman felt that GPH was not aggressive enough. He was tired of supporting dead wood, older partners who were no longer bringing in significant business. Carol could have been part of the breakaway firm if she wanted to be but she was worried that the new firm might fold. Without real roots in the Boston legal community, it might be hard for her to find another job. She and John and Lizzy were happily ensconced in an old, sprawling house in Brookline. John was very happy at his new job at the Massachusetts Department of Education. She didn't want to risk having to uproot them.

Berman opened his new firm directly across the street, as if to thumb his nose at his old partners. His departure left a huge gap in her practice. She had to scramble to find new cases. Berman took with him an array of important clients, including Tyco and The Boston Company. Berman's departure also left her with no one to pave the way for her partnership. "I was socially and politically isolated," she says. For the first time in her career she lacked a mentor.

Trying to ignore her feelings of isolation, Carol threw herself into the new cases to which she was assigned. She worked with a senior litigation partner, Samuel Hoar, son of one of the firm's founders, on a securities case involving Polaroid Corporation. Dr. Edwin Land, the company's founder, was charged with insider trading—making stock trades on the basis of having "inside information" about Polaroid's corporate plans. Land was a demanding client. He often summoned Hoar and Carol to his laboratory in Cambridge. He didn't hesitate to criticize lawyers' work, and Hoar says he knew that Land was impressed by Carol's work because he rarely complained about her memoranda and briefs. Carol was very impressed by Land's total command of science. It wasn't every associate who got to work with one of the captains of American industry.

It was the Iranian assets cases, however, that really launched her reputation as a trial lawyer. In 1979 she won the first preliminary injunction halting the flow of Iranian money from the United States. Two of the firm's most important clients, New England Merchants and Chas. T. Main, a giant engineering company, were involved in disputes with the Iranian government. Working closely with the senior corporate partners who normally supervised all the work for these key clients, she was shuttling between Boston and the multidistrict panel to argue motions. She was elected to a special plaintiffs' lawyers committee that was coordinating strategy on the Iranian cases, as virtually all the major U.S. banks became embroiled in legal battles with the radical new Iranian regime.

She was a relentless litigator who never sacrificed her client's interest to make another lawyer's life easier. If an opposing counsel needed a continuance she often argued against it in court. To Carol, a trial date was a trial date. This did not win her many friends in Boston's tightly knit legal fraternity. One of the senior partners at Goodwin, Procter worried that Carol was too legalistic, that she sometimes lost sight of larger, "political" issues. But she was getting good results. "It was ultimately ironic," Carol responds. "The same partner who told me I was too aggressive told me he loved it on his cases."

She passed the critical fifth-year review at GPH, usually the last cut before partnership. Hoar, a tall, handsome patrician with a mane of silver hair, indicated that he would support her for partnership. The next step was to win the approval of the firm's Legal Personnel Supervision Committee. Some of the most senior and influential partners served on this committee. They were charged with interviewing every partner about every associate who was under consideration for partnership—usually, all seventh-year associates left at the firm. The LPSC then made its recommendation to the firm's Executive Committee about which associates should be nominated for partnership. Once a year the partners voted on the nominees. A two-thirds majority was needed for election, although the votes were weighted so that the more senior partners had more voting power. Once the LPSC and the Executive Committee had given their imprimaturs to a candidate it was rare for the associate to be voted down on the floor.

While she was engrossed in the Iranian cases Carol was unaware that the Legal Personnel Supervision Committee had already done its interviews and rendered its verdict for 1982. She had failed to win the committee's recommendation. Her name was not going to be sent to the Executive Committee, where she had supporters. Two of the firm's most senior partners were unalterably opposed to her election. While one had worked with Carol on the Iranian cases and agreed that her talents were considerable, he felt she was much too aggressive—too gung ho, almost overzealous. She had rubbed a number of senior partners the wrong way. They just didn't like her.

Two partners on the LPSC, one who had backed her and one who had been opposed, called her in one morning to deliver the bad news. She was dumbfounded, caught completely unprepared. Although there had never been any promises, her reviews had led her to believe that her chances were very good. She felt like lashing out at them but she was trying to get as much information as possible. The criticism that she was too aggressive seemed nonsensical. Her aggressiveness was what had won for the firm's clients. Would the partners have ever complained that a male lawyer was too aggressive? She doubted it. In fact several of the male associates who had glided through the LPSC were, in Carol's estimation, even more aggressive than she. "It all seemed so irrational," she says.

When the partners left she went into Hoar's office. Hoar was clearly upset about the decision, fed up with his partners. He was willing to nominate her from the floor when the full partnership met, even though it would be difficult to muster a two-thirds majority. But she was hardly in the mood to start plotting a floor strategy. She called John and went home. Then she did something totally uncharacteristic. She got drunk.

Some of the younger women at GPH were also upset. They might not love Carol personally but it hurt to see a talented senior woman get passed over. Carol's failure might not bode well for their own partnership chances. The firm's women associates began caucusing secretly. They wanted assurances from the firm that there was not discrimination against women—that GPH would make some effort to have women in its partnership ranks. Samuel Hoar was drafted to head a Committee on Women.

A few of the partners were still talking about a floor fight. But Carol didn't want them to ram through her election, even if it was possible to muster the necessary votes. She would have to live at Goodwin, Procter knowing that many partners didn't want her there. It would be a constant battle —for backup, for compensation, for getting her own associates accepted within the firm. Partnership on these terms would not be worth very much. "It's very difficult to live long term in a place where you don't have friends," she explains. "I sat back and said I didn't want to be a figure of controversy in the partnership for the rest of my career. I had a practice and a life to get on with."

Even though Carol had nixed the idea of a floor fight, the partnership meeting to elect new partners had been long and bitter. Hoar vented his feelings about her situation. He thought she'd had a raw deal, that the partners were changing the rules in the middle of the game, trying to hold Carol to a higher standard. Three associates who had been recommended by the LPSC and the Executive Committee also went down in defeat. Only four of the seven nominees were elected.

Carol had already begun to look for a new job, registering with headhunters in Boston, New York and Washington, feeling a bit dejected and unwanted for the first time in her career. Although she had never been completely comfortable at GPH, now she felt like a pariah. Then a lawyer at another firm told her that a lawyer from GPH had called her a "fucking cunt" during a squash game with several prominent members of the Boston bar. She had no idea that the feelings against her had become so vituperative. She determined not to discuss her job prospects with anyone at the firm. It was possible that someone might try to poison the well on her.

Maybe she was being paranoid, but she had been through a very bruising experience.

Lawyers like Carol Goodman, Julia Bonsal and the other women in their class were expected to pursue male standards of success while remaining "feminine" according to traditional male standards, an almost impossible standard to meet. In the ensuing months Carol had ample time to mull over her situation and analyze what had happened. She came to believe that she was the victim of a double standard—that the very qualities for which she had been criticized would have been considered admirable and highly desirable . . . if she were a male lawyer. The drive, ambition and brilliance that had brought her to Harvard Law School in the first place and through Paul, Weiss, where, according to several of her colleagues, she was not noticeably more aggressive or hard-charging than any of the other associates in this notoriously competitive firm, had worked against her in a more traditionally minded institution. Somehow, it seemed to Carol, and to some of the other women in the Harvard Law School class of 1974, if you were an aggressive lawyer and a woman, the sum total of these ingredients often equaled abrasiveness in the minds of male colleagues and senior partners.

Julia Bonsal, of course, had the opposite problem. Her reserve led some of the other lawyers at White & Case to stereotype her as a back-room lawyer. The lawyers who worked closely with her saw beyond this. "Julie is supremely self-confident and at ease with herself and perhaps because of that is less inclined than others, perhaps because of the nature of her disposition, to assert herself," Patrick observes. "I don't think of her as a woman on the make, it's not her presentation. In the case of someone like that, since they're not marketing themselves like others, you have to take a step toward them to see their strengths."

Learning how to "market" themselves was more difficult

for many of the women from the Harvard Law class of 1974 than for the men. "For all the fact that I'd gone to Harvard Law School, I was still very much a child of the fifties," recalls Patricia Nicely Kopf who, like Julia Bonsal, began her career as an associate at White & Case without having had much experience in the business world. "I was brought up to be nice and polite to everyone and a good girl, and I had to learn to be more aggressive and forceful in asserting my own abilities. I had always been able to let people find out for themselves that I could do whatever needed to be done and had always kind of bubbled up to the top on my own without having to be assertive about it or sell myself at all. And in any law firm or business environment you have to do that. You can't expect people to devote the energy and time to find out how smart you are, you have to show them. It took me awhile to figure that out.

"I think in my generation boys were brought up to be a little streetwise and savvy about corporate politics," she adds. "A friend of mine at White & Case once said to me, 'My father told me, "Whatever you do, make sure you're noticed. You can make a fool of yourself and it doesn't matter. Just make sure you get noticed."' That's very different advice than girls were told in the 1950s, at least little girls in New Jersey like me. I was told, 'Be a good girl, don't talk back. Do your job and you will be rewarded.' I think that was much more the ethic that little girls of the 1950s were brought up with. And I think women in general in my generation were a little bit naive about what the corporate world is really like and what the practice of law is really like." Kopf left White & Case and joined Fenwick, Stone, Davis & West, a firm in Palo Alto, California, where she is a partner.

Shy and diminutive, another member of the class, Nancy McMillen, admits her personality was probably more suited to back-room lawyering during her early days as an associate in a Rhode Island law firm. "I liked sitting back and writing a brief," she says. But she was interested in litigation, even though she was extremely tense every time she walked into a courtroom. Naturally soft-spoken and retiring, she forced herself to develop an assertive courtroom style, handling scores of small cases, mostly fender benders, in state court. "Once you get out of Harvard Law School," she explains, "you're just starting to be a lawyer. You learn pressure, speaking, to push yourself a wee bit more. It's gut-wrenching to get up in front of a judge and jury and make it work." Today, as a lawyer in the antitrust division of the Justice Department, McMillen relishes each opportunity to get in the courtroom. But she is also still sensitive to the issue of style and is careful not to come on as too aggressive. "I never raise my voice in court," she says. "It's an advantage to be a woman. Opposing counsel is usually a male, used to fighting and being rude. I always establish that I'm Mrs. McMillen, not Ms. McMillen. Then they have to be somewhat deferential and nice. That will, for a while, throw them off guard. They won't know quite how to argue with you. Whereas, if you come across as hard, bitchy, rude and Ms., they can treat you like anybody else. If you're Mrs., soft-spoken, not rude, and reasonable, they are disarmed."

"You had to adjust your courtroom personality to what you could sense the judges felt about women," observes Carolyn Daffron, who spent the early part of her career as a trial lawyer. "It was a problem because some judges really expected to be deferred to by women and you had to decide—a very complex decision involving a lot of issues of morality and pride and your duty to represent your client and so on— you had to decide how much you were going to act like the stereotypical woman who gets the traffic ticket and cries or whether you were going to go in there and be at least as aggressive as the men. I was pretty good at going with the flow and tended to err on the side of not being terribly feminine and deferential."

Ellen Marshall, a corporate lawyer, observes, "You have to carry yourself in a relatively mature way and I think it's helpful not to be prissy and female. There's the old saying about being able to talk about sports. It really helps. You are dealing with men who have not in many instances previously had an occasion to work with a woman as an equal. It's not because they don't like you as a woman or don't trust you, but they just have to develop their own style of how they should relate to you. It helps if you can put them at ease and the best way to do that is to express knowledge of their business, because that's what they know—inside and out, and if you can ask intelligent questions about their business, you're no longer a female, you're an equal, and that's what it's all about, being trusted by them."

The issue of style, as well as marketing, were also at the heart of the *Hishon* case. By most accounts, Elizabeth Hishon was shy and retiring, as well as technically proficient in her field of expertise, real estate law. Like Julia Bonsal, some of her colleagues considered her a back-room type. Like Carol Goodman, Hishon was socially isolated within her firm, King & Spalding, rarely invited to the country clubs and sporting events where her male colleagues congregated. Yet Hishon's case touched on issues far deeper than these. The former King & Spalding associate charged that she had been underestimated, isolated and, finally, passed over because she was a woman. One member of the class of 1974, who preferred to remain anonymous, also felt she had failed to make partner solely because of her sex. She claims she was told by senior partners that she was one of the most competent and valued tax specialists at the firm. However, when the partnership decision was made, other male lawyers in her department were elected to the partnership and she was not. Her competitors had families to support. She was married to another successful professional and had no children. "There was a false assumption that they needed partnership and I didn't," she explains. "It was totally unfair."

Julia Bonsal's mentor, Casimir Patrick, admits he held this same prejudice when he was starting out in the profession. "I had my third child my first year at White & Case," he explains. "I thought it was outrageous women should be competing with me. I had a wife and family. It was a frolic for them, life and death for me. I just came around. Now I have as many if not more women working for me."

For Harvard Law alumnae of an earlier generation, concerns about making partner were not as great because the chances were so slim. Landing an associate's job was a feat in itself, given the kind of attitude that Patrick describes during his early career at White & Case. The issue of whether or not a female associate was on partnership track was rarely raised. Almost always it was assumed that she was not. At Paul, Weiss in 1967, Doris Carroll was the first woman ever hired in the litigation department. Carroll says she assumed that at the time she was hired she was on the same track as other associates. At some point in her early career, she figures, she was passed over, although she was never formally told about her status. Nevertheless she was content to stay on as an associate with her thriving matrimonial practice, and the firm never hinted that it wanted her to leave. And Carroll didn't feel motivated to go out and look for another job. "It was a comfortable kennel," she says. Instead she remained at Paul, Weiss as an associate and now earns a comfortable $70,000 a year, although this is a small fraction of what she would make as a partner.[7] "I was not terribly ambitious for partnership," she says. "I was scared and I was just as glad that I felt I didn't have to do that." Nevertheless, Carroll admits, her status as a permanent associate has its drawbacks. "The point of up or

[7.] At Paul, Weiss, average per partner profits in 1984 were over $350,000 according to a survey published in *The American Lawyer*. "The Am-Law 50," *The American Lawyer*, Steven Brill, July–August 1985, p. 1.

out," she explains, "is, after a while, How can I take orders from someone who is thirty-two years old? It doesn't bother me but I can see that the older I get it's going to be a bigger and bigger problem. Not necessarily my taking orders but his giving orders; it is sometimes an awkward situation for both."

By the time Julia Bonsal and Carol Goodman had arrived at the point of making partner, the old attitudes were changing, the old prejudices vanishing as more women made their presence felt within firms. Nevertheless the problem of hitting on the right professional style remained and so did the back-room and too aggressive stereotypes that were still used to tag and stymie a number of highly competent women professionals. Both Julia and Carol were determined not to let these hindrances get in their way.

Given the same choice as Julia Bonsal, it is possible that a male lawyer might have had too much pride to stay on. In his seventh year as an associate at New York's Weil, Gotshal & Manges, Robert Weiner was told his department was divided on his candidacy. Weiner, a 1972 graduate of Columbia Law School, left to start his own firm. "Their view was, 'We can't decide,' " he explained to *The Wall Street Journal*[8] in 1983, in an article about the process of making partner. "My view was, 'You've known me a long time!' I, for ego purposes or whatever, wanted to be considered with the other people who were coming up in my class."

By waiting it out, however, Julia Bonsal displayed a tenacity that most lawyers at White & Case admired. She might not be a superstar—the kind of young lawyer who was already adept at bringing in new clients—but few of the firm's associates had proven themselves as rainmakers. Julia was cer-

8. *The Wall Street Journal*, January 3, 1983, p. 1.

tainly willing to apply herself in this direction in her own quiet but determined way.

With her prep school and Harvard Law background, Julia fit into the mainstream at White & Case. Although she was reserved, she had a wry sense of humor that was apparent once she let her guard down. She didn't have a chip on her shoulder or make a point of thinking of herself as a *woman* lawyer. When another woman associate at the firm had insisted on having "Ms." branded on the nameplate outside her office, Julia thought her silly. Julia didn't think her sex was much of a factor in her career progression and didn't believe it had an effect on the partnership decision.

When the partners finally set the date for the partnership meeting, White & Case had never before had so many female candidates to consider. Associates from three classes, 1974, 1975 and 1976, were being voted on. Julia tried to stay calm waiting for the Wednesday meeting, knowing that Patrick and her other supporters were doing everything they could. Although nine other lawyers worked in the leveraged leasing area, none of the other associates were nearly as experienced as Julia and Patrick wanted badly to keep her at the firm. Looking over the competition, there were no clear shoo-ins among the associates, although there were a number of other strong female contenders. Julia couldn't begin to guess how this might affect her chances.

The Wednesday of the vote finally came and she was in the middle of a closing, trying to concentrate on the deal at hand. Suddenly the firm's managing partner was on the phone, having tracked her down at the closing. He had a simple request. Could she find time to work her way downtown to attend the partners' luncheon at Windows on the World, the plush restaurant atop the World Trade Center? So, after all this time, she was to be a partner. Since the luncheon was slated to begin in a half hour she hardly had time to bask in glory before she was out on Park Avenue fighting for a taxi.

Two other lawyers from the firm's midtown office also discreetly made their way down to Windows on the World. They were all waiting in a private dining room that had been reserved for the occasion. It was already past twelve-thirty, and none of the other partners were there. As the wait grew longer the three of them joked, a bit uncomfortably, about whether they were victims of some prank. But finally the partners strode into the room. They had been delayed by odd bits of business that needed to be taken care of at the end of the meeting. The champagne was finally uncorked.

As Julia sipped her drink and glanced around the scenic room, it suddenly dawned on her that four of the seven new partners were women. From what she gathered in later conversations, the partners themselves hadn't realized that this record number of women had made it until the final list was prepared after all the votes. Nobody was keeping a tally by sex. She felt good about the firm's attitude. The partners were not going around patting themselves on the back for electing so many women. It was more as if the partners were looking around the luncheon table, saying quietly, "Goodness. Look what we've done."

She was feeling a bit numb. "You work for a goal like this for so long and it's always just out of reach and then all of a sudden you have it—it's a really amazing feeling."

In the following days and weeks clients kept calling to congratulate her. It was a thrill each time to hear them introduce her at meetings as White & Case's new partner. It was also enlightening to attend the firm's weekly partnership meetings. On those Wednesday mornings she was learning about the firm's finances, how the partnership operated. She was beginning to feel like a real insider.

Sitting in her office several months later, she is explaining the changes in her life now that she is a partner. There are all kinds of new concerns. She has to watch her accounts even more carefully, to make sure clients are being billed and that collections are good. She also has to supervise more of the associates in her department. If she wants to rise up the partnership ranks and really make a place for herself within the firm's structure she also needs to begin developing her own clients, getting out to more places where she can plug the virtues of the firm. "I think women are in a slightly different place than men in doing this," she observes. "Particularly if you call up a man and say, 'Let's go have lunch,' or 'Let's have a drink after work.' I think people are getting more and more used to it, but it's still a funny sort of feeling."

The one thing lacking in her life—a husband and/or children—is not something she really worries about. Reflecting on the changes in her life, Julia says, "I'm very happy with my life the way it is. I'd like to have the other dimension with the right person, but I don't worry about it. I do have the feeling that, now that my future is more set, having more stability does free up my mind to ponder other possibilities."

Under the circumstances Carol Goodman's farewell party at Goodwin, Procter & Hoar was a rather tense affair. Several members of the Executive Committee showed up, and a senior partner even bought some champagne. One of the partners who had opposed her partnership delivered her final check. It contained a generous bonus which, combined with her year-end bonus of $16,000, put her in fine shape economically. As he presented the check the partner told her, almost by way of an apology, "I guess I'm just a prisoner of my history."

Carol had lined up a very good job in the Boston office of LeBoeuf, Lamb, a much bigger firm with a national practice. The firm's main office was in New York, but there were also seven branches in other cities and a London office. When she signed on Carol was promised a percentage of the billings she brought in on top of her associate's salary, and that she would be considered for partnership within eighteen months.

Psychologically, she felt much more comfortable at Le-Boeuf. She not only socialized with the lawyers in the Boston office, she had become close to several litigators and securities lawyers in the New York office, which she visited frequently. The firm's two women partners were also very supportive. They were both, like Carol, strong women in traditionally male specialties, antitrust and insurance. She and the other associates who were coming up for partnership were always trading the latest gossip and prognostications. Carol was coming into her own at LeBoeuf. Although the firm was old-line, it was multi-ethnic. There were several younger, free-wheeling partners and there was no one Le-Boeuf style. Good lawyering, rather than social gracefulness, won people over at LeBoeuf. John even liked a lot of the lawyers there.

But the partnership competition was tough. Among the six candidates under consideration there were two women and two Goodmans. That was a big joke going around the firm. Also, as an associate in the Boston office and as a lateral recruit, she was not well known to most of the New York partners. But she had done her best to be visible.

Almost immediately after she had hung up with the New York associate who had called with premature congratulations the phone rang again. This time the voice on the other end of the line was unmistakably Paul Connolly's. Her name had just been voted on. With almost no discussion, she had been elected. She was a partner.

She and John began phoning friends with the news. They called old colleagues at Paul, Weiss, a few Boston lawyers and their parents. John decided to celebrate by buying himself a new pair of boots.

"For me," Carol explains, sitting in the conference room on the top floor of LeBoeuf's Boston office, "it was almost an empty feeling. I had worked so hard for something and suddenly the goal isn't there anymore."

There are, of course, new hurdles. As a new partner, she is actually at the bottom of a new ladder. Because she brought so many cases with her from Goodwin, Procter & Hoar, developing clients has not really been a problem for Carol. With her abilities as a litigator, and a growing expertise in the corporate side of securities law, Carol is confident that with the necessary time and seasoning she can develop into a rainmaker. Already she was assigned to some of the firm's most important matters, including the reorganization of the Seabrook nuclear facility in New Hampshire. LeBoeuf didn't pigeonhole its lawyers. Although she was still concentrating on litigation, she also did corporate and bankruptcy work.

As self-confident and aggressive as Carol is, like Julia Bonsal, she finds the role of up-front lawyering occasionally confusing. In The Hague she once went with another LeBoeuf partner to a client reception. "There I was," she recalls, "all these women were dressed very elegantly, and I was in my suit and tie being treated as one of the guys. That's the way I wanted it to be. On the other hand, you get pressure from other women and even other women lawyers, almost a sense that you're overstepping, that you're stepping into a different role. The idea is, 'Women do things in a certain way and you don't do them that way.' It makes for a lot of role confusion that is difficult to deal with."

For the most part John is supportive of her career, even though she often works until 8 P.M. and brings work home from the office. For the past year she has been going to Europe often to work on the Iranian cases. "And I was working hard enough," she admits, "that I wasn't really home when I was home." She knows that John would like to entertain more often but Carol's schedule makes planning ahead difficult. Lizzy, an unusually intelligent and independent eight-year-old, doesn't seem to resent Carol's routine. "You can't maintain a traditional relationship with Mom in the kitchen," Carol says of her profession. Having a student live with them helps to keep Lizzy occupied and John is usually home by four each afternoon. It is fortunate that John's career and schedule have the flexibility that hers so lacks.

Recently, after a rough-and-tumble argument in The Hague, her client, the president of the company, came rushing up to congratulate her. As he opened the door for her the client gushed, "You know, you're a real lady." Carol resisted the temptation to bop him over the head. What she wanted to hear was, "You're a real fighter," or, better yet, "You're a real lawyer." But change, in a gentleman's profession, comes slowly.

On May 22, 1984, the U.S. Supreme Court ruled unanimously that law firms may not discriminate on the basis of sex, race, religion or national origin in deciding whether to promote lawyers to partner. "I'm not typically one to march in a parade," the reserved and soft-spoken plaintiff had proclaimed on the day of her victory.[9] "But there comes a point," Hishon explained, "and I reached that point, where you have to take a stand. I hope it will have a wide impact on women and minorities in the profession." Although the decision paved the way for a trial on the merits of her complaint, a few months later King & Spalding settled with Mrs. Hishon for an undisclosed sum.

Carol Goodman and Julia Bonsal have each made partner on their own merits. But there are those who feel that the Hishon case may have given them, and all women coming up for partnership in the next few years, an additional push. With the court's decision that Title VII can be applied to law partnerships, firms may face tough consequences if they refuse to promote qualified women. There could be more Betsy Hishons lining up to storm the barricades.

In reality making partner is only the beginning of a new

9. New York *Times*, May 23, 1984, p. 27.

challenge for Carol Goodman, Julia Bonsal and the fourteen other women in their class who have achieved this status. For the invisible line of exclusion may shift to another plane. The question may no longer be *whether* women have a future in law firms but what kind of future? Once they become partners, will women like Carol Goodman and Julia Bonsal have real clout? Will they be allowed to play an important role in their firms' management? If they fail to become rainmakers will they slip into a new status as "junior partners," not really integral to their firms' growth and survival? Will partnership become devalued as more women attain the goal—as certain specialties of medicine were, once they became heavily populated by women? For Carol Goodman, Julia Bonsal and the fourteen other women in their class who are partners the future may look promising, but the answers to these questions lie many years away.

7

Getting to the Top

Ten years into their professional lives, few women from the Harvard Law School class of 1974 can say, with real conviction, "I've made it. I am successful." They are all, of course, still at an early stage in their careers when this kind of self-satisfied, complacent declaration would seem misplaced. But some of the women display ambivalent feelings toward their profession making their very definition of success confusing, full of conflicting signals. A few, like Ellen Marshall, have always defined success as reaching the goal of partnership at a major firm. "My goal was stated unabashedly," she says. "To become as successful as possible in the profession and to make a lot of money." As a partner at a Los Angeles firm and a recognized specialist in savings and loan corporate work, Marshall has achieved both. Others, like Anne Redman, say that success is abandoning workaholism and striking a balance at work that allows for a personal life, including children, even at the cost of building a big practice. "As a practicing attorney, to the extent that you want to mix in substantial other commitments, you will stunt your practice," says Redman, a partner at a Seattle firm. "But family is an important outlet. It is important to have someone to love. After a while I realized no matter what I did for my clients a certain amount of it is not returned. This is a business practice, these are not orphans I'm saving. That's part of the reason I wanted a baby." And for still others, like Rene Townsend Robinson, success has meant shedding the traditional, Harvard Law School definition of achievement—amassing status, power and money, staying on the fast track, being competitive—accepting, as she says, "that there will always be someone who is just a little bit better than you," and learning how to take a different path.

In every class at Harvard Law School there are the stand-outs, the superstars. Almost everyone from the class of 1974 cites Isaac Pachulski, who graduated with the highest grades, and Barry Simon, president of the *Harvard Law Review*. Both men are today partners in prestigious law firms. As far as the women in the class are concerned, there are no consensus choices among the men and women we interviewed. The names of Margaret Morrow, Diana Daniels, who was an officer of the Board of Student Advisers (the closest thing Harvard has to an honors society) during law school, Karen Katzman and Alice Young were frequently mentioned as women whom everyone remembered as possessing the brains and personalities needed to succeed. And, in terms of having important, prestigious jobs, these four women have succeeded.

Although she is a partner at Los Angeles' Kadison, Phaelzer, Woodard, Quinn & Rossi and is a member of its management committee as well as vice-president of the Los Angeles County Bar Association (normally a steppingstone to the presidency), Margaret Morrow realizes she has a long road to travel before she wields real influence in the profession. "At many firms the partners who control and generate business are the powerful ones and it's very difficult for women to break into the old-boy network. Now that I'm a partner I'll have to focus on developing entrepreneurial instincts, becoming more of a businesswoman."

Morrow knows firsthand that, for the select group of

women from her law school class who have achieved partnership, a whole new set of challenges awaits confrontation. "The really important issues come at the higher level of things, where you begin to get into the power games. It's when you make the challenge to become an equal rather than a subordinate that push comes to shove, and for me that's been in the past four years," she explains. Her former classmate Deena Jo Schneider, a partner in a Philadelphia firm, agrees. "As long as law firms are governed by those who are substantially older, they are not going to treat women the same and the effects of that will be felt for years to come."

In Los Angeles Morrow belongs to an informal group of women partners at different firms who get together to discuss common problems. "It's really interesting to hear that group talk," she says. "They talk about everything from female associates don't get the good work assignments to the fact that female partners don't get asked out to business-client development events like basketball games or dinners, to the fact that their clients aren't viewed as being as important as the clients of a male partner. There is a lot of anger. I don't feel that kind of internal anger toward my firm very much, but I understand it."

At New York's Kaye, Scholer, Fierman, Hays & Handler, where she is a partner, Karen Katzman tries to be accessible to women associates at her firm, realizing, she says, that "women now feel they are no longer a novelty piece but men are still reluctant to be their mentors." And it is still harder for women to fit in. "Women have to walk a fine line between being too aggressive or too reserved," Katzman adds. "I think I've walked that line rather well. It's a plain fact that you're scrutinized more. There are more hoops to jump through. You are under a microscope. Little issues of behavior can become issues of merit and nonmerit." At most firms women have yet to find equal status at either the partnership or associate level. While more women are making partner,

few have made it to the top of the top: becoming rainmakers
or political heavyweights at their firms. Katzman believes it
will take at least another ten years to tell whether she and her
classmates will scale those heights. "That's the really interesting question," she told us. "It should make a good sequel."

There are, however, two women from the class who have
already made it to the very top of the profession, Alice
Young and Diana Daniels. Alice Young is not only a partner
at Graham & James, she founded the firm's New York office
and is a member of a key governing committee. She has not
only built her own practice, attracting enough clients to keep
four other lawyers and herself swamped with work, but also
administrates an entire branch office. Diana Daniels is vice-
president and counsel of *Newsweek* and serves in one of her
company's top corporate posts. She calls the shots on how her
company handles tricky legal issues, including libel suits, and
directs the work of a host of outside firms that handle litigation for the magazine. If there are few women in the partnership ranks, there are fewer still in the executive suites of
major corporations. Diana is part of this tiny elite.

Fierce determination, competence, force of personality and
a variety of other factors have combined to make these two
women so successful. Both readily admit that luck—being in
the right place at the right time—has had much to do with
their respective achievements. And the opening of doors
hitherto locked, the changing attitude toward young women
in the business world, may deserve even more of the credit.

It was an unusual, contrasting scene. Outside, the Manhattan streets were slick with rain, which had been pelting down
throughout the crowded and unpleasant rush hour. Inside the
new, opulent Helmsley Palace Hotel, five hundred guests of
the California law firm of Graham & James were sipping
cocktails as solicitous waiters dashed around the function

room making sure the assembled lawyers and businessmen had their share of hors d'oeuvres and drinks.

At the entrance to the room a striking, thirty-one-year-old Chinese-American woman named Alice Young stood greeting the guests and shaking hands. With her shiny dark hair, dazzling smile and ready wit, Alice projected a confidence far beyond her years. She was dressed, as usual, with a flare that set her apart from other women lawyers who, for lack of imagination or confidence, usually stuck to a uniform of boxy skirted suits. Slim and attractive, Alice had developed a look all her own. "I've never been comfortable in the corporate suit," she often said, "and I've refused to conform to it." She managed to appear completely professional and at ease with herself while wearing more original dresses with unusual accessories. Some of her clients were the young Japanese designers who were revolutionizing the fashion industry.

This elaborate fete at the Helmsley Palace was Graham & James's formal introduction of Alice Young to the New York legal community. Just a few months earlier, in September 1981, the firm had plucked Alice from New York's Coudert Brothers, where she was an associate, and in one bold stroke had not only offered her partnership but had given her the plum assignment of launching the firm's brand-new New York office. And while Alice Young certainly made a favorable first impression, there were plenty of lawyers at the Helmsley Palace that night who probably thought the firm had been foolhardy to entrust such an important mission to a young and relatively untested woman.

The job of heading a branch office, particularly in a competitive marketplace like New York, usually went to a firm elder or a proven rainmaker, to draw new clients and build a strong practice in a new city. Launching a successful satellite office required top management skills, the ability to attract and hire other skilled attorneys, oversee billings and collections, manage staff, purchase expensive office technology for

Graham & James's worldwide network and coordinate with its other offices. As an associate, Alice had not had a chance to prove her capabilities in most of these areas. Indeed there were few women lawyers anywhere, even those in their fifties, who had been called on to perform such an important role in firm management. Graham & James appeared to be offering Alice Young a ticket to the very top of her profession. What was so special about this young woman? the guests had to be wondering.

In New York, even in 1981, it was still unusual to find women at the partnership level at all. Several of the city's most prominent firms were still all-male preserves at the partnership level. Although the situation was beginning to change in the 1980s, as more women associates were making it to the finish line, there were still only a handful of women lawyers who could truly be characterized as heavy hitters within the profession. Alice Young was on the verge of breaking into this very select group.

"There is little doubt in my mind that ten years ago this wouldn't have been possible," Alice told a reporter during one of the many press interviews that followed her elevation as head of Graham & James's New York office. "I feel particularly fortunate as a woman and as an Asian-American. It's the kind of opportunity that rarely comes to white males in their fifties, and I'm particularly honored that someone of my background was able to do it."

Before accepting Graham & James's offer Alice had spent months agonizing over whether she was up to the task. Although she had always enjoyed good relationships with the clients she serviced at Coudert Brothers, most of them were institutional clients of the firm. She had not really had to go out and develop her own. "I wasn't coming from total inexperience," she explains, "but it is different watching than shouldering." While the senior partners at Graham & James had indicated their willingness to be patient, Alice knew the success or failure of the New York office would rest in large part on her abilities to attract and keep business. Although she had rarely failed at anything she set her mind to, Alice had occasional moments of anxiety when she pictured her newly furnished offices at Rockefeller Center sitting empty and silent, bereft of clients. Given the presence of many established Graham & James clients at the cocktail reception, including the officers of several leading Japanese electronics and trading companies, she knew that the New York office would not fail. But neither would it really succeed—and Alice had set very high standards—if it remained simply a service office for existing Graham & James clients. Alice would have to bring considerable new business through the door if the venture was going to be the smashing success she very badly wanted.

In the past few weeks she hadn't really had time to sit around worrying or second-guessing her abilities. Ever since she had accepted Graham & James's offer of partnership she had been busily attending to the mundane details of opening and equipping a small law firm. Although the firm's librarian had been dispatched from San Francisco to help out, Alice had to be involved in virtually everything, from picking out the furniture, selecting the telephone and photocopying equipment, to staffing. She had conducted interviews for the position of office manager while sitting on a telephone book in one of the many empty offices in her new suite. It had been weeks before a telephone system was put in. Although the doors of the office had officially opened on October 1, 1981, during her first week in operation Alice was calling her clients from the telephone booths in the lobby of the building. "It was sort of an Outward Bound experience," she jokes. "Here's one match. Now you have to figure out how to survive."

So, on this rainy but festive evening at the Helmsley Palace, Alice was in a celebratory frame of mind. She had been on board at Graham & James for six weeks, and Phase I of her assignment was almost completed. Furniture and phones had finally arrived. Clients, both of Graham & James and from her days at Coudert, already had active files in New York. She had also been successful in hiring two of her former colleagues from Coudert, Dan Mathews and Bill Campbell, to work as senior associates for Graham & James in New York. At last she had a real, functioning office and this party, replete with clients and various luminaries of the legal and business worlds, seemed to be an auspicious beginning.

Although she felt elated and very much on display, Alice was also extremely tired. She knew when she had decided to take it that the job would require a hundred and twenty percent of her energies. "It was like having a child," she says. "It took tremendous responsibility and I watched over and worried about it all the time." Focusing almost all of her energies on work was an adjustment. Unlike many young lawyers, and many of the women from her law school class, Alice's life hadn't revolved around work exclusively. She was a junior member of the prestigious Council on Foreign Relations, active in women's business organizations and on several boards. As head of a new office for a large international firm, Alice knew some of these outside interests would be neglected, particularly since she would be traveling constantly. During her first year at Graham & James Alice would spend more than sixty percent of her time traveling back and forth to the firm's main office in San Francisco and throughout the Far East, where many of her best opportunities to develop business lay. She was prepared to spend much of her time on the road. The major burden of all of this traveling, she realized, would fall on her relationship with Tom Shortall, the man with whom she had been involved for several years.

Tom, an investment banker with Smith Barney Harris Upham & Co. had been tremendously supportive throughout her transition from a relatively obscure associate to a prominent young partner. Although he also realized that Alice would be taking a tremendous risk—if the New York office was a flop the failure would be an intensely personal one for her—like Alice, he viewed the Graham & James offer as a once-in-a-lifetime opportunity. If she turned it down there might always be regrets.

When Alice began talking to Graham & James she had not contemplated such a large-scale project. She had grown restless at Coudert Brothers and was considering other options. A professor friend from Columbia Law School had been asked by Graham & James to recommend attorneys with expertise in East Asian practice. He suggested Alice and mentioned that her fluency in both Japanese and Chinese would make a natural fit with Graham & James, which had an active practice in the Pacific basin. She had initially been contacted by managing partner Conger Fawcett. Alice had made it plain to him that she was not interested in moving out to San Francisco. Fawcett had urged her to visit the firm anyway, hoping that Graham & James, combined with San Francisco's beauty and charm, might lure her away from New York. Fawcett had also mentioned that Graham & James had periodically considered opening a New York office but the right combination of legal talent and clients had failed to materialize. Alice certainly hoped to rekindle the firm's interest in New York but thought this was a long-shot. After all, an established law firm like Graham & James was unlikely to trust her to carry off a venture that the firm, with more than fifty partners, had doubts about doing itself.

She arrived in San Francisco on an early summer evening in 1981 and stayed up until three in the morning talking with Fawcett and other members of the firm's Executive Committee. They spent about fifteen minutes trying to coax Alice out to California and the rest of the time chatting about how she would go about setting up a New York office. Alice was surprised by how seriously interested they seemed and wished that she had prepared more thoroughly for the encounter. She didn't even have a rough budget in mind.

The next morning she was back at the firm at nine in the morning to begin a round of whirlwind interviews with partners and associates. While Alice was busy meeting the other Graham & James lawyers Fawcett placed a call to Sandy Calhoun, a senior partner who was out of the country on business. He briefed Calhoun about how excited he and the other members of the Executive Committee were about Alice Young. Fawcett thought she was the perfect person to build a New York practice. At dinner that night, at the elegant Stanford Court, Fawcett made the offer official. The Executive Committee was prepared to recommend to the partnership that Alice become a partner and launch a New York office. Alice was stunned to have an offer so quickly. "I make no guarantees whatsoever on clients," she told Fawcett and the others and added that she needed time to think everything over.

She took all summer to decide, weighing the pros and cons with Tom. There was no question in her mind about leaving Coudert Brothers but she was unsure of what she wanted next. She had spent seven years training to be a competent business lawyer, working very hard. Part of her yearned to just drop what she was doing and make a dramatic change—perhaps going off to write a novel or taking a more entrepreneurial job in the business world itself. Yet, during her more practical moments, both she and Tom realized this was her chance to really seize success. At thirty-one, as head of the New York office, she would be catapulted into one of the most important positions at Graham & James. She would be running the show. It was all too tempting to turn down.

In September 1981 she gave the firm a definite yes and gave notice at Coudert. She tried to be scrupulous about not wooing new business while she was still at Coudert. "I didn't want to get into a push-pull contest over clients," she recalls.

Just six weeks later, at the Helmsley Palace, some of these old clients had turned up to congratulate her on the opening of her office. The party had also attracted a few reporters, who were anxious to chronicle this young lawyer's unusual rise to the top of her profession. When such a young woman catapulted into a top management position at a major firm it was an important and unusual story for those who covered the legal profession. Now, as Alice stood greeting more guests, trying to think of something memorable to say to each one, she realized that the job of proving herself had only just begun.

The proverbial "big break" had come to Diana Daniels even earlier. At age twenty-eight, after spending only two and a half years at Wall Street's Cravath, Swaine & Moore, Diana was plucked from the corporate department to fill a plum position as assistant general counsel of the Washington *Post*. With its famous coverage of the Watergate scandal, which Diana and most of her classmates had followed closely as students at Harvard Law School, and its unparalleled investigative reporting staff, the *Post* was the hottest newspaper in the country. It was also one of the first major dailies to put together a first-class, in-house legal department. Because she was a corporate associate with no experience in either litigation or libel law, the choice of Diana Daniels to fill the job struck some of her colleagues at Cravath, and Diana herself, as unusual.

Then, after barely a year, lightning struck again. In July 1979 the Post Company announced that Diana was being promoted to become vice-president and counsel of *Newsweek,* a position that put her directly in charge of the magazine's legal affairs. The *Post* had purchased *Newsweek* in 1961 and the news weekly was one of the jewels of the *Post*'s growing media empire. Ensconcing a twenty-nine-year-old woman in the executive suite on the tenth floor of *Newsweek*'s headquarters on Madison Avenue seemed an unusually bold move, even for a hard-charging, progressive company like the *Post,* which was itself ruled by Katharine Graham, one of the most powerful women in the country.

Diana's rise was meteoric but not because she had set a clear goal for herself to become a star in the glamor field of First Amendent law. Like most lawyers, Diana was cautious by nature and when the *Post* offer first presented itself she had been reluctant to uproot herself from New York, where she had a job she liked and a group of close friends, to move to Washington and start all over. While other, more ambitious young lawyers might have killed for such an opportunity, Diana was not, for all her competence and outstanding credentials, extremely driven. She had never been entirely sure that she wanted a career as a lawyer, and she had attended law school mostly because it seemed to close off the fewest options. She had gone to Cravath for similar reasons, not because she was hungering for a long-term career at a prestigious firm, but because she thought the training she would receive would equip her to move in several directions, once she had a clearer idea of what she wanted to do with her life. It would never hurt to have either Harvard Law School or Cravath on her résumé. And, despite her initial reluctance, she had taken the job at the *Post* because it seemed like an interesting opportunity. "I guess I've gone through most of my life looking for what would close the fewest number of doors," she explained in 1984, sitting in the comfortable office where this reserved, attractive woman, with shoulder-length dark hair and almond-shaped brown eyes keeps watch over *Newsweek*'s legal affairs. "The idea is to leave yourself the most numbers of options at all times."

Eight years earlier, she had been fortunate to find herself as a Cravath associate at a time when several leading corporations, following new affirmative action guidelines, were looking to hire qualified women for management-level positions.

In fact when Donald Graham, the soon to be young publisher of the *Post,* had started making inquiries about filling the new legal job at his newspaper he had made it plain to Christine Beshar, the Cravath partner who handled the Graham family's trusts and estates work, that he preferred to hire a minority. Christopher Little, the newspaper's general counsel, wanted to hire a woman to be his deputy if the right candidate could be found.

Cravath was a natural recruiting ground for the *Post,* and not only because of the firm's reputation for training good lawyers. Although the newspaper relied on several firms to handle its work, the relationship with Cravath was particularly close and of long standing. Katharine Graham's father, Eugene Meyer, a prominent financier, had been a Cravath client and the firm had represented the *Post* in virtually all of its important corporate moves, including the *Newsweek* acquisition and taking the company public. A senior Cravath partner, Frederick Beebe, had served as president of the Post Company and another senior partner sat on its board of directors. Alan Finberg, the Post Company's top legal officer, had once been a Cravath associate. And Beshar, the firm's first and at that time only woman partner, handled estate planning for the Graham family.

Diana occasionally had lunch with Beshar who, one afternoon in 1978, broached the idea of Diana's considering the job at the *Post.* When Beshar outlined the qualifications for the job, Diana was skeptical. "I didn't have any of the qualifications they were looking for," she admits. The company was searching for someone with four years of experience and a litigation background. Diana had been at Cravath less than three years and hadn't even looked at the First Amendment since taking constitutional law her first year at Harvard Law School. Also, while she was unsure of her long-term future at Cravath—out of the twenty-one associates who had graduated from law school in 1974, Diana knew only two or three would make partner, perhaps even less—she wanted to complete her apprenticeship there. "I hadn't had the experience of working for the different areas of Cravath that I thought would be worth having under my belt," she explains, "but I wasn't sure whether I wanted to stick it out and become part of the race for partnership."

Her hours at the *Post* were certain to be just as long but the work might be more interesting. Diana loved politics and the *Post* seemed to be at the center of every major political story. Like many of her classmates, Diana had studied for the bar exam while glued to the television set watching the Watergate hearings. Although she was dubious about her qualifications for the *Post* position, Beshar had piqued her interest. After all, she had nothing to lose by flying down to Washington to meet Chris Little and some of the other *Post* executives.

Although one of the important aspects of being his deputy would be reviewing fast-breaking stories for libel considerations, Little was looking for someone who could handle a broad range of corporate matters, from contracts to employee relations. The fact that Diana was doing well in Cravath's notoriously competitive and male-dominated corporation department impressed Little. Even in the late 1970s there were, Little knew, lingering beliefs on Wall Street that women couldn't really be trusted to handle the huge sums of money at stake in the deals that firms like Cravath handled. Diana obviously hadn't let any of this get in her way. What she might lack in experience, Little was sure, she would make up in drive. When he met Diana during her first interview in Washington he was sure she was right for the job. Diana, meanwhile, was frank about her lack of litigation experience. "I gave them every opportunity to say no," she says. But the newspaper wanted her. She took a month to consider the offer. On the one hand, she was doing well at Cravath. The partners in the corporate department had made it plain that if she didn't take the *Post* offer they would be happy to have her stay. "I just decided that I had two opportunities," she explains. "I could sit there and wait it out, maybe four, six or eight years, and I still would not know one way or the other whether I'd become a partner. The opportunity at the *Post* was only going to come around once in a lifetime. It wasn't an opportunity I was going to get a second chance at."

So she moved to Washington. She had been on the job only six weeks when Little took two months off to attend a prestigious business training seminar at Stanford University, leaving Diana virtually in charge of the newspaper's legal department. "It was a very fast breaking-in period. I had to learn in a hurry. It meant you were really responsible and having to rely on yourself very quickly without knowing much about the company or their procedures." She did everything that summer: covering the newsroom and reading copy, drawing up contracts, handling real estate deals, supervising the outside firms that handled the newspaper's litigation and dealing with a subpoena order or two. Although Diana had been studying libel law since her arrival, by coincidence only one libel suit was filed against the newspaper during the time she was at the *Post.*

In Little's absence she was forced to dive into the legal work, to trust her own judgment and start putting out brushfires. There were at least four or five stories a week that needed to be reviewed for potential libel problems, and at the beginning of her tenure, when Little headed down to the giant newsroom on the fifth floor, Diana followed. The two of them would stand together reading copy, and Diana would listen carefully as Little began to question an editor or reporter about the text. She would try to follow his train of thought, why certain points were important and others were not. Sometimes Diana reviewed copy on her own and took it into Little's office to analyze the problems she had found, to see if Little agreed with her reasoning. To refresh herself in

First Amendment law, Diana also pored over the landmark libel decisions and read the briefs in more recent cases.

She enjoyed the give-and-take with the editors over the phrasing of certain stories. Since her job was to protect the newspaper from being vulnerable to libel claims, she often had to question an editor or reporter on his facts, his thoroughness and his choice of words. Even though they were on the same side, Diana realized there was a built-in friction between the editorial side of the newspaper and the legal department. By nature, most journalists have big egos and they don't like being picked apart by lawyers. And at the *Post* big egos were legendary. Although Watergate luminaries Carl Bernstein and Bob Woodward were not around the newsroom the year she was there (Woodward was writing *The Brethren* and Bernstein had taken a new job with ABC News), Diana met a number of reporters who thought they knew absolutely everything about the subjects they were covering. She knew the paper had a terrific editorial staff but she refused to hold any reporter or editor in awe. She thought it was part of her job to question everything and not acquiesce just because she might be dealing with a well-known journalist.

For the most part her relations with the editorial side were very smooth. The newspaper's famous executive editor, Ben Bradlee, had enjoyed a good relationship with Little and his good feelings toward Chris seemed to rub off on Diana too. Occasionally she and managing editor Howard Simons had lunch together with some of the other editors.

She gave some valued advice on the corporate side of the newspaper. The *Post* was in the process of purchasing new presses, a multimillion-dollar transaction. Diana was instrumental in drafting and reviewing the contracts to make sure the newspaper was getting the most favorable terms. Her corporate abilities had impressed the newspaper's hierarchy, but she was still surprised when Alan Finberg, general counsel of the Post Company, the newspaper's corporate parent, approached her about yet another opportunity: to become vice-president and counsel of *Newsweek*. Finberg felt the magazine's current in-house counsel, Ed Smith, lacked the corporate experience the job now demanded. *Newsweek* had expanded, launching book and video divisions, and was on the verge of starting a sports magazine. Finberg wanted a lawyer with a strong corporate background to oversee the magazine's legal affairs. Peter Derow, *Newsweek*'s president, also stopped by her office on the way to a *Post* board meeting, to encourage her to take the job.

It was a clear promotion, a chance to move from a support role into the number one position. There was really no way she could turn down such an offer. Ironically, she was now reluctant to leave Washington, just as she had resisted leaving New York the year before. She had a new circle of friends, and had bought a nice apartment and a car. Also, she knew that replacing Smith, who was extremely popular with *Newsweek*'s editorial staff, would be a delicate matter. It might be perceived that Diana—a young attorney whose star had risen at the parent company, the *Post*—was being sent to elbow Smith aside. Although she had had nothing to do with the changing of the guard, she was prepared for some backlash. At Harvard Law School, Cravath and the *Post* she had learned to handle herself with confidence, poise and tact. She was determined to win over her new colleagues at *Newsweek* by being the best counsel the magazine ever had.

Something special about both Diana Daniels and Alice Young equipped them to take on tremendous responsibilities at an early age and give them both a level of self-confidence far greater than most of the women who attended law school with them had attained. Neither Alice nor Diana displayed the reticence that some male lawyers claim often cripples the careers of young women lawyers. Roscoe Trimmier, a classmate who made partner at Boston's Ropes & Gray, perceives the problem in an interesting light. "There have been occasions," he says, "when women haven't been as eager to accept responsibility which they don't think they could discharge, like asking the assigning partner, 'Do you think I could do that?' full of self-doubt. Whereas a male contemporary would take it and run with it. He may screw it up, but at least would give it a try. It may be that some women just lack self-confidence, but males at least play the game. It is a very crucial factor in success in law practice. If you fail to demonstrate self-confidence, if there is not that aura of self-confidence, you come off as wishy-washy." Alice and Diana both projected the aura that Trimmier has found lacking in some of the women lawyers he has observed.

Rita Hauser, a member of the Harvard Law School class of 1958, says that she can literally "smell" the qualities needed for client-getting in young lawyers and that women rarely exude this special scent. Hauser is one of the nation's leading international corporate lawyers, and her name has often appeared on the short list for high government office, including the U.S. Supreme Court. For some reason, because of cultural or personality traits, Hauser believes, women make excellent technicians as lawyers but are inept at generating clients. Until the situation changes, Hauser warns, women lawyers will not really rise to powerful positions within their firms, as leadership roles tend to be awarded to the partners who bring in the bacon. At Stroock, Hauser has tried to hold rainmaking tutorials for younger women lawyers, but whatever makes Hauser so successful at wooing clients—either her gutsiness, charm or drive—is impossible to transfer to others. Her special qualities were apparent even when she was a new associate at another large New York firm, Proskauer, Rose, Goetz & Mendelsohn, where senior partner George Shapiro recalls, "She was just a stripling of a girl, but even back then she had unusual potential for leadership. She had sparkle."

Similarly, Alice Young's potential exhibited itself early in her career. Just as Hauser attributes part of her drive to her childhood, during which she was always compensating for being tiny (today she stands barely over five feet tall and weighs less than a hundred pounds) and battling with her father over her career plans (he did not support her desire to have a profession), Alice finds the explanation for her success in her early life.

She had, in effect, grown up in two cultures and by the time she was in college she had lived on two continents as well as Hawaii. This experience equipped her, as she demonstrated at the opening party for Graham & James, to seem perfectly at ease in a roomful of strangers. Although Alice was born and raised mostly in the United States, her parents were first-generation Asians who had come to the United States in their adulthood. Because of her father's academic career, she was used to being uprooted, learning about new cultures, and adept at meeting people. These early experiences would serve her well during her hectic first months at Graham & James.

Alice's father had hoped she might pursue a doctorate in East Asian studies and follow in his footsteps as a university professor, and for a short while this seemed like a probable route for her. Her father's specialty was history and sociolinguistics, which he had studied at several universities after his arrival in the United States in the late 1940s. In Asian culture, lawyers were not nearly as esteemed as they were in the United States, and as a profession law had seemed to her father less worthy of her talents than academia. But he respected Alice's independence and knew she would make her own career decisions.

When she was twelve the family moved to Tokyo for two years while her father administered the foreign language programs for the University of Maryland in Asia. Although it was wrenching for her to leave the security of the Washington suburbs, Alice was fascinated by Asian culture and quickly picked up bits and pieces of the language.

Then her father was named chairman of the Department of Asian and Pacific Languages at the University of Hawaii. The family moved to Honolulu, where Alice attended a large public high school called Kalani. Part of what made her high school career in Hawaii interesting was being exposed to people completely different from herself. Few of her friends at Kalani, where she was an honor student and vice-president of the student body, planned to go on to college. Alice, on the other hand, was an early admissions student at the University of Hawaii. Her freshman year she was not only on the dean's list but was also voted Outstanding Freshman Woman for her academic and civic achievements. Despite her successes at the University of Hawaii, Alice was restless for a more challenging academic program. She applied and was accepted into Yale's first undergraduate class of women.

Socially, Yale was far more homogeneous than the high school and college populations to which Alice had been exposed. "At Yale people were from one or two dimensions," she says, "they'd been so sheltered." Between living on the East Coast, in Hawaii and abroad and going to Kalani and the University of Hawaii, Alice felt that she came from, as she puts it, "about twenty different dimensions." Academically, however, Yale was everything she hoped for. She became fluent in Japanese and Chinese, studying East Asian history and literature. In 1970 she won a Bates Fellowship to study Japanese literature under Nobel Prize laureate Yasunari Kawabata. With a stellar academic record, Alice easily won scholarships to both law school and several PhD programs. Although she had had limited exposure to it, she was intrigued by the world of business and its faster pace. Opportunities for women in the field of international law were not that great but Alice was hopeful she would find a place for herself in the profession. She decided to go to Harvard Law School.

If Yale channeled her professional goals it also had a major impact on her personal life. She fell in love with one of her classmates, who was also planning a legal career. While Alice was starting Harvard her future husband would be attending Boston University Law School, just across the river.

As a married student living off campus, Alice had a built-in distance from the pressurized, one-dimensional existence of most Harvard One Ls. At Harvard Alice was determined to keep an emotional as well as physical distance between herself and the school. "It was a neurotic environment," she recalls. "Half of my energies were spent trying not to get swept up into it." A friend of Alice's once joked that it got ten degrees colder every time she walked onto the Harvard Law School campus and Alice had to agree. If you let yourself get swept up in the Harvard Law, *Paper Chase* mentality, Alice was convinced, you would lose your basic humanity. She had entered law school with a strong sense of her own identity and she was not going to lose it now. "I proved to myself that you could be successful and still survive with your personality and values intact," she says.

When she became involved in the East Asian Legal Studies program, she developed more of a sense of community at the law school. She also worked part-time for a professor at the law school and for the federal Office for Civil Rights, reviewing the affirmative action plans of Harvard, Yale and other universities in the Northeast region. The three years passed relatively quickly. Although she had been offered a clerkship for the chief justice of the Supreme Court of Hawaii, which could have led to a promising future in Hawaii, Alice decided to work in a law firm after graduation. Part of what had attracted her to law school in the first place was the chance to work in a business rather than an academic setting. With her fluency in foreign languages, Coudert Brothers, the venerable New York firm, which had a significant international practice, was a natural fit.

At the time she joined Coudert Brothers the firm was in the process of expanding its East Asian practice. In the early 1970s Coudert had opened offices in Singapore, Tokyo and Hong Kong. The firm was looking for an associate, fluent in Japanese, to work in a new Hong Kong office and to handle assignments in Tokyo. With her academic credentials, background and language abilities, Alice was a perfect candidate. The prospect of working abroad excited her, but her husband had already been offered partnership in his father's New York practice. A New York–Hong Kong commute was out of the question, so Coudert made a unique proposal: during the time Alice was overseas, the firm would employ both of them in the Hong Kong office.

Going overseas immediately meant that there would be no "coddling period" for Alice, time when new associates were slowly introduced to the art of drafting legal documents and to clients. Instead, she was sent to Coudert's most distant provinces, to work in a three-lawyer office with very little backup staff. Although she didn't realize it at the time, pioneering in a small office was exactly the training she needed to prepare for opening a satellite office herself in the future.

For someone with less experience or guts, the new environment would have been unsettling but Alice thrived in Hong Kong. She loved getting out and around the city, studying the new culture and meeting the Chinese, Japanese and American businessmen who were key clients. Although she had little background in it, she found she was fascinated by the business world and she tried to master the details of each of her clients' businesses as well as the legal aspects of their problems. As a new associate in New York, she knew she would not have had the extensive client contact she enjoyed in Hong Kong and might have been stuck in the library, stapling memos. Since the supervising partners were often out of the office seeing clients throughout the region, Alice learned to be a self-starter and to dispense legal advice with confidence. By her second year in Hong Kong she was handling some transactions by herself.

Alice was fortunate that her immediate superiors were willing to give her important work once she had demonstrated her competence. Diana Daniels had had the same experience at the *Post*. Their respective bosses were men in their thirties who were comfortable dealing with women colleagues and used to seeing women in a professional setting. There was no one standing in the way of either Alice or Diana, telling them they couldn't work on any particular deal, looking over their shoulders. Both women were encouraged to take on as much responsibility as they wanted.

Alice's fluency in languages gave her a big edge. Sometimes she was the only lawyer working on a deal who could communicate directly with all the parties. Although Asian businessmen were reputed to be sexist and very reluctant to deal with women lawyers, Alice discovered that if you understood their business considerations, gave solid and practical legal advice promptly and also happened to be able to communicate in their language, being a woman made her unique as a lawyer. "These older Japanese businessmen really seemed to get a kick out of dealing with someone young and bright, attractive and charming," says another Coudert associate who watched Alice in action.

By the time her two years in Hong Kong were over Alice not only knew how to handle clients and work on complex corporate transactions, she also knew how to attract new clients. By watching Coudert's more experienced partners operate in East Asia, Alice learned that developing clients wasn't so much a matter of making cold calls or going out and knocking on doors. If she did good work for existing clients they often referred her to others. Making rain wasn't all that difficult.

Coming back to New York gave Alice a chance to increase her exposure to different types of legal transactions. In Hong Kong she had worked primarily on financing projects, involving shipping, petroleum production facilities, iron ore plants, manufacturing as well as multicurrency syndications. In New York she was able to expand her general corporate experience, handling joint ventures, acquisitions, license and distribution agreements and contracts for foreign and domestic clients. In addition to her Asia-based work she also began to travel to Europe on a variety of matters. Coudert's clientele stretched across Europe, into the Middle East, the Far East, California and South America, which made practicing there an exciting opportunity for anyone interested in international work.

In 1981 the firm's leader, Alexis Coudert, died. The political atmosphere at the firm worsened precipitously after the patriarch's death. Partners in different practice groups suddenly had competing agendas. Charles Stevens, a young partner in Alice's East Asian group, was threatening to defect, taking a number of lawyers and clients with him. "It was a very unsettled atmosphere," Alice recalls. "The political and internal strife made it impossible to service clients." None of the associates knew where they stood and Alice was unsure whether she had a future at Coudert Brothers or even if she wanted one. With the intense personal rivalries that had developed within the partnership, being a Coudert partner might not be all that pleasant, even if the goal was attainable. Partners and associates began leaving the firm. Alice was approached to join some of them, and headhunters began calling to ask if she was interested in other firms.

Coudert had only one woman partner, which added to her uncertainty about the future. During her early career there were no women role models to emulate or to act as mentors.

The firm had held some of its functions at the then all-male Sky Club, and when Alice had had to attend meetings there she had been ushered into the private dining rooms through a side door. Although more women were filtering up through the associate ranks, they were still a distinct minority. "I remember worrying about what you had to do to be accepted," Alice recalls of her early life as a Coudert associate, "whether to wear the gray suit or the black suit, whether to talk in a strident voice or a soft voice."

It did irk her that lawyers often applied a double standard. If a male lawyer was tall and good-looking the assumption was that he was socially graceful and knew what he was talking about. With a woman the assumption was that she wasn't a serious lawyer. Alice was troubled by the fact that women lawyers were usually stereotyped as overly aggressive or quiet, efficient back-room types. Fitting neither of these stereotypes, Alice, as her experience and confidence grew, found it easier to relax and set her own style. If you reached a certain level of expertise and assurance, she believed, people would be embarrassed to make clothes, attractiveness, or anything else related to her sex, an issue. As her career developed, she found that being a woman could, in fact, be a distinct advantage. "If a client is impressed by your legal work he is more likely to remember you than all the male lawyers he usually deals with," she observes.

Alice was determined to leave Coudert before the whole house of cards fell apart, as there were rumors that the firm was in failing economic health. Thus the offer from Graham & James had appeared to come from a deus ex machina. She worried that all big firms might be like Coudert Brothers, filled with petty rivalries and complicated internal politics. This was part of the reason why she took so long to accept Graham & James's offer. She wanted to make sure the partners at Graham & James were different. In one respect, Graham & James was nothing like Coudert: there were large groups of women in the senior associate ranks. In fact during Alice's early years at Graham & James four women were elected partner. After several trips to California she was convinced that Graham & James would be a far more supportive atmosphere for professional growth and she went ahead and did what her first instincts had told her to do—grab the job.

The Coudert chapter of her life was ending and it had been an important one, both personally and professionally. During these years she had undergone rapid changes, both good and bad. Her marriage had ended midway through her associate training. She had lived abroad and become steeped in East Asian culture. Most important, she had become an experienced and effective corporate lawyer. Without that certainty she would never have accepted Graham & James's offer.

Without being sure in exactly which direction she was heading, Diana Daniels pursued every challenge that came her way. Her record before arriving at Harvard was impressive, even by the law school's standards. As an undergraduate she had zipped through Cornell University in just three years, winning election to Phi Beta Kappa. College had been topped by a prestigious one-year Sloan Fellowship that took her inside New York City Mayor John Lindsay's administration, where she studied the workings of New York City government. She emerged from the experience torn between a career in law or urban planning. All the young movers and shakers in the Lindsay administration seemed to be lawyers. "Looking at the number of people in city government," Diana recalls, "the people who held positions of real authority were all lawyers."

Like Alice Young, Diana was a first-generation American. Her mother, a nurse, was born in Hong Kong and her father, a college professor, was German. When she was growing up, first in rural Montana, then in suburban New Jersey, Diana's parents had not pushed her in any direction. She was not

greatly influenced by the political events of her high school
and college years. At Cornell she participated in a number of
student demonstrations against the Vietnam War. But Diana
was not one to holler and scream and although she agreed
with some of its principles, she was put off by the strident
tone of the feminist movement. "In the longer term," she
explains, "I think it is going to be the activities of women
who achieve their successes and do so quietly and without
much fanfare that will sustain whatever gains the women's
movement has tried to achieve. I think if you just have
women running around and making a lot of noise they might
make momentary gains but the long-term goals won't be
much."

At Harvard Law School Diana attended a few of the meetings of the Women's Law Association but she wasn't really
involved with the organization. Her first year she spent most
of her time studying or socializing with a group of students
who lived in her dorm, Hastings Hall. She lucked out in her
pick of roommates and was assigned to a suite with older
women from the classes of 1972 and 1973. Diana felt her
roommates helped her to keep a level head, particularly her
first year. "They gave me a lot of advice about how to be
calmer about the whole situation. First year could be a trau-
matic experience because everyone was the same as you
were, overachievers who had all done very well, and so you
were being pushed very hard to succeed." Although she
didn't make *Law Review,* she earned extremely respectable As
and Bs.

Her second year, Diana was selected to join the Board of
Student Advisers, the panel that helped teach the required
One L writing course, legal methods, to new law students.
She was also an official of the Law School Forum, a speakers
bureau and was elected vice-president of the Board of Student Advisers her third year. The Board provided a social life
within the law school community.

Her roommates admired her energy. In addition to her extracurricular activities, she was also carrying an unusually heavy academic load. At the beginning of her second year at Harvard Law she also enrolled at MIT to earn her master's in urban planning, hoping to earn a joint degree by the time she graduated from Harvard in 1974. She was also a teaching assistant for courses at both MIT and the law school. "I always marveled at her ability to do both," remembers Karen Nelson, one of Diana's law school roommates. "It was a superhuman job to do it in three years."

When she did graduate from Harvard Law in the spring of 1974, Diana was still unsure which career to pursue—law or urban planning—or how she might combine the two. Having worked throughout college and law school, she felt the need for a break. So she applied for a Rotary Fellowship, which provided funds for outstanding scholars who wanted to study abroad, and spent a year at the University of Edinburgh in Scotland, doing more course work in urban planning and traveling.

Before accepting the fellowship Diana had interviewed at a few large firms, unsure of whether she really wanted to work at one but wanting to explore the option. Many of her classmates had found themselves in a similar state of confusion when faced with the reality of making a first job choice, and many of them had taken the same path of least resistance. Diana had some idea of what large firms were like from working one summer at New York's Milbank, Tweed, Hadley & McCloy, the firm that represented the Rockefellers. Although she had briefly considered moving out to San Francisco, where her parents were living, she ended up having serious interviews at a handful of the largest and best-known New York firms and accepted an offer from Cravath. "There the idea was again that Cravath closed the fewest number of doors. It had a name and at least in the legal profession, if you mentioned you worked at Cravath, everybody knows what it is," she explains. Diana's vague plan was to stay at Cravath for about four years, the time she thought was necessary to receive a thorough training, and then move on to something else, perhaps back in urban planning.

Although some of the young lawyers who worked there found Cravath hopelessly stodgy and too highly pressurized, Diana was characteristically lucky in her draw of assignments. She was assigned to work for corporate partner John Hunt but spent most of her time working with a new partner named Richard Allen. Allen seemed to be cut from a different cloth than the typical Wall Street partner. Although Diana hadn't paid much attention to these details, other associates poked fun at Allen's polyester suits and loud jackets, so different from the impeccable blue serge uniform of Wall Street. Perhaps because he had so recently been an associate himself, Allen often had lunch in the firm's cafeteria with Diana or the other associates who worked for him rather than repairing to the elite Wall Street Club, the private luncheon club atop 1 Chase Plaza, the skyscraper that housed Cravath. Diana admired Allen for his brilliance as well as his easygoing manner, which made learning the ropes a lot easier for her than for some of the other young associates who were working for more imperious senior partners.

At Cravath lawyers were notorious for their huge egos and eccentricities. One corporate partner, who often had as many as ten associates working for him, was an incurable mumbler. But he had put his associates under strict orders not to ask him to repeat anything. Instead they were forced to turn to the partner's male secretary, who had worked for him for years, for a proper translation. Diana avoided many of these problems. "Working for a young partner," she explains, "I escaped the feeling of being a lowly associate, getting the worst lowly tasks. I worked as hard as any of the associates, came in on weekends. But I didn't feel particularly put upon.

I didn't feel I was having to do anything somebody else wouldn't do."

Still, being a junior associate at Cravath had its difficult moments. "I think about it almost like hazing or Army boot camp," Diana says. "If you can go through this, you can go through anything. It's a good training ground. They really push you as hard as you can be pushed." Cravath was, as one of its lawyers described it, the kind of place where partners, not just associates, "stayed up all night checking for commas on the fortieth page."[1] The quality of its work product was what had won Cravath an unparalleled array of clients, from top investment firms like First Boston and Paine Webber to corporate behemoths like IBM. The hours were very demanding and the deals on which Diana worked were extremely complex.

One of Allen's major projects involved the mining of iron ore, in which a consortium of large banks and insurance companies, represented by Cravath, were lending money for the project in different stages. There were more than three hundred documents in some of the closings Diana handled. Her job was to see that all the documents were there, all correct and all properly signed. One of the most important closings was scheduled for right after Christmas in 1976. An associate needed to be in Cleveland the day after Christmas to be at the printer's to proofread all the documents. It was going to be either Diana or Edward Cox, who was also an associate in the corporate department. The two ended up splitting the assignment; Diana was stuck in Cleveland through Christmas Eve and Cox arrived the day after Christmas. Diana spent much of the rest of the winter shuttling back and forth from Cleveland to work on other aspects of the deal.

Although she was anxious to succeed at Cravath, she was not perceived by other associates who were there at the time

[1] *American Lawyer*, September 1982, p. 116.

as being overly ambitious. She wasn't one of those who sat around gossiping obsessively about which associates were thought to be "doing well" or who was in the doghouse. When, after two years, she was rotated to work for corporate partner Benjamin Crane, it was interpreted as a good sign, since Crane handled important clients and matters. Still, Diana realized her chances for partnership—like those of the rest of the fifteen or so associates who were left from the class of 1974—were remote. Nevertheless she thought she was learning the most valuable lesson—how to apply good judgment. If this was all Cravath gave her it would be enough.

Some of the women with whom Diana worked at Cravath found her distant and difficult to get to know. She rarely discussed her Chinese ancestry or any aspects of her personal life. It wasn't that she was unfriendly, it was just that her coolness went beyond the "professionalism" that many young lawyers tried hard to project. Although she occasionally socialized with groups of women from Cravath, Diana seemed to adopt a "one of the boys" attitude. She didn't make a big deal out of the fact she was a woman or seek out women as friends. Her closest friends at Cravath happened to be men. Years later she would often say that she thought her sex had had little impact on her career.

While she was weighing the *Post* offer, she discussed her future with a few close friends, like Karen Nelson, but didn't go around the firm boasting about her great offer, the way a more insecure person might have. As news of her new job spread through the firm there was a predictable amount of envy. Some of the other associates speculated that Diana was not getting along well with Crane. Others claimed she had got the job simply because the *Post* was looking for a woman. Neither was accurate. The *Post* was hoping to hire a woman but if Diana's background hadn't impressed the newspaper's hierarchy she wouldn't have been hired. And, while Crane was an altogether different cup of tea from Allen, Diana didn't think there were any problems between them. She had been invited to stay at Cravath if she decided against going to the *Post*, although she wasn't going around broadcasting this to the other associates either. Diana preferred to be a bit quieter about her successes than the average Harvard Law or Cravath lawyer.

The trappings of Alice Young's success since she joined Graham & James in 1981 are everywhere. Her suite of offices, no longer in Rockefeller Center but on Madison Avenue, are elegantly decorated, covered with lush jade-green carpeting and filled with tasteful furnishings. The overall look of the New York office is sleek and modern, with a slight oriental ambience.

On a rainy July afternoon in 1984 Alice stands at the telephone near the side of her desk, on which a vase of delicate fresh flowers is poised. She is wearing a striking gunmetal-gray two-piece dress. A thick black belt hangs loosely around her waist and, in a special flourish, is buckled at her back. Her long fingers, which are highlighted with brilliant red nail polish, are curled around the receiver. She is in the middle of an animated conversation, in Japanese, with one of her clients —the son of the president of Toyota. Most of her sentences end with a soft lilt. In Tokyo her client is telling her all about the rigors of being in the Toyota training program. Although he is the son of the president, he has been living in one of the company dormitories, working on the assembly line and learning the business from the ground up. He has called because he wants to know when Alice will next be in Japan, as he needs to consult with her on a variety of legal matters. She has not been in East Asia in several months and knows she should plan a trip soon. But as she glances forlornly at her red engagement book she sees that her schedule, as usual, is hopelessly clogged. And in the next few weeks she had promised to block out time to plan her wedding to Tom and their honeymoon.

As head of Graham & James's now successful New York office, there are constantly competing demands on her time. Handling the administration of the office, which has grown to five lawyers, in addition to a support staff, is a demanding job in itself. Additionally, she heads the work on most of the transactions that are handled in the office and, even when she is not the lawyer directly responsible for the matter, she must keep abreast of the key developments in all the legal work that flows to and from the office. She also maintains an exhausting schedule of speaking engagements and meetings that frequently take her out of the office during the day and carry on late into the evenings. Recently she was elected to full membership in the Council on Foreign Relations, an honor usually reserved for senior corporate leaders, and participates in leadership seminars at the Aspen Institute, another refuge of the corporate elite.

Operating at the top level of the legal profession, it is difficult for Alice to describe a "typical" day, since her life as a lawyer is far from routine. When pressed, she describes the following hectic, though challenging twenty-four-hour cycle:

7:30–8:30 A.M.: Breakfast meeting with a Singapore lawyer interested in retaining Graham & James as special counsel in reorganization deal.

8:30–9:30 A.M.: Since most New York firms don't begin office hours until nine-thirty, this is Alice's quiet time in her office. She tries to read the *Wall Street Journal,* New York *Times, Asian Wall Street Journal, Far Eastern Economic Review, Business Week, Japan Economic Journal* and *International Trade Alert,* and marks any articles that may be of interest to clients.

Telexes from Europe must be handled immediately, since the clients are five to six hours ahead.

During these hours Alice also tries to take care of administrative matters—signing checks, reviewing budgets and going over Advisory Board plans.

10:00–Lunch: By ten the office is in full swing. On a normal day Alice takes twenty to sixty calls, meets with clients and consults with other lawyers in her office. She is usually juggling ten to thirty ongoing projects at any one time. Simultaneously she may be called on to: prepare a letter of advice on antitrust issues involving the purchase of a division of a U.S. chemical company, review documents for a syndicated loan to construct and manage a hotel in China, negotiate the acquisition of shares in a medical research high tech company, incorporate another company for a real estate acquisition, revise an employee handbook for a chain of stores, prepare documents for a joint venture in the United States involving Japanese and South American interests and negotiate a licensing agreement for a bottle-manufacturing plant in the Middle East. Projects take from a few minutes for quick advice over the telephone to several hours or days for negotiations, research and drafting.

Lunch: It is either skipped altogether to give Alice more time to work or spent with a client or at one of her outside groups, like the Council on Foreign Relations.

Afternoon–8 P.M.: Calls to the firm's West Coast offices are placed after lunch because of the time difference. The afternoon is much like the morning, with an acceleration of incoming calls. The calls begin to taper off at seven, but many clients know they can reach her until eight or nine. Telexes to Asian clients are sent in the early evening, since it is early morning there.

Sometimes there are cocktail receptions for visiting clients that she must attend. Often she has dinner meetings with clients.

8:00–10:30 P.M.: Dinner with a client from Hong Kong to discuss a new investment his company plans to make in the United States.

10:30–Sleep: Alice heads home to see Tom, skims the Japanese prints and paintings catalogue a friend at Sotheby's has sent, reads a few chapters of a novel by Paul Bowles and calls it a day.

Other women lawyers from her class, either because of a lack of experience and confidence or because their firms provide less support and opportunities for client development, or perhaps because family demands leave them with less time for outside activities, stay within more circumscribed areas, often limiting their roles as lawyers to servicing established clients of their firms. Alice cannot, even if she was so inclined, afford the luxury of being only a service lawyer. She has to build a practice, one that is large enough to support an expanding office.

Although she is, like many lawyers, reluctant to provide a list of her clients, she has brought major Asian clients to Graham & James in the computer, telecommunications, shipping, banking and trade industries and a number of domestic companies as well. In 1983 she was selected, from a number of lawyers competing for the business, to represent Comsat's television satellite subsidiary in a new multimillion-dollar project that involved advising the company on dealing with major Japanese equipment manufacturers. Over the past few years she has handled a variety of matters for NEC Corporation, the large Japanese electronics firm, and for a number of textile and fashion clients, including Itokin, the Japanese-based company that represents a consortium of French, Italian and Japanese designers and operates several boutique-concept stores, including one in midtown Manhattan. Alice has attracted many of these new clients through referrals from other lawyers, clients and business acquaintances who know and respect her work. And her new clients, in turn, have referred yet more business her way.

Alice obviously enjoys getting out of the office, meeting new people and trying to generate new business for her firm.

The whole process feels entirely natural to her. For others, however, learning to generate clients has been harder. "Business development is probably the most difficult issue for women," observes Mary Nelson, one of Alice's former classmates who is a partner at Boston's Hill & Barlow. "I think many women, myself included, are very bad about keeping up old school ties and exploiting relationships. Sometimes women see it as offensive to exploit a relationship. They don't milk a situation for all it's worth in getting clients. Men don't think that way. If they meet someone on the golf course, 'fair game', they think, 'Go after anyone you meet.' "

Alice developed these instincts early in her career, as an associate in Hong Kong. Mary Faith Higgins, another classmate, also happens to be a partner at Graham & James and also enjoys the challenge of pursuing clients. In 1984 Mary Faith was tapped by Graham & James to open a new Hong Kong office, and she is in the process of trying to replicate the kind of success Alice Young has scored in New York. "I network relentlessly," says Higgins. Something basic to their personalities makes both women "real go-getters," to use the words of their senior partner Sandy Calhoun.

When Alice joined the firm as a new and untested partner Graham & James had, as was customary practice with lateral partners, placed a sunset clause on her partnership. If the firm hadn't been satisfied with her performance it could have canceled the deal within the first two years. Alice not only survived the sunset period, she has been awarded discretionary bonuses above her partnership draw every year since she joined the firm, and the New York office, less than five years out, was close to operating at a profit. Its performance has far exceeded the firm's original economic forecast, considering the enormous start-up costs involved in launching a new enterprise in the world's most competitive legal marketplace, New York. She was elected to the firm's Advisory Board, an influential group of partners who assist the firm's Executive Committee in making policy decisions.

Alice gives much of the credit for her success to Graham & James. The firm has supplied her with all of the backup she needs. The top partners in all of the firm's offices are always willing to help out on large transactions or to provide her with more associates. She is especially gratified that both of the senior associates whom she brought over from Coudert have been elected partners. Most of all she is grateful to her firm for placing such faith and responsibility in a young woman. "We were all going against stereotypes of what does and doesn't work," Alice says.

With nine women partners, Graham & James is unique. Alice, Mary Faith Higgins and Susan McCarthy all speak glowingly about the firm's working atmosphere. The leading partners, particularly Calhoun, have helped these three women develop new clients, trying to nurture their talents as lawyers. At many other firms, however, young women partners still feel that they are not yet part of the club.

At Graham & James, Alice, if anything, has the opposite problem. She has become so important to her firm's inner workings that she has less and less time for her life outside work. She is still spending at least thirty-five percent of her time traveling, to San Francisco for meetings of the Advisory Board and to see clients in the Far East. In September 1984 she took off for Asia exactly one day after she returned from her honeymoon in the South of France. If Tom were a more insecure person, or a more selfish one, their relationship could not have survived. "He is completely unthreatened by how important my career is to me, and very supportive," Alice says proudly. "I make a lot of demands on a relationship," she admits. "I don't have very much personal time and I live under a tremendous amount of stress." Tom is also heavily involved in his career as an investment banker, although his hours are more predictable. So in the early evenings Tom has his own, separate life, exercising at the New York Athletic Club, seeing friends and going out to dinner. But the little personal time the couple have together is sacrosanct, as are family and friends. "I think it is important in a career to have a balanced family life," Alice says. She and Tom were looking forward to starting a family of their own.

Occasionally someone visiting the office still mistakes Alice Young, so youthful-looking at 34, for the office manager. At cocktail parties people sometimes make comments, like, "Isn't it sweet that you're doing this." "It isn't sweet," Alice bristles to herself, "it is damn tough." But she doesn't let herself take offense at every clumsy remark. "People are still surprised," she observes. "It is still a real rarity to have a woman partner at all, let alone one founding an office. That shows we haven't come that far."At some business meetings Alice still has to face "the unfortunate reality of being the only woman." Until there are a lot of women out there who are the heads of corporations or holding powerful positions like her own, there will be these annoyances. Already, as more women have begun rising to the top, Alice notes that there are more varieties of women professionals. The super-aggressive or retiring technocrat caricatures of women lawyers no longer typify most of the women with whom she deals. Although the range is still somewhat limited, women feel less constrained and under less pressure to conform to old stereotypes. Few, however, have reached Alice's level of self-confidence and style.

Diana Daniels occupies today an equally rarefied position in the legal profession as one of a handful of women corporate counsels. Although some of her former cohorts from Cravath days expected to find Diana on the corporate fast track after she joined the *Post*, her rise was rapid-fire. At twenty-nine, while many of her old New York friends were slogging through their fourth and fifth years as associates,

Diana was giving the marching orders to the firms that did *Newsweek*'s outside legal work, including Rogers & Wells and other respected firms across the country.

Following her promotion to counsel at *Newsweek,* Diana didn't have time to bask in glory. For three months she shuttled between New York and Washington, while Ed Smith, the outgoing counsel, introduced her around *Newsweek.* In many ways, Diana knew, Smith would be a tough act to follow. "Any time there's a change it takes both sides time to get to know one another," she reflects. An affable man in his forties who had worked as a reporter and editor at the Associated Press, Smith was a corny punster with an avuncular manner of dealing with reporters and editors. "At first, editors were not predisposed to like anyone who replaced Smith," one *Newsweek* editor admits. Diana's toughness and business-like manner contrasted sharply with Smith's jolliness. "Diana could be pretty tough," reports another editor. "Smith seemed more permissive." Diana would sometimes ask to see a reporter's files and she would question editors closely about the sources for their information. Sometimes dealing with Diana was more like dealing with an opposition lawyer than someone on the in-house team. "We've been smarting under her education," says a *Newsweek* official. "She wants us to appreciate legal minutiae we don't think we have to follow. We may think she's too picayune and scrupulous. She probably thinks we're too cavalier. Her function is to hold us to higher standards and she does a very good job."

During her early months at *Newsweek* Diana did have a few clashes with the editorial side of the magazine. Lester Bernstein, who was editor when Diana assumed her duties, had defied her legal advice by putting dollar bills on the cover of one issue. The Treasury Department, Diana warned, had extremely strict rules prohibiting the reproduction of money, and shortly after the issue hit the stands the Secret Service came calling. The U.S. attorney's office also warned that the offense was prosecutable, although the matter eventually was dropped. "We sweated a bit," Bernstein remembers.

Diana was willing to risk being thought of as too literal-minded by the magazine's writers and editors. "I think you'd be remiss as a lawyer if you weren't cautious and if you did not try, as you're reading a story, to look for the kind of interpretation someone else might have. I don't think that's a negative. I think it's a positive that you are in fact cautious but don't say no. I try to look at the job as being one of trying to make sure that the articles or the matters be publishable, and you look to see how you can fix the story, refashion the sentence in a way that will protect you as best you can and allow the story to be published." Given the increasing number of highly publicized libel cases, particularly the case against rival *Time* magazine brought by Ariel Sharon, in which *Time*'s fact-checking procedures were criticized by both the judge and jury, Diana's rigorousness was probably justified. But some of the magazine's researchers dreaded the Saturday afternoon sessions in her office when most of the copy was reviewed and approved so the magazine could be "put to bed" and printed the next day. They preferred it when her warmer and more easygoing assistant, Peter Fitzpatrick, was on duty.

Trying to position her office as an ally of the editorial department, Diana began holding periodic tutorials on libel law for editors, writers and researchers so that they could understand her concerns. "I really wanted the editorial people to look at the legal department not as a nay sayer but as somebody who could help them move things along and help the business of the company," she says.

If the editorial department was a bit slow in warming up to her, Diana was always highly regarded by the top executives at the Post Company. Shortly after her arrival at the *Post*, Donald Graham telephoned Christine Beshar at Cravath to rave about Diana's work. He joked that Beshar should think about setting up an employment agency since the match she had arranged between Diana and the *Post* had worked so perfectly.

As a corporate officer of *Newsweek,* Diana did a good job of keeping her eye on the bottom line. From a business point of view *Newsweek* was going through a difficult period during Diana's early tenure. Profits were down sharply from the 1970s and the magazine had launched a very expensive spin-off called *Inside Sports,* which was supposed to go head to head with Time Inc.'s wildly successful *Sports Illustrated.* Circulation figures had been terrible the first year and the Post Company was losing millions on *Inside Sports.* In 1982 Diana negotiated the sale of the magazine to Active Markets, Inc., getting the white elephant off the company's hands for good. When Active Markets went bankrupt a year later Diana succeeded in recouping $200,000 still owed to *Newsweek* for the purchase of the magazine.

The short-lived sports magazine provided Diana and *Newsweek* with some of their most nettlesome legal problems. *Inside Sports* did not publish the usual puff pieces on established sports stars. It frequently ran critical pieces that tried to pierce the mythology of the sports world. While several of the magazine's in-depth profiles won editorial praise, they also precipitated several lawsuits that landed, naturally enough, in Diana's lap. In August 1980 the magazine ran a catty, scathing exposé on the troubled marriage of Los Angeles Dodger star Steve Garvey and his wife Cyndy, replete with the wife's complaints about the couple's sex life. The Garveys sued for $11.2 million when the article, called "Trouble In Paradise," was published. Diana turned to William Masterson, a veteran litigator at Rogers & Wells, to handle the case. What looked like a nuisance suit to many outsiders proved to be a very thorny case.

First the judge granted the Garveys' request for a restraining order to stop the Los Angeles *Herald Examiner* from serializing the piece. Masterson eventually succeeded in having the order lifted by the Ninth Circuit Court of Appeals. Then, in a surprise move, *Newsweek* was approached and agreed to settle the case. Since the stipulations of the settlement required the parties to keep the specifics of the arrangement secret, neither Diana nor Masterson could talk about the reasons why *Newsweek* had opted to settle. Press reports at the time estimated that *Newsweek* paid the Garveys around $100,000 to get rid of the case, and there was speculation that the Garveys had sought the settlement because of mounting legal fees. Soon after the case was settled the Garveys separated.

Diana claimed that the settlement represented only a partial payment of the couple's legal fees. What puzzled observers, however, was not the size of the settlement but the fact that *Newsweek* had settled at all. For years virtually all of the major publications had adopted a no-settlement policy when it came to libel suits. Although the costs of taking a case to trial were potentially greater than reaching an out-of-court settlement, most publications felt that a more lenient policy toward settlement would only invite more lawsuits. The *Post* was one of the strongest adherents to this principle, which is part of why the Garvey settlement seemed so surprising.

At the time of the settlement a few prominent First Amendment lawyers had criticized *Newsweek* for settling and there were unflattering press stories. The decision to settle certainly hadn't been Diana's alone, but she had agreed with *Newsweek*'s top corporate officers that there were good reasons to settle. Not being able to reveal those reasons had been very frustrating for Diana, but she didn't let the situation get to her. "I look at it from the perspective that I work for a media organization. One has to be fairly thick-skinned about these things and take it as it comes. My getting upset about things is not going to change what's been written and it only adds fuel to the fire and makes it seem bigger than it should be," she says. She considered the whole Garvey affair to be the low point of her career at *Newsweek.*

Another, potentially far more damaging lawsuit against *Inside Sports* ended far more favorably, in large part because of Diana's judgment calls. In another 1980 exposé, entitled "The Fix," *Inside Sports* alleged that Willie Pep, a former featherweight boxing champion, had "dumped" an important fight. Pep sued the magazine for $75 million. Rather than turn to a traditional First Amendment litigator to handle the trial, Diana decided to retain Peter Fleming of New York's Curtis, Mallet-Prevost, Colt & Mosle, a litigator with a specialty in white-collar crime. Steve Froling, another litigator whom Diana retained, helped devise a brilliant strategy for the case. Fleming's performance in court was flawless, and it took the jury just ten minutes to find in favor of *Newsweek* after two weeks of testimony. Diana had been right to place her faith in Fleming and it was thrilling to see the magazine vindicated so completely.

Since her arrival at *Newsweek,* Diana has taken steps to be more visible in her field. "As few other people have done, she has gone out on the lecture road telling groups the reality of life in the newsroom. She is very savvy and a heavy hitter in the field," says Floyd Abrams, the dean of the First Amendment bar. Diana was a member of the Communications Law Committee of the New York City Bar Association and she has been on the faculty of the Practicing Law Institute, lecturing on First Amendment law at several conferences sponsored by PLI, the most popular continuing legal education program for most private practitioners.

But her responsibilities extend far beyond First Amendment work. At one moment she may be confronting problems about moving currency from one of the foreign countries where *Newsweek* operates overseas bureaus. Another unanticipated crisis may bring a contractual problem with a division of employees. Diana deals with many delicate personnel matters. And increased responsibilities have brought more power and influence.

Diana has found a comfortable niche within *Newsweek*'s corporate hierarchy. She sits in a roomy office down the corridor from Chairman Katharine Graham and Washington *Post* President Richard Simmons. She survived a changing of the guard at *Newsweek* in 1981 when Mark Edmiston became the magazine's new president. "When somebody comes in at a position of authority they canvass the field and she is one of the good people. She is very secure in her job," says the Post Company's general counsel, Alan Finberg. In 1984 Diana was selected to attend an eight-week Senior Executive Program at the Stanford Business School. Several up-and-coming young executives at the *Post* including Chris Little had attended the prestigious program.

Diana is usually in the office six days a week. Although she is reluctant to talk about her private life, she says, "I work very hard at my job but I have enough other things to do that I am not hopelessly driven." Life outside of work includes a strong relationship with a man who is a partner at a law firm. She has not come close to marrying and says she is not troubled by the prospect of not having a family of her own. "I look at it in terms of the fact that I haven't found anybody I'm particularly interested in or have been interested in long enough to want to make that kind of commitment," she explains.

Although she had not precisely planned to be where she is at age thirty-five, the success she has achieved has required tremendous self-discipline and determination. Diana appears to be one of those professional women who is very much married to her career and *Newsweek* is the central focus of her life. For the time being, her demanding job has brought Diana what she considers to be a fulfilling life. "I think I'm reasonably successful," she reflects. "I have an interesting job which, fortunately, pays well. It provides a lot of stimulation."

Given the vast array of top credentials that they held collectively (summas from Yale, Phi Beta Kappa keys, impressive fellowships) when they arrived at Harvard Law School, should more women from the Harvard Law School class of 1974 have achieved the superstar status of a Diana Daniels or an Alice Young? After all, these seventy women were the crème de la crème of the law school population, entering the profession just as the old barriers were falling. Why did so few of them attain partnership at major firms, and fewer still become real insiders in the corporate world?

The answers to these questions raise uncomfortable and touchy issues for a group of women who want to believe that those women with the ability and training to be the best lawyers in the country are at least on the brink of gaining parity with men. The statistical discrepancies—the fact that more than half the men in the class are partners and fewer than one quarter of the women have achieved that status and that even fewer of the women have gained any real degree of power and influence in the world of corporate law and business—are difficult for many of the women from the class of 1974 to talk about.

"Damn it all," exclaims Debbie Stiles, who is anxiously awaiting the partnership decision at her firm, New York's Debevoise & Plimpton, "I'm not going to say something now that will hamper my chances to get my foot in the door because I think the way these places will ultimately change will be by getting people who are different. Women have different views about how law firms should be run." If she becomes a partner, Stiles says, she will try to change her firm from the inside, hoping to make her firm more sensitive to what she calls "environmental issues." But when a New York *Times* reporter called her and several other senior associates to comment on the ramifications of the Hishon case, she was unwilling to talk for the record.

The women from the class who have already made partner or reached the upper echelon of the profession are more willing to be candid. And most agree that whatever statistical differences exist between the men and the women in the class, they are attributable more to the nature of the legal profession itself than to individual failings or any lack of talent or perserverance among the women. Even though the entry barriers had started to fall by 1974, as Margaret Morrow observes, "I think when I started you had to be extraordinary rather than just above average, to make it in a firm."

Besides accepting increasing numbers of young, entry-level women, the firms and corporations at which many of the women from the class of 1974 went to work did relatively little to make real changes in their organizations and power structures. The kind of opportunities that presented themselves to Diana Daniels and Alice Young were the exception rather than the rule. Larger numbers of women were filtering into the bottom of the pyramid. In order to rise up, the men in the class could fit into readily established patterns, finding mentors among the senior, powerful partners and clients eager to help them rise to the top. As Karen Katzman observes, "It's more difficult for women to get close to people who can help them with their careers." So many of the women we interviewed, while not citing overt instances of discrimination, cited general feelings of isolation. And many of them left.

For the ones who remained, there were more clearly defined problems as they became senior associates. Clients were occasionally reluctant to let a woman take lead responsibility for their affairs. And partnership did not necessarily bring solutions. Again, the conservatism of clients, the closed doors of elite luncheon clubs where deals are struck and new clients met, made generating business—the key to attaining real influence within the firm—extremely difficult.

Still, many women from the class are willing to persevere,

to fight on to win acceptance in the corporate boardroom and law firm conference room. They want success just as much as Diana Daniels and Alice Young. What will eventually determine whether they find it is whether more of the Dianas and Alices of the world attain positions of real power and influence and become the ones who are running the firms and doling out lucrative legal work.

8
Where They Are Now

In choosing to study the seventy women from the Harvard Law School class of 1974 we consciously selected a very elite, highly motivated, success-oriented group for scrutiny. Knowing the accomplishments of various Harvard Law alumni whose illustrious ranks include Supreme Court justices, senators, leading practitioners and outstanding academicians, we would not have been totally stunned if our project had evolved into a chronicle of seventy success stories. However, knowing what we did about the nature of the legal profession, and having covered the profession as journalists for several years, we expected to find more subtle shadings. Frankly, we were not surprised to find as much uncertainty as self-satisfaction among the women we interviewed. Although very few of them express disillusionment with their choice of careers, or regret going to Harvard Law in the first place, the women of 1974 are far from complacent about their jobs or lives ten years after graduation.

With only ten years of experience under their belts, it is impossible to reach sweeping conclusions about this class of women. They are still a group in transition and a substantial number of them are in the process of evaluating their careers and making changes in their lives. In the months between the time we finished our research for the main text of our book and then compiled the chart at the end of this chapter, nearly 10% of the women had changed jobs or made alterations in their careers, some opting to work part-time because of the birth of a child, others considering what changes to make in anticipation of having a first child or more children. Eager for a break, one woman, Mary Kathleen Hite, took a leave of absence from her job as an associate at a small Washington firm almost certain that she did not want to return to the practice of law. Another, Janine Wolf Hill, had left her job at Time, Inc. to stay home with her two children. Relatively few of the women can say with real confidence that what they are doing today is what they will be doing ten years from now.

These women are, however, acutely aware that they are part of a historic change that is taking place within their profession. Coming out of Harvard Law School in 1974, most of them did not realize that they were in the vanguard of a veritable population explosion within the legal profession— leading the charge of young, ambitious women toward the most elite and traditionally male corners of the law. "We didn't know it but we were right in the middle of this historic event," observes Molly Munger.

It is true that the women of Harvard Law School who graduated in 1974 entered the profession at a time of widening opportunities for women. They were no longer pioneers, as the Harvard Law women from the 1950s and 1960s had been. But the world they entered was still a traditional one where women were seldom seen at the highest levels. Some felt put off by the clubbiness of law firms they entered. Others felt shut out from the camaraderie of the courtroom and local bar cliques that can win a young trial lawyer a prize referral. At some point during their first ten years in the profession most of the women from the class brushed up against the reality that, while it was easy to land a job out of

Harvard Law School, it was quite another thing to become a real insider, part of the decision-making structure.

From our vantage point, the women from the class were caught in the middle between the pioneer era and a modern one that may be just dawning. They were on the cusp and unable to take full advantage of the changing times. They entered the profession at a point when the women's movement was steaming ahead, leading some to believe that women could, for the first time, "have it all." But in the ensuing ten years the effort to fit the superwoman stereotype has taken its toll on some of the class members, many of whom have concluded that it is simply not possible to run a household, raise children and bill 2,000 hours annually.

In fact, while a substantial number of women from the class enthusiastically devoted all their time to developing their careers in the years immediately following graduation, by 1984, approaching age thirty-five, several were rigorously reexamining their priorities. "I think it's really something internal," says Margaret Morrow, who has centered her life around her firm, where she is a partner, and her local bar association. "You've got to reevaluate your internal decisions. In a sense I feel I've compromised the personal aspects of my life up to now and so I have to make a decision. Am I willing to continue to do that?"

Other women in the class wrestled with this same dilemma at earlier points in their careers. But the one-dimensional life of a workaholic lawyer is only part of the reason why the dropout rate is so high among the majority of women who joined private firms after graduation and why so few made partner. We find it difficult to accept the stereotypical explanations for why so many young women leave firms—that women have less drive than men, that they are less willing to put up with "shit work," that they leave to have babies and lose their desire to work once motherhood blooms. As one of our chapters details, the women in the class left firms in droves for a variety of reasons—there was no single one. Many of them did find the associate lifestyle unpleasant (as did many of the men). But a crucial difference between the men and women was that, if a male graduate from Harvard Law School decided to stick it out for the requisite eight or nine years, he could be confident that his sex would not be a factor weighing against him in the intense competition for partnership. Seeing so few women in the partnership ranks, and seeing capable women leaving or being passed over, had to have a dampening psychological effect on young female associates, for whom an eight- or nine-year commitment was a far riskier proposition.

And for those who stuck it out there was the lingering problem of how to compete in a male-dominated world. As another chapter of this book emphasizes, it was all too easy for women lawyers to be tagged as "too aggressive" or "too mousey," regardless of their legal talents. Without female role models, it was difficult for women to know how to prove they were partnership material.

Family concerns did play a major role in determining the career paths many of these women followed. Some of the women we interviewed feel their profession has failed to make really significant accommodations to working mothers. Candy Fowler, a government attorney, works part-time so that she can spend time with her daughter. Hopes of career advancement have been put on hold. "I do worry about staying at the same level," she confessed to us. "Working part-time could hurt me. My situation and the limits on my career could be perceived as systemic discrimination because the workplace is still not very receptive to raising a family and having a career."

The women from the Harvard Law School class of 1974 want to be on the cutting edge of change. Many of them are aware that it is their responsibility to forge ahead, blaze new trails and try to make the profession a more hospitable one for women. This is the main reason why many of them were willing to talk to us. "I feel an obligation to talk to you," one woman from the class told us before our interview, "not because I want to but because I think some of the problems and issues we face as women lawyers are so important." Whether it was discussing the embarrassment of having a senior partner make a pass, the difficulties of breast-feeding on the job, the awkwardness of negotiating against an older male or dealing with a condescending judge, most of our subjects were extremely candid. Given the pain generated by some of these experiences, we were surprised to find few traces of bitterness in our conversations. One woman from the class had been job hunting for more than a year after being laid off as a corporate staff attorney. She was clearly worried that she would not find a similar position (indeed, she never did and pursued an alternative legal career) because most corporations seemed more interested in hiring junior-level women or promoting from within. But even she remained hopeful, wailing in mock horror, "This is not supposed to happen to graduates of Harvard Law School!"

Although a few superstars are earning in excess of $100,000, the women from the class of 1974 lag behind the men in their class in terms of both the earning and prestige levels of their jobs. Many are doing legal work historically deemed appropriate for women—teaching, public interest and defender work, or working in government. Relatively few can say that they have made it to the top, although their prime earning years are yet to come. In short, it is impossible to say what the future will hold for these seventy women.

And if it is impossible to predict how these women from Harvard Law School will ultimately fare in the legal profession, it is harder still to draw any hopeful conclusions about the status of women in the law generally. Although more and more women continue to flood the profession (in 1984, 14% of the nation's 650,000 lawyers were female and women comprised 30% of the law school population), their status within the profession has not changed as dramatically as their numbers. A survey conducted by the American Bar Association in 1984[1] revealed that 65% of male lawyers had no female colleagues at work. The median income for male lawyers was $53,000 and $33,000 for women. Forty-five percent of the men queried said that the influx of women into the profession was only a "somewhat favorable" development and would have only minor consequences. (In contrast, 70% of the women surveyed called it an "extremely favorable" development and predicted major consequences.)

And another recent survey[2] revealed that, while 30% of the associates at the hundred largest firms in the country were women, only 5% of the partners at these same firms were women. While the managing partners of these firms explain away these figures by saying that large numbers of women have not been in the profession long enough to be reflected in the partnership ranks, this is plainly not the case. In fact one third to one half of the partners of these major firms graduated after 1970. After all, 60% of the women from the Harvard Law School class of 1974 began their careers at law firms. Given how their male counterparts (who joined in roughly the same percentages) fared, it is a reasonable expectation that the same proportion of men and women would become partners. As our research underscores, this plainly didn't happen. And while the reasons relatively few women made it past the finish line are highly individual, institutional barriers were an underlying factor in many cases.

As long as women, even women from Harvard Law School, are not fully embraced as valuable members of the business community at large, as long as they are excluded from prestigious clubs, as long as they are frozen out of the inner workings and power centers of their profession, the law

[1] *American Bar Association Journal,* October 1983.
[2] *National Law Journal,* May 21, 1984.

will be a difficult career for women to pursue. Even in 1984
Harvard Law School itself was still a tough environment for
women, as our interviews with women students underscored.
In a negotiation workshop, one woman from the class of
1984 told us, a female student made a forceful point but was
ignored by the six men in their seminar. "A man made the
very same point a few minutes later," she says, "and the class
took off on his point. It was as if she had been speaking into
air. It appalled me. It was clear they didn't respect women."
Lewd drawings ridiculing Harvard Law women are still mainstays on the bulletin boards.

And what will the women who graduated from Harvard
Law School in 1984 find once they begin to establish themselves in their jobs? Never again will the legal profession be
the kind of gentlemen's club depicted in the novels of Louis
Auchincloss. But there are so many unanswered questions.
Will the profession do more to assist working mothers? Will
larger numbers of women make partner? Will women lawyers develop into successful rainmakers? In the next ten
years, will there be more women who can honestly be characterized as leaders of the profession?

"A lot of women my age are grateful to these pathbreakers
and hope things will be somewhat easier," reflects Barbara
Fischbein Berenson, a member of the class of 1984. The next
decade will prove whether it has become easier for women to
succeed in the law, and women from Harvard Law School,
beginning in 1974 and continuing for the rest of this century,
will be in the vanguard. They are the generation of women
who will leave their mark on the style, substance and shape of
the nation's most elite profession.

STATISTICAL PROFILE OF 1974 HARVARD LAW WOMEN

	Title	Time	Married	Children
Claudia Angelos	Clinical law professor, New York University School of Law	FT	Yes	Yes
Theresa Arnold	Staff attorney, Amoco Corporation Chicago	FT	No	No
Roberta Baruch	Deputy assistant director, Office of Evaluation, Federal Trade Commission, Washington, D.C.	PT	Yes	Yes
Patricia Bass	Associate director National Health Plan, Inc. Washington, D.C.	FT	No	No
Carolyn Beck	Unable to locate			
Sheila Bell	University legal counsel, Northern Kentucky University	FT	Yes	Yes
Judith Berkan	Professor, Universidad Interamericana Facultad de Derecho, San Juan, Puerto Rico	FT	No	No
Julia Bonsal	Partner, White & Case, New York	FT	No	No
Bari Boyer	Part owner of real estate and development company	FT	Yes	Yes
Mary Brody	Partner, Craig & Macauley, Boston	FT	Yes	Yes

	Title	Time	Married	Children
Renee Chotiner	Full-time mother		Yes	Yes
Carolyn Cotsonas	Assistant professor, University of Massachusetts Medical School, Worcester	PT	Yes	Yes
Alice Welt Cunningham	Associate professor of law, New York Law School	FT	Yes	No
Carolyn Daffron	Writer, civil practitioner, law and social work professor, Rutgers University, New Brunswick, New Jersey	PT	Yes	Yes
Ellen D'Alelio	Partner, Steptoe & Johnson, Washington, D.C.	FT	Yes	No
Diana Daniels	Counsel, Newsweek, Inc., New York	FT	No	No
Roslyn Daum	Partner, Choate, Hall & Stewart, Boston	PT	Yes	Yes
Jane Eng	Associate, the law firm of Arnold Kawano, New York	FT	Yes	Yes
Francesta Farmer	President, Operation Crossroads Africa, Inc., New York	FT	No	Yes
M. Candace Fowler	Staff attorney, Administrative Conference of the United States, Washington, D.C.	PT	Yes	Yes
Sandra Froman	Visiting assistant professor, University of Santa Clara Law School	FT	Yes	No

	Title	Time	Married	Children
Mary Gallagher	Consultant on linguistics and trial attorney, Federal Defenders of San Diego, Inc., San Diego	FT	No	No
Anne Wolman Geldon	Solo practitioner, estate planning (home)	PT	Yes	Yes
Shelley Green	General counsel, University of Pennsylvania	FT	Yes	No
Ann Lambert Greenblatt	Executive director, Massachusetts Correctional Legal Services, Boston	FT	Yes	No
Barbara C. Haldeman	Housewife and mother, Wayne, Pennsylvania		Yes	Yes
Bernice Heilbrunn	Teaching assistant and graduate student in history, Rutgers University, New Jersey	PT	Yes	Yes
Christine Hickman	Court commissioner, Los Angeles Superior Court	FT	Yes	No
Mary Faith Higgins	Partner, Graham & James, Hong Kong office	FT	No	No
Janine Wolf Hill	Full-time mother		Yes	Yes
Rosemary Williams Hill	Supervising attorney, Roxbury Defenders Committee, Boston	FT	Yes	Yes
Mary Kathleen Hite	On Leave of Absence Amram & Hahn, Washington, D.C.		No	No

	Title	Time	Married	Children
Toby Hyman	Associate, Proskauer, Rose, Goetz & Mendelsohn, New York	FT	No	No
Karen Katzman	Partner, Kaye, Scholer, Fierman, Hays & Handler, New York	FT	No	No
Patricia Nicely Kopf	Partner, Fenwick, Stone, Davis & West, Palo Alto	FT	Yes	No
Sophie Krasik	Associate counsel, Naval Supply Systems Command, Office of Counsel, Department of Defense, Washington, D.C.	FT	No	No
Bernadine Layne	President, Consolidated Broadcasters, Inc., Atlanta, Georgia	FT	Yes	Yes
Judith Lindahl	Solo practitioner, Boston	FT	No	No
Susan Chan McCarthy	Partner, Graham & James, San Francisco	FT	Yes	Yes
Margarita McCoy	Policy analyst, Seattle City Council	FT	No	No
Mary Ann McGunigle	Graduate student in architecture, Columbia University	—	—	—
Nancy McMillen	Trial attorney, Antitrust Division, Department of Justice, Washington, D.C.	FT	Yes	No
Ellen Marshall	Partner, McKenna, Conner & Cuneo, Costa Mesa office	FT	No	No
Joyce Miller	Lecturer/clinical supervisor, Clinical Programs, University of Pennsylania Law School	FT	No	No

	Title	Time	Married	Children
Phebe Miller	Vice-president and counsel, Discount Corporation of New York	FT	Engaged	No
Margaret Morrow	Partner, Kadison, Pfaelzer Woodard, Quinn & Rossi, Los Angeles	FT	Yes	No
Molly Munger	Founding partner, Baird, Munger & Myers Los Angeles	FT	Yes	Yes
Judith Neibrief	Assistant/attorney adviser to the Administrator, Food, Safety and Inspection Service, USDA, Washington, D.C.	FT	No	No
Mary Nelson	Partner, Hill & Barlow, Boston	PT	Yes	Yes
Joan Markey O'Connor	Vice-president/Legal, Paine Webber, Inc.	FT	Yes	Yes
Anne Redman	Partner, Foster, Pepper & Riviera, Seattle	FT	Yes	Yes
Paula Rhodes	Associate professor, Howard University Law School, Washington, D.C.	FT	No	No
Rene Townsend Robinson	Special projects coordinator and director of equal opportunity, Administrative Office of the U. S. Courts	FT	Yes	Yes
Barbara Sard	Managing attorney, Greater Boston Legal Services	PT	Yes	Yes
Carol Schepp	Associate, Morgan Stanley & Co.	PT	Yes	Yes

	Title	Time	Married	Children
Deena Jo Schneider	Partner, Schnader, Harrison, Segal & Lewis, Philadelphia	FT	Yes	Yes
Enid Hochstein Schultz	Solo practitioner, Great Neck, New York	PT	Yes	Yes
Bari Schwartz	Legislative assistant, Congressman Howard Berman (D, Cal.), Washington, D.C.	FT	Yes	No
Juliet Shepard	General counsel, Mobil Exploration and Producing Services, Inc., Dallas	FT	No	No
Wendy Singer	Associate, Gibson, Dunn & Crutcher, London office	FT	Yes	Yes
Gail Sticker	Solo practitioner, New York City	FT	Yes	pregnant (due Dec. '85)
Deborah Fiedler Stiles	Associate, Debevoise & Plimpton	FT	Yes	Yes
Susan Thorner	Partner, Hughes, Hubbard & Reed, New York	FT	No	No
Elisse Walter	Associate general counsel, SEC, Washington, D.C.	FT	Yes	Yes
Roberta Watson	Associate, Trenam, Simmons, Kemker, Scharf, Barkin, Frye & O'Neill, Tampa	FT	Yes	Yes
Marley Sue Weiss	Assistant professor, University of Maryland School of Law	FT	No	No
Susan Roosevelt Weld	Researcher, East Asian Legal Studies, Harvard Law School	PT	Yes	Yes

	Title	Time	Married	Children
Cecilia Wirtz	Assistant general counsel, Office of Management and Budget, Washington, D.C.	FT	Yes	Yes
Lois Wood	Directing attorney, Land of Lincoln Legal Assistance Foundation, Inc., East St. Louis, Illinois	FT	Yes	Yes
Alice Young	Partner, Graham & James, New York office	FT	Yes	Yes
Carolyn Lewis Ziegler	Of counsel, Flemming, Zulack & Williamson, New York	PT	Yes	Yes

BIBLIOGRAPHY

Harvard Law School

Osborn, John. *The Paper Chase.* New York: Warner Books, 1983.

Seligman, Joel. *The High Citadel.* Boston: Houghton Mifflin Company, 1978.

Stevens, Robert. *Law School.* Chapel Hill: University of North Carolina Press, 1983.

Turow, Scott. *One L.* New York: Penguin Books, 1978.

Women Lawyers

Couric, Emily, ed. *Women Lawyers: Perspectives on Success.* New York: Law & Business, Inc., Harcourt, Brace, Jovanovich, 1983.

Epstein, Cynthia Fuchs. *Women in Law.* New York: Basic Books, 1981.

The Woman Lawyer Within the Firm. Chicago: LawLetters, Inc., 1984.

The Legal Profession

The American Lawyer Guide to Leading Law Firms. New York: Am-Law Publishing Co., 1983.

American Lawyer magazine, 1979–85.

Hoffman, Paul. *Lions in the Street.* New York: Saturday Review Press, 1973.

———. *Lions of the Eighties.* Garden City, N.Y.: Doubleday & Co., 1982.

Stewart, James A. *The Partners.* New York: Simon & Schuster, 1983.

INDEX